The Roots of Antisemitism in
SOUTH AFRICA

Milton Shain

University Press of Virginia

Charlottesville and London

To the memory of my father
and to my mother

The University Press of Virginia
Copyright © 1994 by the Rector and Visitors
of the University of Virginia
First published 1994

Library of Congress Cataloging-in-Publication Data

Shain, Milton.
  The roots of antisemitism in South Africa / by Milton Shain.
    p.   cm. — (Reconsiderations in southern African history)
  Includes bibliographical references and index.
  ISBN 0–8139–1487–6 (cloth). — ISBN 0–8139–1488–4 (paper)
    1. Antisemitism—South Africa—History.   2. Jews—South Africa—
  History.
  3. South Africa—Ethnic relations.   I. Title.   II. Series.
  DS146.S6S53   1994
  305.892'4'068—dc20   93–33137
                                                                      CIP

Printed in the United States of America

The Roots of Antisemitism in
SOUTH AFRICA

RECONSIDERATIONS IN
SOUTHERN AFRICAN HISTORY
Jeffrey Butler and Richard Elphick, Editors

Milton Shain, *The Roots of Antisemitism in South Africa*

Contents

Foreword

*H*ISTORIANS, *LIKE* other mortals, are shaped by and reflect their times. In both obvious and subtle ways social and political changes affect their assumptions, outlook, choice of materials, and indeed the subject matter itself. Milton Shain's study on the foundations of anti-semitism in South Africa presents a case in point. This is the first systematic historical account of the genesis, development, and dynamics of anti-Jewish sentiment in South African political culture. It is no coincidence, perhaps, that it appears during a period in which the established South African order and its welter of underlying assumptions are being questioned (and undermined) as never before. Political transformation and the accompanying breakdown of old taboos render previously opaque structures increasingly transparent. This is a situation in which the complexity of historical inquiry thrives. Indeed, in South Africa history is presently undergoing a kind of renaissance, having over the last few years replaced a more static, preindustrial, tribal-oriented anthropology as the relevant science.

While this trend most obviously applies to the overall study of the racial dynamics of South Africa, especially the problem of the historical domination and persecution of its black population, Shain's work demonstrates its percolation to the analysis of Jews and their place within South African society. The study of any particular national antisemitism typically presents a delicate problem for resident Jewish communities whose sensitivities need to be attuned to their vulnerable minority situation. For this reason many such inquiries contain an (understandably) apologetic tinge. Within the present South African context, however, as the old order wanes and as the issue of the place of the Jew in the new, still unborn order takes on greater relevance, more critical, long-range, and less apologetic approaches to this problem become possible. This is not to say that South African antisemitism has never been properly analyzed or that it has inevitably been apologetic. It is rather to argue that Shain's work represents the first serious investigation into the deeper roots of the phenomenon and its changing functions over a sustained period of time. This study documents not only the overt political antisemitic activity of the 1930s and the early 1940s but, more concentratedly, its socioeconomic and stereotypical foundations as they took hold and developed from the last third of the nineteenth century on. Shain uncovers the varied attitudinal expressions of anti-Jewish sentiment and its discrete functions for the differentially situated English and Afrikaans communities against the backdrop of the tensions and conflicts attendant upon a rapidly industrializing economy and nationally contested polity.

Through the imaginative use of previously unmined popular sources—novels, plays, caricatures, and so on—derived from various realms of the South African experience, Shain provides us with a "thick" description of the way in which Jews were perceived within a changing political culture. Moreover, through his extensive knowledge of the wider literature on modern Jewish history and antisemitism he sheds comparative light on the more generalized experience of Jews and non-Jews undergoing the strains of modernization.

Shain's focus on the foundations and continuous dynamics of anti-semitism in a peculiarly South African context has rightfully drawn our attention to a phenomenon heretofore never fully documented or analytically assessed. Without a long period of attitudinal preparation, he argues, the organized political antisemitism of the 1930s would hardly have been possible. Yet, as his work makes abundantly clear, despite the ongoing antipathy to Jews, organized political antisemitism was more the exception than the rule. In the final analysis, it may be that neither the category of "philo" nor "anti" semitism may best fit the totality of the Jewish experience in South Africa. Structurally and experientially South African Jewry fitted into the context of a society based upon rigorous racial, ethnic, and multicommunitarian divisions and definitions. Jewish "otherness" (whether negatively or positively conceived), its "South Africaness," indeed, its very self-definition flowed from this wider social context, a reality in which otherness was a generalized, not a uniquely Jewish, property. It is precisely this reality that is today undergoing challenge. The significance of such changes for the non-white population is obvious. With regard to the question of antisemitism and the continued vitality of Jewish collective life in South Africa, as Shain points out in his conclusion, the matter remains far less clear.

Steven Aschheim

The Hebrew University of Jerusalem

Preface

ALTHOUGH SOUTH AFRICA is universally regarded as a metaphor for racism and bigotry, there has been surprisingly little scholarly focus on antisemitism in that society. Perhaps it is precisely because South Africa's race problems have assumed such overwhelming proportions that attitudes toward the Jew have received so little academic attention. South Africa, after all, has not been immune to Judeophobia or, in the parlance of late nineteenth-century Europe, "Judenhetze." In fact, the 1930s and early 1940s witnessed a popular surge of antisemitism, ensuring a prominent position for the "Jewish Question" on the public agenda. Historians examining this period have hitherto focused essentially on the impact of Nazism interacting with the social traumas being experienced by Afrikaners in the 1930s. While these factors are certainly important, they fail to explain why antisemitic ideas resonated so forcefully at the popular level and why they provided such a useful means of political mobilization for the Afrikaner right wing. This is the essential issue addressed in this study.

In the search for explanations, I have been assisted by numerous colleagues and friends. In particular, I am indebted to Edna Bradlow, who supervised the dissertation upon which this book is based. At all times she tempered my more outrageous intellectual flirtations and ensured that my feet were firmly planted on the ground. I also owe a great deal to Millie Pimstone, Harry Saker, Mohamed Adhikari, Hermann Giliomee, David Welsh, Basil le Cordeur, Bernard Steinberg, and Colin Bundy for their comments on parts of, or the whole, manuscript. In addition I am indebted to Richard Mendelsohn and Sally Frankental for enduring my ongoing intellectual probings and questions. I was also fortunate to benefit from the insights of scholars at the Hebrew University when I spent a year as a Fellow of the International Center for the Teaching of Jewish Civilization in Jerusalem. In particular I wish to thank Gideon Shimoni and Steven Aschheim for their constructive advice and encouragement. It was extremely useful for me to be able to present an outline of my dissertation to a seminar under the auspices of the Hebrew University's Vidal Sassoon International Center for the Study of Antisemitism. I benefited similarly from two seminars which I presented to the Department of History at the University of Cape Town.

Of course, in the final analysis it was my dialogue with the printed word, housed in a range of libraries in numerous cities, that enabled me to reach the conclusions presented in this study. I therefore wish to extend my sincere gratitude to the staffs of the following institutions: the Archives of the South African Jewish Board of Deputies, Johannesburg; the South African Library, Cape Town; the State Library, Pretoria; the Cape Archives, Cape Town; the State Archives, Pretoria; the Unisa newspaper library, Pretoria; the Standard Bank Archives, Johannesburg; the Manuscript Division of the Jagger Library, University of Cape Town; the Gitlin Library, Cape Town; and the Wiener Library, London. I also wish to thank my typists, Diana Prince and Anne Grant; my research assistant, Gideon Pimstone; and Marjan Hull and Biebie de Villiers, who assisted me with translations. Credit is also due to Richard Holway, Editor at the University Press of Virginia. And to Richard Elphick and Jeffrey Butler, Series Editors, for their constructive comments, concern, and support.

Lastly, I wish to acknowledge the financial assistance received from the Isaac and Jessie Kaplan Centre for Jewish Studies and Research at the University of Cape Town, the Memorial Foundation for Jewish Culture, Solm Yach and the Mauerberger Foundation, the Human Sciences Research Council, and the University of Cape Town. Needless to say, the opinions expressed and conclusions reached are those of the author and are not to be regarded as a reflection of the opinions and conclusions of these institutions or of any other person.

The Roots of Antisemitism in
SOUTH AFRICA

*To take only the subject of the Jews, it would be
difficult to find a form of bad reasoning about
them which has not been heard in conversation
or been admitted to the dignity of print.*

George Eliot

Introduction

> Anti-semitism was not a natural growth in South Africa—in view of our traditions, our traditions of a religious outlook and reverence for the Bible, of hospitality and of the love of freedom, it might have been expected that it would never get a foothold here. . . . But during the last twenty years our traditional attitude towards the Jew has been widely breached. . . . It is with the Nazis that anti-Semitism took on a particularly aggressive form, and the anti-Semitism of Nazism was an article meant for export. The seeds of this evil thing were blown over the oceans even to South Africa. The stock libel of Nazi propaganda came to be sedulously disseminated among us, sometimes skillfully adapted to our local circumstances, and anti-Semitism grew apace.
>
> —*J. Hofmeyr, Hoernlé Memorial Lecture, 1945*

*H*OFMEYR'S ARGUMENT that anti-Jewish manifestations in South Africa during the 1930s and early 1940s were an aberration, a departure from traditional patterns of interaction between Jew and Gentile, accords well with the dominant thrust of South African Jewish historiography.[1] That historiography has underplayed, if not entirely ignored, antisemitism in South African society.[2] Historians writing before the 1960s, in particular, turned a blind eye to anti-Jewish manifestations and instead lauded the pioneering decades as years during which Jews were accorded great respect and hospitality.[3]

Afrikaners especially were singled out for their kindness and courtesy toward the "people of the Book." The itinerant Jewish pedlar, or *smous,* was commonly identified as a welcome addition to society.[4] Jewish pedlars, notes Abrahams, "supplied almost all the requirements of the farming population, from agricultural implements and patent medicines to low-priced furniture and oleography." The smous, writes Saron, "brought to the isolated farmer living in semi-primitive conditions the material goods and also some of the cultural wares of civilization." For these services, it is argued, the farmer was forever grateful. Indeed, writes Abrahams, there are innumerable authenticated stories of the kindly hospitality that the Jewish smous received at the hands of the *Boerevolk* (Afrikaner people). To them the Jew, "irrespective of his occupation or appearance, was a member of the People of the Book and as such deserving of a cordial welcome." "My Joodje," writes Aschman, a historian of Oudtshoorn Jewry, was a term of endearment applied by Boers to those pedlars who had for years brought news of the "outside world," "produce markets," and "gossip from the town and the rest of the countryside." The Boer farmer, he continues, "came to rely on that information and to seek the advice of the *smous* or *makelaar* [broker] who was in touch with the world beyond the aching Swartberg range." Jan Smuts also recalled fondly the smous's visit to his father's farm. "It never entered our heads that they were any but the Lord's people of whom we read in the Bible."[5]

No doubt, by comparison with their coreligionists in eastern Europe, the newcomers did enjoy much affection and—for the white community at least—an enviable civil order. But relations with the non-Jewish majority were not without conflict. Nor indeed were perceptions of the Jew as favorable as those portrayed by historians who, eager to challenge anti-Jewish rhetoric during the relatively insecure decades after 1930, emphasized the Jewish community's contribution to South Africa and the comfortable environment within which it could exercise its talents.[6] In their standard history, for example, Saron and Hotz concentrate mainly on communal origins and the contribution of Jews to the broader society. Scant attention is devoted to conflict, and anti-Jewish outbursts in the 1930s and 1940s are characterized as a deviation from "traditional attitudes of tolerance and fairplay." In Saron's view, economic, political, ideological, and spiritual turmoil made the Afrikaner susceptible to Nazi propaganda emanating from South West Africa.[7]

Thus, in its early phase South African Jewish historiography sought to minimize conflict and maximize accommodation between Jew and Gentile. Since the 1960s, however, a new generation of historians, professionally trained and perhaps more comfortable with their South African (and Jewish) identity, has begun to focus on conflict between Jew and non-Jew. Michael Cohen has examined the wide-ranging nature of antisemitism in the 1930s; Edna Bradlow, the measures to restrict the entry of Jews into the Union; and Gideon Shimoni—albeit obliquely—the precarious nature of Jewish well-being in South Africa. A previous study by the present writer focused on antisemitism in the Cape Colony and its impact on Jewish communal organization.[8]

The new historiography has neither denied nor ignored the many instances of hospitality accorded Jews in South Africa and the manifold ways in which Jews have been accommodated within and have benefited from the South African body politic.[9] It has, however, provided an important and a necessary antidote to what one might call the "accommodationist" or "hospitality" school of South African Jewish historiography. Nevertheless, the new historiography continues to depict antisemitism in the 1930s and early 1940s as essentially an alien phenomenon, a product of Nazi propaganda at a time of great social and economic trauma. Shimoni, for instance, while more nuanced and certainly more ambivalent in his description of Jewish-Gentile relations, still seeks an explanation for anti-Jewish outbursts within the Afrikaner's existential condition and his receptivity to Nazi propaganda. Acute race consciousness, anti-British sentiment, disillusionment with British parliamentarianism, frustrations with industrialization, and a vague sense of racial affinity with the Germans are all forwarded by Shimoni as factors facilitating the Afrikaner's receptivity to Nazi ideology. A fundamentalist Calvinism, moreover, predisposed him to Christian-rooted prejudice. However, this prejudice was operative only in the urban context. In the rural setting, argues Shimoni, Calvinism encouraged a sense of "fellow feeling" with the descendants of the "Biblical children of Israel."[10]

Recent studies have thus uncovered conflict between Jew and Gentile. Indeed, a new book by Furlong on the Afrikaner radical right during the fascist era devotes substantial attention to antisemitism and demonstrates unequivocally its importance in the Afrikaner's weltanschauung in the 1930s and 1940s. However, in line with Shimoni and other historians referred to above, Furlong fails to explore the roots of South African antisemitism and explains anti-Jewish outbursts purely in terms of circumstances peculiar to the era: political confusion, increased Jewish immigration, and Nazi propaganda.[11] Nonetheless, the overstretched canvas of Gentile hospitality has been breached, and it is now acknowledged that South Africa did have a "Jewish Problem." In accounting for this problem, however, historians have sought explanations only within the confines and contingencies of the 1930s and early 1940s.

This study argues that antisemitism was an important element in South African society long before 1930 and that anti-Jewish manifestations were related to a consistent and widely shared Jewish stereotype, the roots of which were deeply embedded in the South African experience. That is to say, while South Africa may not have experienced organized antisemitism before the 1930s, it was not free of anti-Jewish sentiment and ideas.[12] A study of these ideas as manifest in the Jewish stereotype is pertinent and, as argued in this book, essential for an understanding of the later period.

The stereotype, therefore, was both a barometer and facilitator of prejudice; it prepared the way for the growth and dissemination of antisemitism. The rhetoric of the 1930s cannot be divorced from deeply entrenched negative images of the Jew that had undergone a long maturation process. An initially ambivalent image had, by the 1920s, become overwhelmingly negative.

The reasons for this transformation will be explained in subsequent chapters as will widespread support across language and party divides for legislation in 1930 that curtailed the influx of eastern European immigration. "The Bill will commend itself to most citizens of the Union and has not been introduced a day too soon," noted an editorial (which perhaps best captured the public mood) in the *East London Daily Dispatch*. Irrespective of political party, claimed *Die Burger,* the overwhelming majority of South Africans supported the legislation. In the opinion of the *Sunday Times,* the newcomers were "ignorant people of the peasant class who have neither the ability nor the experience necessary to make a living." The *Cape* reminded its readers that the Dutch and English were the real pioneers, and they had "a right to say whom they would have as fellow citizens." According to this weekly, there were too many traders and too few producers. Eastern Europeans, moreover, had a considerably different commercial morality. In similar fashion the *Daily Representative* applauded the government for taking "a firm stand in the matter, for a young and growing country cannot afford to allow itself to be used as a dumping ground for immigrants from Southern and Eastern Europe." Even those who recognized and appreciated Jewry's role in the development of South Africa supported the legislation. Clearly it would be a blatant denial of contemporary evidence to maintain that eastern Europeans (and virtually all were Jews) were perceived as a welcome acquisition to society, notwithstanding their often-acclaimed contributions.[13]

By examining perceptions of the Jew in South Africa from the late nineteenth century to 1930, this book attempts to explain the apparent contradiction between the many instances of support for the Jew (and praise for his contribution), on the one hand, and immigration legislation in 1930 curtailing his entry into the Union on the other. The relationship between popular Jewish stereotyping before 1930 and anti-Jewish outbursts in the 1930s and 1940s is also considered.

I shall examine only the perceptions of the white population. Anti-Jewish outbursts and movements belong exclusively to the realm of white parliamentary and extraparliamentary politics. The majority black population—including Coloreds and Indians—has never focused specifically on the Jew when articulating grievances and aspirations. For them the issue has always been one of white oppression and domination. Insofar as we know something of black attitudes toward the Jew—and evidence for the late nineteenth and early twentieth centuries is scant—these are dealt with in the concluding chapter.

Besides being concerned with only white perceptions of the Jew, comment focuses on the male stereotype—a reflection of sexist assumptions of the day. The reader will also note that extensive use has been made of direct quotation from the sources. Paraphrasing often dilutes the sentiments, tone, and temper of the times. In addition, the reader should appreciate that, although opinions about and attitudes toward the Jew are inferred by and large from the literate middle classes, it is reasonable to assume that the sources used do not seriously distort popular views.

Images and Stereotypes

In his study of the emergence and dissemination of the modern Jewish stereotype, Isaiah Schachar defines images as "single words and images which spring associatively to mind whenever the relevant subject is mentioned." In this work *image* refers to a broader and more elaborate construct. The "single words and images which spring associatively to mind" are pertinent, but only partly so. Here we attempt to delve deeper and to examine that complex mental construct (or set of images) underpinning what Lippmann has referred to as those "pictures in our heads." When such a construct is widely shared in society we refer to it as a stereotype.[14]

Identifying and conceptualizing an image or stereotype is a task fraught with methodological problems. With the range of sources virtually unlimited and the danger of preconceptions inherently acute, the selection and organization of material assumes a critical importance.

Preconceptions or preconceived paradigms must not determine the final synthesis. How then does the historian gauge a popular or conventional image?

Images are inferred from a range of published and unpublished comment. This includes ideological pronouncements, opinions, attitudes, cartoons, letters, literature, theater, and so forth. The process of inference is problematic. Comments are often less important for the ideas expressed than for the purposes intended or served. The historian, for instance, should remember that those commenting were involved in contemporary social issues. The encomiums showered upon Jews by Lord Alfred Milner on the occasion of the formation of the Transvaal Jewish Board of Deputies, for example, tell us more about Milner's desire to settle the Transvaal with pro-British white immigrants than his perceptions of the Jew, particularly those from eastern Europe. Similarly, those praising Jews for their enterprise and thrift may well have appropriated them as exemplars of bourgeois values, desirable in an age of reconstruction. In short, the historian must enter into what Winthrop Jordan calls a "reciprocal relationship" with the sources, to approach these "with mind and eyes open" and to ensure that the "thoughts and feelings of their authors" are fairly reflected.[15]

Adhering to Jordan's precepts for a period spanning more than six decades is no easy task. Fortunately, the sensitive antennae of the Jewish press reveal clearly the crisis periods in Jewish-Gentile relations.[16] For example, comment in the Jewish press during the Rand Rebellion of 1922 indicates a concern by Jews that as a group they were associated with Bolshevism. Formal Jewish responses, contemporary newspaper comment, periodicals, cartoons, parliamentary speeches, commissions of inquiry, and private papers reveal the extent to which Jews were associated in the popular mind with Bolshevism. Legislation, and perhaps more importantly, responses to legislation serve to confirm or undermine general impressions. As noted above, responses to the 1930 Quota Act affirmed a pervasive anti-Jewish stereotype. In essence, then, one gauges the stereotype by investigating in depth as wide a range of sources as possible.

The image of the Jew as it relates to the legacy of European history and its intellectual traditions cannot be ignored. White South Africans, after all, are among the heirs to those traditions. And, of course, the period dealt with in this study was an age of increasing literacy, improved communications, and large population migrations, specifically between Britain and South Africa. The penetration of European ideas (including the deeply rooted anti-Jewish stereotype) was inevitable. Moreover, "a vaguely racial definition of Jewishness" ensured that those traits traditionally associated with Jews would be ascribed to their coreligionists in South Africa. One has, therefore, continually to bear in mind the possible impact of external ideologies. For example, eugenicist notions (as shown later) have influenced South African perceptions of the Jew.[17]

However, notwithstanding outside influences, the image of the Jew in South Africa must be placed within the context of South Africa's own historical reality and intellectual traditions.[18] Throughout this study I have attempted to characterize essential South African worldviews and to understand their changes through time. Perceptions of the Jew, in other words, have been related to the entire social system, including patterns of South African public life. Those equating Jews with Bolshevism, for instance, were doing more than labeling. A significant influx of eastern European Jews had occurred in South Africa after the First World War and many had settled on the Witwatersrand. Their alien appearance could readily be associated with an alien ideology. But this was not the only reason for equating Jews with Bolshevism. I have argued that the presence of Jews enabled a threatening ideology to be personified, captured, and deflected. The association of Jews with Bolshevism was a way of dealing with ideological conflict and opposition. At this level, then, focusing upon the Jew was a means of furthering political and ideological interests. Of course, it was only possible to use the Jew because he had earlier been perceived as the archetypical subversive or outsider.

In addition to their function in contemporary ideological struggles, these stereotypes should also be understood at the psychological level. They serve to interpret the world and fulfill a psychological function. The poor white farmer, for instance, seeking an explanation for his plight, could easily blame the visibly alien Jewish creditor or supplier. Here was a readily available symbol of change and upheaval. In this sense stereotypes have, as Banton puts it, "critical emotional significance for those who hold them and they fit together in a twisted but ordered pattern of social relations."[19]

Thus stereotypes are complex constructs relating both to the individual's psychological needs and to the wider polity. Rooted as they are in a social reality, they possess, moreover, what social scientists refer to as "a kernel of truth." This study makes no attempt to confirm or deny their validity. Nor does it wish to categorize individuals commenting about Jews as either philo- or antisemitic, despite the blatant antisemitism of some commentators. The complex nature of the human psyche precludes such a simple correlation. As Peter Gay reminds us, the nineteenth-century German novelist Gustav Freytag depicted the Jews as villainous in his *Soll und Haben* and yet only a few years later repudiated Richard Wagner's antisemitism. Gay correctly points out that it would be absurd to single out the "anti- or philosemitic strand" constituting the real Freytag. This study heeds Gay's warnings and passes no judgment upon individuals. Its aims are more modest. It attempts to outline images of the Jew in South Africa from the late nineteenth century to 1930, to contextualize these images, and to explain their formation. By illustrating the evolution and maturation of the stereotype, the inextricable relationship between popular Jewish stereotyping and anti-Jewish manifestations and movements in the 1930s and early 1940s is demonstrated. Antisemitism in South Africa rested upon firm and solid foundations embodied in the Jewish stereotype.[20]

CHAPTER ONE

Gentlemen and Knaves: The Ambivalent Image, Beginnings to 1885

Fulfilling the Emancipation Contract

*A*LTHOUGH JEWS were among the early explorers who circumnavigated the Cape of Storms, they and other non-Protestants were denied the right to settle at the Cape during the rule of the Dutch East India Company (1652–1795). This practice was abrogated under the relatively enlightened Batavian administration (1803–6) and maintained thereafter by their administrative heirs, the British, in 1806. A handful of Jews, mainly of English and Dutch origin, availed themselves of the new circumstances. The majority settled in Cape Town, although a contingent of seventeen among the 1820 Settlers located themselves in the eastern Cape. Within a few years most of these settlers had gravitated toward Grahamstown, an eastern Cape military and trading center.[1]

Without formal structures, meager in number, and outwardly assimilated, the Jewish settlers made little impact on the popular consciousness. Such observers as the American missionary George Champion and the German naturalist Ferdinand Krauss failed to mention Jews when commenting on the variety of groups and sects found in Cape Town in the 1830s. Such oversights were hardly possible following the establishment of the Cape Town Hebrew Congregation in 1841. Seven years after the congregation's formation, its moving spirit, Benjamin Norden, welcomed—specifically on behalf of the Jewish community—the triumphant Cape governor, Sir Harry Smith, on his return from the Battle of Boomplaats.[2]

The exchange of pleasantries on that occasion reflected both the

Jewish community's good standing and the tolerant and liberal ethos of Cape society. All religious denominations, noted the governor, were "equally valid" and Jewish interests were "as blended with the people at large, for whether a man is a Jew or a Christian, he is equally protected by the law, and I believe equally acceptable in the eyes of God." Smith's sentiments succinctly reflect classical nineteenth-century British liberalism, rooted as it was in respect and admiration for the Judeo-Christian tradition.[3]

Prejudice, bigotry, and anti-Jewish sentiment were, of course, not entirely absent from the settlers' cultural baggage. For instance, even before the arrival of Jews, the English explorer John Barrow described a certain exploitative element in the South African hinterland as "a kind of Jew broker defrauding the simple boors," while Charles Boniface, a Cape Town belles lettrist, referred in 1834 to his rival—the misshapen apostate Jew, Joseph Suasso de Lima—as a "Joodse Dwergje" (Jewish dwarf).[4] The power of latent antisemitism emerging at times of stress was even more evident in the "Neptune affair" of 1849. In this instance, Benjamin Norden's contravention of a pledge not to service the convict ship *Neptune* resulted in the stigmatization of the entire Jewish community. In fact, accusations were so serious that the president of the Cape Town Hebrew Congregation, S. Rodolf, found it necessary to state

> that no member of the Jewish persuasion with the exception of those already known have acted against the wishes of the people of this Colony, nor have been implicated in any way whatsoever to thwart any steps taken against the introduction of convicts. Though some malignant persona, out of men [*sic*] malice, are exciting the public mind to condemn a whole community for the unworthy act of one or two, for conclusion I beg to say on behalf of the Jewish community, that they are grateful to their Christian brethren for the benevolence shown towards them in contributing so liberally in their cause.[5]

Even though the synagogue was placed under police protection during the High Festivals of 1849 and Norden was the victim of riotous behavior, the tarnishing of relations between Jew and Gentile was short-lived. Sir Harry Smith immediately condemned the unruly behavior and prohibited large meetings. Jews, in fact, continued to be welcome. In the 1850s A. J. van der Walt of Middelburg in the Cape Colony advocated the establishment of a Jewish and German colony in the Free State. The proposal was not taken up but its sentiments are indicative of a favorable image of the Jew. Certainly there were many instances of goodwill between Jew and Gentile. For example, financial support from the non-Jewish community in the building of synagogues was often forthcoming as was support for distress calls and the plight of Russian Jewry. Jews and Gentiles, then, enjoyed amiable contact that included substantial social intercourse. Governor Frere's presence at the wedding of the Reverend Rabinowitz's daughter, Rose, was symptomatic of a sound relationship.[6]

In all likelihood Jews were generally perceived in much the same way as were their coreligionists in mid-Victorian England. While that image included some negatively charged dimensions, it was on the whole benign. Certainly the 170 Jews in Cape Town in 1855 and the increasing number of Jewish traders in the southern and eastern Cape thrived in a society that separated church and state. An act of 1860 empowering the government to appoint Jews as marriage officers and another act eight years later proscribing any differentiation or penalties on account of religious belief were further indications of tolerance and goodwill.[7]

This tolerance survived the initial influx of Jewish fortune-seekers following the discovery of diamonds in 1869. Indeed, despite the historian James Froude observing among the diggers, "a hundred or so keen-eyed Jewish merchants . . . gathering like eagles over their prey," the image of the Jew in the 1870s remained overwhelmingly favorable.[8] This was evident in Governor Barkly's generous and philosemitic speech when he laid the foundation stone of Kimberley's new synagogue in 1875:

> None I am well aware more thoroughly and sincerely participate in the feelings of whole hearted loyalty which is characteristic of the British nation than Her Majesty's subjects of Jewish lineage and faith. I have had opportunities of becoming acquainted with them as a body obedient to the law, ready to take their part on all occasions as good citizens and to cooperate in works of benevolence and mercy. In Griqualand West, especially it has happened, from the first, that some of the most energetic and enterprising members of society have been Jewish.[9]

By the time of Barkly's speech, Jews comprised a mere fraction of South Africa's white population. The majority resided in the Cape Colony where they made up a paltry 0.23 percent of the entire white population. Cape Town (169), Port Elizabeth (123), Graaff-Reinet (36),

Grahamstown (25), and Victoria West (22) were the only centers in the Colony with significant concentrations of Jews. Kimberley (at that time not part of the colony) had approximately 120 Jews. A handful of Jews resided in the South African Republic, Natal, and the Orange Free State.[10]

Most South African Jews were of Anglo-German origin. They were acculturated (modeling themselves on the British), bourgeois, and, by and large, well ensconced in Cape and Orange Free State society. As Lady Duff Gordon, a visitor to the Cape noted in 1860, they had "abandoned the peculiarities of their tradition if not the features of their race." The Jewish community, in other words, reflected the lifestyle and communal patterns of their "enlightened" coreligionists in western Europe. Religion was a private matter and primary allegiance was accorded to the state. The community, moreover, personified the values and norms dearest to nineteenth-century English liberals: loyalty, obedience, civic virtue, charitableness, and, above all, enterprise. In the words of Bill Williams (writing about Mancunian Jewry of the 1870s), the Jewish vanguard had "fulfilled their commitments" to the "emancipation contract."[11]

Fortune-Seekers and Knaves

Pogroms in Russia that followed the assassination of Tsar Alexander II in 1881 sparked an influx of Jewish immigration. Waves of newcomers—the overwhelming majority from Lithuania—sought security and opportunity in South Africa, its attraction further enhanced by the discovery of gold on the Witwatersrand in 1886. The new arrivals differed from the Anglo-German vanguard in speech, manner, religious customs, and even dress. A relatively homogeneous community was transformed into a motley combination of cultures bound by a common religious heritage.[12]

Many of the newcomers settled in Kimberley where, by the late 1870s, Jews had attained prominence in commercial and financial affairs. By October 1881 the *Diamond News* was writing of a Sunday atmosphere in Kimberley on the Jewish Day of Atonement: "All the houses of business were closed and the diamond market was deserted, a proof of how strong a hold the Jewish people had succeeded in establishing in Kimberley."[13] Certainly names of Jews such as Lewis, Marks, Beit, and Barnato had become synonymous with entrepreneurial skill and success. Of course, few Jews were as successful and many were casualties of Kimberley's 1881 financial collapse. The early 1880s, marked by straitened economic conditions, were not a propitious time for the influx of more fortune-seekers and refugees. In a competitive and economically depressed climate, it was not long before the new arrivals attracted the type of opprobrium evident in the comments of Lewis Michell, general manager of the Standard Bank: "The departure of hordes of hook-nosed Polish and Lithuanian Jews whose evil countenances now peer from every little shanty and cigar divan would be a distinct gain to the community. Under cover of keeping a 'winkel' [shop] they at present flock to Kimberley from afar, like as-vogels [vultures] to a dead ox, and their villainous faces enable one easily to understand the depth of hatred borne to them in Russia and elsewhere."[14]

One specific dimension of the stereotype that evolved in Kimberley and would persist for decades was the association of Jews with illicit diamond dealing. As Turrell notes in his study of early Kimberley: "If Africans were labelled diamond thieves by mineowners, 'Cape Boys' and Jews were most commonly associated with illicit dealing." These generalizations are corroborated in contemporary fiction as well as in memoirs, satire, and cartoons.[15]

Many of the eastern European newcomers avoided Kimberley or other urban centers and instead chose to settle in the mushrooming hamlets of the hinterland. These isolated towns were not unlike the villages of Lithuania and Poland where Jews had for centuries functioned as middlemen between the landed aristocracy and the peasantry. In the new South African setting, their presence as shopkeepers and itinerant traders was keenly noted, particularly since their arrival coincided with the disruption of traditional agrarian life and the emergence of the "poor white" problem.

Although the emergence of the poor white problem is usually associated with the late nineteenth century, already in the 1860s a severe economic downturn had ruined many farmers in the eastern Cape, substantially eroding white living standards in that region. There are indications that merchants were identified as at least partly responsible for impoverishment. Certainly the smous, a traditionally welcome asset to the rural economy, appears to have lost favor. In 1865 the *Burghersdorp Chronicle* characterized him as only marginally superior to the *meester* (itinerant teacher), described by this newspaper as "the very lowest occupation an unfortunate wretch can apply himself to."[16]

Bearing in mind the fact that the smous was not necessarily Jewish at this time, this statement cannot be accepted as irrefutable evidence that perceptions of the Jewish trader had taken a turn for the worse. Nevertheless, there are indications that Jews were beginning to be disparaged. For instance, in 1873 the travel writer Frederick Boyle reported the Cape to be "a great hunting ground for the [Hebrew] tribes. They fatten on its heavy, credulous boers, especially the German variety." In similar vein the *Era* of Richmond suggested in 1875 that "Israelitish Boereverneukers" (Jewish swindlers of farmers) tried to persuade farmers not to improve their properties but simply to confine themselves to sheep rearing. A few years later English and Jewish shopkeepers were accused in the Dutch press of influencing elections in favor of English candidates through their hold on country commerce. Clearly the rural trader represented—at least for some—the vagaries of commerce and, as shown below, the binding power of credit.[17]

As alien traders became more prominent in the 1880s, the voices of protest grew louder. This was a period of severe economic distress following drought on the frontier and a slump in both the wool and diamond trades. In these conditions observers were quick to note the burgeoning Jewish presence. That this was not always a welcome one is evident in a *Uitenhage Times* editorial following a complaint by "Afrikander" to the *Tarka Herald,* a rural eastern Cape newspaper. "Afrikander" had deplored the imprisonment of an English clergyman, the Reverend B. B. Kett, for a debt owed to a firm of Kimberley auctioneers, Rothschild Brothers:

> We don't know the Rev. Kett, nor have we the least idea who "Afrikander" may be, but we have met many Shylocks in our time of the tribe of Benjamin, and we can fully sympathize with the English clergyman and his Afrikander defender. These are the kind of Afrikanders we want in the Colony; if we had more like the Tarkastad "Afrikander" and few Hebrews of the Rothschild type, the Colony would be better off than it is. It is a fact which few will be found to state publicly—but none the less true for that—that the Jewish race has been one of the greatest curses to South Africa. Of course we know that there are Jews and Jews, and that some of the Yeddin are generous and straightforward, and far more generous than most Christians, but they are the very infinitissmal [*sic*] minority. . . . If a few of those slightly bloodthirsty peasants could be imported . . . from South Russia, they would have gay times in Kimberley and the

neighbouring villages—and the Jews wouldn't. All Houndsditch, Petticoat Lane—Pilomet as the people called it—and Seven Dials rolled into one could not produce such an aggregate of knavery and vice as the Hebrew fraternity of the Fields exhibit. The Afrikander Bond should, as the old Kimberley song has it—"Bar the Jews."[18]

Besides reflecting an obvious knowledge of conditions in London and Russia, the diatribe openly reflected a growing antagonism toward Jews in the rural areas where they were believed to be responsible for economic hardship. The comments in the *Uitenhage Times* also indicate the ease of transmission of ideas, in this case between London, the diamond fields, and the South African hinterland.

One observer who certainly noted the Jewish presence was Martin James Boon, an expatriate Englishman. Together with Germans and Hollanders, Boon ensconced Jews in his pantheon of hate. His invective displays notions of social Darwinism and Anglo-Saxon superiority but little is known of the man himself, apart from his arrival in 1874. Eastern European Jews, whom he accused of having driven the Dutch (Boers) from their land "by craft," obviously made a marked impression upon this inveterate racist:

> In the early days in almost all the villages the only storekeepers were Polish Jews and German or Dutch Hollander men, who prided themselves on their ability to cheat with impunity the real Dutch families of their neighbourhoods, and who, to continue their position, did all in their power to make the name of Englishmen hateful in the eyes of the farmer, and while stating what the English would do, took great care to make the farmers their dupes and their victims, driving them by craft from their lands. Thus it happens that so many German-Jew storekeepers have the lands of the Colony, Free State, and the Transvaal in their possession. The Boers, like the English farmers have no faith in towns.[19]

Jewish traders—or as Boon referred to them, "'vaatch' vendors"— allegedly overcharged the Dutch and then begged "shamelessly." He was, however, pleased to note that the Dutch were beginning to recognize "that under the sneaking 'ferneuking' [swindling] Jew, German and Hollander, they are in the hands of Shylocks, and that in having their pound of flesh, they lose their farms and that the Hebrews were their masters."[20]

Besides maligning Jews in the hinterland, Boon also identified Jews as the villains of Kimberley. The "sons of Israel" had made fortunes on the fields and nothing, he contended, was beyond their shrewd and cunning ways: "During the night I passed the celebrated Lakers Kraal Diamond Fields, the last speculative effort of the Jews. Owned by a Jew, who by concession had Jewed a Boer out of it, in trading on their usual cent per cent style, it was conceived as a master-stroke by another Lev-us-see-her of the capital who was the head of the Abramic Order of the Hebrews in Bloemfontein, due to the fact that he had been the most successful manipulator of the Boers."

In one passage Boon describes how Jews had fraudulently claimed that "the largest diamond yet" had been found at Jagersfontein in the Free State. This, of course, was just another devious move by the "illicits of Kimberley."[21]

Boon's comments, although unusually flagrant, were not unique. Even a *Cape Punch* satire managed to blacken the Jew when jocularly identifying a range of thoughts held by Dutch farmers at the time: "All Jews to be banished. A Jew or 'Boereverneuker' may always be known to a farmer by the shape of his nose, by the many rings on his fingers, and by the tongue being too large for his mouth. Avoid such. The Bible says they are a stiff-necked and perverse generation."[22]

In a more serious vein, *De Zuid Afrikaan* alluded to Jewish power in the Transvaal and the Jew's money-grubbing ways.[23] Clearly the substantial involvement of Jews in speculation and trade on the diamond fields and in the hinterland had aroused the resentment of both Afrikaner and Englishman. Antagonism was of course exacerbated by the influx of unmistakably alien Jews from eastern Europe who were also frowned upon by the Anglo-German Jewish establishment.[24] It would, however, be historically inaccurate and misleading to see the negative Jewish stereotype simply as a product of the eastern European influx.[25] After all, we have seen how the role of certain Jews in the *Neptune* affair led to aspersions being cast upon the Anglo-German Jewish community. Similarly, Boyle commented unfavorably on "Hebrew tribes" in the early 1870s and Boon castigated "German-Jew storekeepers." Moreover, when the *Lantern* suggested in 1880 that the increase of burglaries across the country may have been a product of the influx of the "Children of Judah," it too could not have had only eastern European Jews in mind.[26] And, of course, the association of Jews with illicit diamond buying was not limited to Jews from eastern Europe.

Reconciling Contradictions

Despite the emergence of an unflattering and invidious Jewish stereo-type in the early 1880s, favorable attitudes toward the Anglo-German Jewish establishment continued to be manifest. Gentiles still contrib-uted liberally to Jewish charities, and a number of Jews enjoyed promi-nence in public life.[27] Discrimination on religious grounds clearly re-mained unacceptable. Indeed, at the very time antagonism toward eastern European Jews was mounting, the *Cape Times* published a powerful editorial condemning pogroms in Russia. These disgraceful acts, it noted, had been wrought "on a people guiltless of anything but a difference of race and religion."[28] While primarily concerned to portray Russia as a bulwark of reaction, the *Cape Times* sentiments reflected those liberal British values alluded to earlier. It was that ethos which underpinned spirited praise of the Reverend Joel Rabinowitz on his departure from Cape Town in 1882, after twenty-three years' service to the Cape Town Hebrew Congregation. Prominent Capetonians pub-licly lauded Rabinowitz for his "zealous and effective services" to "the poor, the suffering and the down trodden." Rabinowitz's successor, the Reverend A. F. Ornstien, was fully justified in proclaiming, during a New Year sermon in 1883, that Jews in South Africa enjoyed the "free-dom to make an honest livelihood, undisturbed by the persecutions to which their race was being exposed in the other parts of the world." Ornstien expressed similar views five years later when he laid the foun-dation stone of the Oudtshoorn synagogue: "The Jew and his Christian neighbour," he told the gathering of between 400 and 500 persons, "worked together in harmony."[29] This happy position for the Jews was almost certainly helped by the multiethnic and multireligious character of Cape society. Jews, in other words, were not the only minority or sole nonconformists.

By the 1880s one notices that two embryonic but nevertheless dis-tinctive images of the Jew in South Africa had emerged: the gen-tleman—characterized by sobriety, enterprise, and loyalty, and the knave—characterized by dishonesty and cunning.[30] These contradic-tory perceptions were easily reconciled in class terms, the lower class fortune-seekers and the newcomers from eastern Europe providing the negative polarity. This view was best captured by the *Uitenhage Times* following a complaint by a Jewish Town Councillor in Port Elizabeth,

J. Marks, about its anti-Jewish diatribe (quoted earlier) in support of "Afrikander."[31] The editor made it clear that his newspaper "had no intention whatever of ruffling the feelings of respectable Jews by a generic condemnation of their race." It was, he pointed out, a "certain class" of Jew that concerned him, "those who are mixed up with illicit diamond traffic on the Fields." Those who doubted the editor were recommended to look at IDB (illicit diamond buying) trial statistics or go to the Cape Town breakwater. However, the editor was adamant that not all Jews were alike. "What we did and do mean to convey is this—that the lower class of Jews in Kimberley are not profitable to the country or to their neighbours, and that if they could be exported the moral atmosphere of the camps would be much improved, the honest men would have a much better chance of making a living." He concluded his response to Marks by asking his ostrich-farming readers their opinion of smouses who visited their farms periodically. "We are constantly hearing complaints," he noted, "that feathers disappear mysteriously from birds and many farmers say the *smouses* are simply an itinerant market for stolen feathers."[32]

Antagonism toward Jews, then, was not articulated in racial or biological terms.[33] Jews, in other words, were not ascribed inherent or immutable characteristics. On the contrary, in line with nineteenth-century Victorian or Whiggish assumptions, it was anticipated that lower-class Jews would emulate their acculturated and bourgeois coreligionists. Freedom and opportunity would ensure this. These expectations echoed the optimism and hopes of eighteenth-century European emancipationists like Christian Wilhelm Dohm and Abbé Gregoire, both of whom advocated Jewish emancipation in anticipation of assimilation.[34] These hopes would be sorely tested as the eastern European influx gained momentum.

CHAPTER TWO

Pedlars, Peruvians, and Plutocrats, 1886–1902

"Where the carcass is, there shall the eagles be gathered together," and where speculation is rife, and carries in its train the digging up of diamonds, or the production of gold, the Hebrew, with his quick wits and wonderful faculty for using them, comes to the forefront and claims and secures success. They are everywhere in Johannesburg. In the share market, keeping hotels, auctioneering, running cafes, owners of stores, brokers, theatre proprietors, and bar keepers, we meet with the descendants of Moses and Aaron.

—*Charles H. Du-Val, "All the World Around"*

Early Days in the Transvaal

THE CENTER of Jewish life moved to the Witwatersrand following the discovery of gold in 1886. Indeed, having visited the Witwatersrand in 1895, the noted English parliamentarian and historian James Bryce referred to Johannesburg as an "Anglo-Semitic town"[1]—an observation no doubt based upon the substantial number of Jews among the financial elite and the inclination of Jews, who constituted approximately 6 percent of the total white population in 1896, to congregate in specific areas of the city.[2] Of the more than 6,000 Jews in 1896, about half were of Russian origin.[3] Whereas many of the Jewish settlers who came in the 1880s were able to penetrate the crusty layers of competition, those who arrived in the 1890s found fewer economic opportunities.

Inevitably, Jews attracted comment, both favorable and unfavorable.[4] Perceptions were, of course, influenced by cultural stereotypes brought to the Witwatersrand, including negative and positive images nurtured on the diamond fields and in the southern and eastern Cape. However, they were also influenced by conservative and deeply insular views that characterized the Boer population who constituted the majority of whites in the South African Republic. These views, a legacy of the Cape's slave society and long isolation, were underpinned by a strong Protestant tradition that informed the values, norms, and institutions of society.[5] Indeed, the *Grondwet* (constitution) of the South African Republic bound the Dutch Reformed Church inextricably to the state.[6] Thus non-Protestants were without the franchise and unable to hold public office. More specifically, Jews and Catholics were precluded from holding military posts, and from the offices of president, state secretary, and magistrate. Nor could they become members of the first or second *Volksraad* (National Council) or superintendents of natives or of mines. In addition, Jewish children were not permitted to attend government schools, and government subsidies were granted only to Protestant schools that were conducted in the Dutch language.[7] In effect the constitution reflected a determined resolve on the part of the Boers to maintain a hard-won independence and to keep control of the country and its morals.[8]

Notwithstanding the exclusive nature of the constitution, Jews in practice enjoyed cordial relations with the state and even held positions within its machinery. Johannesburg's onetime rabbi, Dr. Joseph Hertz, was correct when he recalled, some years after he left the Transvaal, that discriminatory laws had been treated as a "dead letter." He was referring to the myriad of articles in the constitution that discriminated against non-Protestants and not to the fundamentally discriminatory nature of the constitution in which Jews (and Catholics) were clearly second-class citizens. This policy, however, was not motivated by antisemitic intent but was rooted in the Boer's desire for sovereignty. In fact, at the time the constitution was drafted, non-Protestants were hardly a visible presence.[9]

The reluctance of Boer leaders to change the constitution, despite substantial pressure, was similarly motivated by mistrust—a product of the *Uitlander* (foreigner) problem—and not by anti-Jewish sentiment. The government, in fact, went out of its way to extol Jewish virtues. For instance, at the opening of the Johannesburg Synagogue in 1892, President Paul Kruger made it clear that he respected "the Jewish and other faiths without distinction" and that Jews would "attain civil rights if they proved their trustworthiness." On the same occasion, a very favorable picture of Jews was portrayed by other prominent Boer leaders. Smuts, for instance, reminded the gathering—in an obviously underhanded jab at the British—that Jews had never annexed the Transvaal nor robbed the country. They were, moreover, trustworthy, paying the treasury all they owed, dutiful, law abiding and "faithful subjects of the state." Dr. W. Leyds, the Transvaal state secretary, acclaimed the manner in which his mother country, Holland, had treated the Jews and suggested that people should appreciate Jewish virtues rather than concentrate on their vices only. Another speaker, J. F. Cilliers, Johannesburg representative on the Volksraad, advocated expunging the distinction between Jew and Gentile.[10]

It would seem, then, that the early Jewish settlers in the Transvaal made a favorable impression upon the administration. Kruger gave generously to Jewish charities and even courted publicly two prominent Jewish entrepreneurs, Sammy Marks and Isaac Lewis. It was, ironically, his flirtation with "foreigners" (mainly Hollanders) that generated antagonism toward his administration during the early 1890s. That antagonism was spearheaded by Kruger's arch political rival, Piet Joubert, and Eugene Marais, editor of the Dutch-language weekly *Land en Volk*. For these two, Kruger's predilection for Hollanders and Jews was tantamount to treason; that he courted Jewish capitalists to boot was an even greater crime.[11]

Consequently an anti-Jewish tone was evident in *Land en Volk* from as early as 1889. In that year the newspaper expressed dismay that the Kruger administration had helped to finance a Jewish-run Pretoria newspaper, the *Press*. "We would have thought," complained *Land en Volk*, "that the President of the Republic had already had enough experience in the past about the sons of Israel by who *The Press* was called into life." Kruger was warned that "every rightminded and patriotic burger will not envy his choice if he made *The Press* an organ to ventilate his grievances and interests." "Show me a man's friends," proclaimed *Land en Volk*, "and I will tell you who he is."[12]

By using the voteless and essentially irrelevant Jew to mobilize opposition to the Kruger regime, *Land en Volk* was exploiting a deep-seated Boer xenophobia. Such fears were again aroused during the presidential campaign of 1891. A prominent Transvaler, "Afrikanus Junior," for instance, denounced the president in an open letter for "surrounding himself with speculating Jews and Hollanders and granting them concessions." One week later the same correspondent was more specific: "At your right hand stands Nellmapius, at your left Lippert, behind you Ekstein, Sammy Marks and a whole gallery of Jews. And if I speak to you, Leyds answers me, because he stands for you. Fine company indeed for the President of the South African Republic. . . . The Hollanders rule us and the Jews rule the Hollanders." *Land en Volk* supported these views for patently political reasons, arguing that the president was to be rejected because he preferred Hollanders and Jews "who encircle him like vultures, to loyal sons of the soil."[13]

Quite evidently, Jews and Hollanders were easily exploitable for political purposes. As *Land en Volk* put it on 5 May 1891, they were "dronkaards en modernes" (drunks and modernists). Only the Boer, rooted in the soil, was worthy of praise. One week later, in an approving reference to aspirant presidential candidate P. Joubert, it thanked God that "we have some honest and upright Afrikaners who will withstand Kruger and his Jews." In what one historian of the South African Republic, Gordon, refers to as a fairly typical letter to Joubert, J. D. Bosman, of Krugersdorp, similarly thanked God that the general was "independent of the President, the Hollanders and the Jews." It is therefore no surprise that Joubert threatened to "do all in his power to counteract the Hebraic influence that is making itself felt in this land."[14]

Strangling the Farmer

This "Hebraic" influence was also very evident in the northern, southern, and eastern Cape by the 1890s. There, the prominence of the Jewish smous and shopkeeper was increasingly commented upon. Although some saw the smous as a figure of fun or ridicule, many saw him as a scheming and cunning threat. "Always on the make and ready to turn his head to anything (except, of course, hard work) to earn an honest penny—when he could do it any other way, or make it more," was the way one contemporary, Oliver Osborne, described him. Like Boon and many others, Osborne contended that the smous's greatest prey was the uneducated Dutch farmer. In one passage he describes how two Jews had manipulated a Dutch farmer into paying them off not to construct a railway line through his farm.[15] Clearly the smous was perceived as having a cunning and a wanton ability to exploit. Unwittingly he helped to fashion the anti-Jewish stereotype.

The contours of this stereotype were clearly manifested in an 1893 Commission of Enquiry into Labour in the Cape Colony. Taking into account that this was an enquiry into labor and not immigration, it is noteworthy how regularly the issue of eastern European immigration was addressed and the "set in," or influx, of Polish and Russian Jews mentioned. In essence the newcomers were characterized as paupers (often filthy) who shunned physical work. "They do not work with their hands, they live by their brains," noted J. C. Faure, one of the commissioners. The member of the Legislative Assembly (hereafter M.L.A.) for Cape Town, T. E. Fuller, contended that the fact they did not "beg for food" was of little consequence. For instance, Auguste Albrecht, a Constantia wine farmer, considered them "a pest to the country." In the opinion of D. E. Hutchins, the conservator of forests, "they were simply unsuitable immigrants, the equivalent of Chinamen and Coolies." J. X. Merriman, one of the colony's prominent liberals and a future prime minister of the Cape Colony, opposed such generalizations. With typical Victorian rectitude and piety, he claimed that some Polish Jews were enterprising and at least "believe in God." And yet, notwithstanding these virtues, Merriman believed the colony had accommodated enough of these people.[16]

It is therefore little wonder that a newspaper report referred to the commission as "wholly unanimous against the introduction of Russian Jews . . . a most undesirable people, as already found out in the Uitenhage District, where these people have pushed out many poor shopkeepers and have obtained property intensively."[17] Similar views were expressed about the Oudtshoorn District, where Jews were increasingly prominent in the ostrich feather industry.[18] The *Oudtshoorn Courant,* for instance, published the names of those who had taken licenses in the Oudtshoorn division during January of 1893. These names, it noted, were "interesting and instructive" because they revealed "what a complete hold the Jews have on the business of the district": "Out of the 86 General Dealers Licenses, 51 had a Polish, Russian or Hebrew patronymic, besides these there are 15 Hawkers, which give a total of 66 Jewish traders in general goods in the division. When we come to Ostrich Feather Buyers we find that the Jews have the feather business wholly in their hands, no less than 62 feather buyers were registered during January."[19]

These sentiments were confirmed in contemporary Standard Bank reports, filed by district inspectors. The reports were confidential and as such provide a particularly useful barometer of opinion. One such report for the Oudtshoorn District in 1892 reveals very clearly that Jews were viewed with great ambivalence, if not outright hostility. The inspector warned that vigilance must be maintained when dealing with ostrich feather businessmen. "An unpleasant feature of the trade," he wrote, "is the hold which the Jews are obtaining upon the District—the farmers (mostly Dutch) apparently falling into their hands!" The inspector expressed uncertainty about the effect the Jewish "presence may have upon the business of the branch at this point." Nevertheless, business was conducted with Jews, many of whom appeared "to be doing well and to be establishing confidence."[20]

One year later misgivings were again expressed about "the Hebrew fraternity" in the ostrich feather trade. For the most part, noted the inspector, "they comprised a very shady and undesirable class of men" against whom "it behooves the bank to exercise the utmost caution." The inspector warned that "under no circumstances should the manager be permitted to advance to any of them a penny of the Bank's money where their assets were of a moveable and perishable nature." Managers were warned not to "run the slightest risk with people of this class, who have neither character or means to lose." The inspector suggested that it would "be better for the bank that their business should go elsewhere." By 1894 the fear of farmers "getting into the hands of Jews and being quietly but steadily brought down" was being expressed by the bank's inspector. In considering advances to Jews, the bank was to be especially vigilant. This indeed appears to have been the case. In commenting, for instance, on an advance to one Lazarus, the inspector noted: "For a country Jew shopkeeper, whose statement of position is verbal only, and whose character is admittedly bad, too much accommodation seems to be given to this party."[21]

A particular source of tension between Jewish feather merchants and farmers was the practice of buying ostrich feathers three or four years in advance. This, argued *De Volksbode,* strangled the farmer and gave the Jew inordinate power.[22] The practice, moreover, was riddled with legal problems as recalled by the novelist and onetime magistrate for the Oudtshoorn region, W. C. Scully:

> Competition was so keen that the [Jewish] traders used to buy the pluckings in advance, sometimes months before the feathers were to be plucked. If the crop turned out to be a failure, the trader could endeavour to repudiate the bargain, if on the other hand, it turned out to be exceptionally good, the farmer would cry off the deal; so it came to a suit anyway. Consequently I used to sit in court almost everyday and all day long trying such cases. I think there were then twenty-six lawyers practising in the Magistrate's Court, and most of them appeared to be doing fairly well.[23]

It is not without significance that Scully created Nathan Steinmetz, a onetime smous turned illegal feather merchant, as a central character in his novel, *Between Sand and Sun,* published in 1898. Steinmetz was indeed a quintessential caricature of the Jewish trader and diamond dealer. "His features were of the lowest Hebrew type—his lips were full and shapeless, his nose large and prominent, his eyes small and colourless, but exceedingly bright and glittering . . . money was the only god worth worshipping."[24]

Commenting on the novel, Leveson has correctly identified Steinmetz as "a full-blown anti-Jewish stereotype, ugly and avaricious, connected with shopkeeping and diamond trading." She also perceptively points out that, while Scully's portrait of Nathan's good brother, Max, appears initially flattering, "stereotypical suggestions of avarice and decadence are deeply embedded in the text":

> Max had a face, which, had Raphael seen it through the bars of the Ghetto gate at Rome, would have made him take pains to secure the young Jew as a model. It was one of those faces which one only—and that but very rarely—sees in the youth of Israel. Its shape was a pure oval. The skin was a clear olive, and the eyes were large, dark, and melting. His jet-black hair clustered over a broad low forehead, and his full, red lips were arched like the bow of the Sun-God. As yet the stress of trade had not awakened the ancestral greed which would one day dominate his blood and modify his physiognomy.[25]

The negative attitude regarding feather merchants seems to have been articulated about eastern European Jewish traders in general by Cape parliamentarians, especially those representing rural constituencies. The stereotype usually depicted the newcomers as subversive, dishonest, and exploitative. For instance, P. J. du Toit (Richmond) talked of pedlar Jews spoiling "true trade especially in the Northern and Midland Districts." As J. T. Molteno (Namaqualand) put it, "They were able to exist where others could not." For M. M. Venter (Colesburg), the pedlars were "a danger and a menace to the country." Polish and Russian "loafers" were, in his opinion, "refugees for political offences." T. P. Theron (Richmond), in turn, referred to them as "blood suckers of the farmers" avoiding honest labor and not engaging "in the cultivation of the country." In his opinion, they interfered with honest and legitimate trade in the Colony. Even C. T. Jones (Port Elizabeth), who condemned those who negatively labeled the newcomers as "paupers," "criminals," and "lazy," admitted that the pedlars were doing a "great deal of harm in certain districts like Oudtshoorn." Perhaps the most blatant and vicious antagonist of the eastern Europeans was Thomas Upington (Swellendam). Pulling no punches, the onetime prime minister of the Cape Colony objected to Russian, Polish, and German Jews who "walked about with packs on their backs and tried to earn a livelihood." "The proper way to deal with these people," he argued, "was for farmers to warn them off their land."[26]

It is certain then, that by the 1890s, many viewed the eastern European trader negatively—in the northern, southern, and eastern Cape Colony at least. Increasingly he was being sseen as an exploiter of rural society, a perception vividly encapsulated in an account by a correspondent to the *Cape Times* after a trip to Bushmanland:

> I noticed on my trip to these parts that the Jewish traders exercise a great deal of influence and have these squatters in Bushmanland altogether in their power. Not a day passes but there is either a Jew with his cart or wagon coming to the squatters tent or hut, and making himself at home there for several days, eating their food without paying for it, or doing or giving anything in return, and as they as a rule give unlimited credit and "tick" to the Dutch and half-caste squatters, they thus have them altogether in their power, and the latter are bound to them, as their stock is nearly if not all mortgaged to the Jewish smous.[27]

The coincidence of Jewish penetration into the rural economy and the disruption of traditional agrarian life explains, to a large extent, the crystallization of an anti-Jewish stereotype in the hinterland. The Jew, in his role as creditor and supplier of the struggling farmer, enabled to develop the image of an avaricious shopkeeper, living by his wits and bent on exploiting the Boer.[28] Most farmers did not realize that social changes of a structural nature—brought on by the commercialization of agriculture and aggravated by cattle disease and drought—were undermining their former well-being and security. Disturbing feelings of alienation and displacement were instead projected onto the Jew, a readily available symbol of change.[29]

Pariahs and Peruvians

In the late 1890s, the eastern European Jew became an even greater symbol of change and upheaval in the urban centers, arriving as he did at a time of severe economic upheaval and stress. In Johannesburg, in particular, these newcomers formed a conspicuous segment of the mining city's lumpenproletariat as well as a sector of the much maligned Uitlander community. In the case of eastern European Jews, their foreign appearance was an added component of rejection. This was well expressed in the following extract from the *Critic*'s "Diary":

> The chief objection to this particular class of humanity is, after all, founded on purely sentimental grounds. If the Israelite, who is claiming Russia as his birthplace, were clean, amiable and well-proportioned he would be hailed in the ranks of labour. Being ill-developed, snuffy, unshaven and averse to ablutionary exercises, and bearing also the appearance of an injured outcast, whose hand is against everyone, and against whom every man's hand is, this specimen of humanity is not popular and never will be. It is not his fault, it is his misfortune that clean and respectable people would like to see him fenced in like the Chinese ought to be, in a location.[30]

These hapless victims of tsarist oppression and discrimination, residing mainly within a three-mile radius of the Market Square, were soon "the unhappy recipients of the most vicious class and race prejudice that society could muster."[31] It was not long before they acquired the pejorative label "Peruvian," a term of obscure origin. The first known description depicted the Peruvian as follows:

> To the ordinary members of the public he presents the apparition of a slovenly, unkempt and generally unwashed edition, in various numbers, of the wandering Jew. As a sort of commercial shield, he carries a basket of eggs on his right arm, while holding his money tightly clenched in his sinister hand. He wears no socks. He is a pariah among his own people and among the gentiles. He is only recognized, *en passant*, by the educated part of the Jewish population as a necessary evil . . . in tatterdemalion garments, until he has made his pile. Then he transforms like the butterfly; he eschews his garments of many fluttering rags; he dons the everyday, but more romantic, if less dirty raiment of the civilized populace; he forgets all about the magnanimous generosity of Baron Hirsch; and he blooms forth on the Stock Exchange as a man and a brother, willing to do unto others as others would do unto him. And presently he may rise a stage higher; he buys unto himself with great advantage. . . . If some restraint is not imposed upon the operations of these unwashed peregrinators, it will be necessary to consider some legislative means for the isolation of the

species, and for the protection of those who, whether English or Dutch, have to earn their bread by that most unwholesome of all exertions—the earning of one's bread by the sweat of one's brow.[32]

The Peruvian rapidly became associated with the evils of Johannesburg and more especially with the city's problematic liquor trade—one specific barometer of depravation and degeneration. The extent of the liquor trade in a mushrooming mining town, such as Johannesburg, certainly was enormous and a cause of great social concern. Already in 1892 the Reverend James Gray of Pretoria had appealed on behalf of Johannesburgers and Pretorians for the limitation of liquor licenses. There were sixty-five licensed houses for 2,500 adult whites, according to Gray, who added: "If the salaries payed to employees and the general expenses of these establishments were taken into consideration it was very clear that a very large number of them manage to exist by means of illicit trade only, and by encouraging gambling and debauchery generally." Similar appeals were made by more than a thousand women of Johannesburg and by Wesleyan ministers in Pretoria. The Johannesburg Chamber of Mines, recognizing the debilitating effects of liquor on its black labor force, added its voice to the chorus of protest. It noted that relative to its population, Johannesburg had more licensed houses than any city in the world.[33]

At first "foreigners" were singled out as the purveyors of this social evil.[34] It was not long, however, before such veiled references gave way to specific accusations against eastern European liquor dealers.[35] The latter achieved particular notoriety toward the end of 1894 when the government inspector of mines, J. H. Munnik, publicly castigated them in a conference paper, "Mine Accidents on the Rand, Their Causes and Prevention." In his presentation, Munnik highlighted the difficulty of "getting" at the real owners of the dens of iniquity and vice. He claimed that "the Polish Jews who look after them are the most blackguardly race of men in existence, but until we can trace the evil to its root it is no use trying to depose them. These Polish Jews have not the slightest sense of decency or modesty in them, and a more depraved race never existed."[36]

Munnik's outbursts were followed approximately one year later by a number of editorials devoted to the Temperance Crusade, licensing laws, and the liquor traffic in general. In 1896, *Land en Volk* specifically identified Jewish canteen-keepers as the chief beneficiaries of the African liquor trade. More significantly, the newspaper referred to the decay of Boer society at the expense of Polish and Russian Jewish "money suckers." Articles regularly associating "Peruvian Jews" with the liquor evil were also published in the *Transvaal Critic.*[37]

Under enormous pressure from the antiliquor lobby, the South African Republic prohibited the sale of liquor to blacks, who comprised an important market, from 1 January 1897. Faced with possible ruin, liquor merchants began trading illegally, exploiting their unemployed and impoverished fellow Jews in these operations. Judging from the alleged comments of Johannesburg *Landdrost* (magistrate), N. P. van den Berg (and ensuing correspondence in the *Standard and Diggers News*), this was well known.[38] In the following months, the question of Jewish involvement in illicit liquor dealing assumed greater prominence. According to *Land en Volk,* one source of illegal sales was the *kaffir eethuis* (African canteen), controlled by Jews. In this newspaper's view, Jews had placed pressure on Kruger to abolish the prohibition on African canteen licenses.[39]

By 1899 mining interests could no longer tolerate the impact of illicit alcohol on the black labor force and, in a series of sensationalist exposés, the pro-magnate *Transvaal Leader* definitively linked the Peruvian Jew with the liquor underworld. Glaring publicity followed the gang murder of a Mrs. Appelbe for allegedly supplying information about the liquor gangs. "How long," ran an editorial, "is the community to be ridden by these monsters, by these NATHANSONS, the KATZENS, the LEDIKERS and SCHLOSSBERGS and the rest of the off-scourings from a degraded European race whom they employ. . . . There is blood, the blood of an innocent woman, upon the hands of the KANTOR syndicate of Fordsburg." "Low class Jews," the newspaper warned, were spoiling the name of "clean minded and honourable Jews." It feared that continued Jewish involvement in crime could precipitate an anti-Jewish outburst even more terrible than had occurred in Europe.[40] When a correspondent informed the *Transvaal Leader* that "a very small proportion (I should even say insignificant) number of Jews were involved in the liquor trade," he was challenged by another correspondent who provided a list of local liquor wholesalers, the majority of whom, judging by their names, were Jewish. The negative label was difficult to refute and would survive for many years.[41]

Predictably, the *Transvaal Leader*'s "fearless and effective exposure of the corruption and inefficiency of the Liquor Law" was welcomed by the Witwatersrand Church Council. The latter assured the editor and staff that "they have the hearty support of all Christian Churches represented by the Council." The degree of contempt for the Peruvian was reaffirmed at a public meeting in Boksburg when the Reverend Fagan warned that the Peruvian was a greater "curse to the land" than "Chinese cheap labour." "Peruvians," he exclaimed, "made the name of the white man stink in the nostrils of all men, and were moral pariahs. This was partly the fault of the Russian Government, who for centuries had persecuted the Peruvians." "What right," asked Fagan, "had the Government to thrust them out here. The country was too new for Peruvians, and they could not stand that leaven. A Peruvian was too acute and sharp in his liquor dealings to be a good citizen, the Afrikaner was a child beside him." Clearly, by the late 1890s, the antiliquor crusade had indelibly associated eastern European, or Peruvian, Jews with the liquor underworld.[42]

Besides illicit liquor dealings, the Peruvian was also associated with unsanitary living and the seamier side of Johannesburg's nightlife. It was well known, claimed the *Standard and Diggers News,* that amongst Johannesburg's "ladies of the night" was "a large and thriving colony of Americanized Russian women . . . controlled by an association of macquereaus of pronounced Russian pedigree." Undoubtedly, Russian Jews—many of them schooled in the New York underworld—made a notable impact on this dimension of the city's life, much to the chagrin of the church and the respectable middle class.[43]

The latter's sensitivities were similarly violated by the decrepit condition of Peruvian neighborhoods. In an unusually detailed article, "Awful Hovels: Peruvian Uncleanliness," the *Star* described the nature of these dwellings as well as the associated style of life. It warned that unless drastic measures were taken to get rid of them the town could be faced with an epidemic that would cost many valuable lives. In addition it recommended its readers to stroll through the poorer areas to assess the desirability of having these newcomers in their midst. The rest of the article encapsulated the animus aroused by the alien and impoverished eastern European Jew:

> On Sundays they are to be seen in groups of from twenty to forty. These gatherings take place in what is known as Diagonal Street at the lower end of Market and President Streets [the central business area of Johannesburg]. In this locality no less than thirty old clo'dealers have their business place, and carry on a lucrative trade. They don't

confine themselves to buying cast-off clothing. They purchase any-thing and everything. Their method of book-keeping is beyond de-scription. A small pass-book serves to record all dealings.

Hop and ginger beer and fruit venders etc. herd together in hovels which are sinks of abomination. Here the delectable drinks are man-ufactured in vessels which are filthy. These people are also largely responsible for the sale of the vile decoctions whereby so many natives are driven to the verge of madness, and in which state they commit the hideous crimes daily reported in the columns of the various papers, and many others which are never recorded. Cheap brandy is purchased by the Peruvian in large quantities, and after going through the process known as "doctoring" (a process in which dirty water, cayenne pepper, tobacco and vitriol are freely used), is sold at 5s to 6s per bottle. It is unquestionable that a greater part of the clothing, etc. which is daily being filched from houses in all parts of the town finds its way into dens of iniquity which own these Peru-vians as masters.

The auctioneers business in Marshall Square is hampered in every way by them. They pay no licenses, and no security, evade the law and yet they buy and sell stock and produce with impunity in opposition to those who desire to carry on a legitimate business. They are despised by the better class of Jews almost as much as they are by the rest of mankind. Their morning ablutions (when they do indulge) consist of taking a tin pennikin of water outside their hovels, their utilizing their mouths as a means of partially warming the water and then as a means of conveying a continuous stream on their heads. A rub on the face finishes the process.

Their food consists principally of dried fish and bread, and conse-quently in cases where they are mechanics they are able to work for a far lower rate of wage than any average workman. Their womankind of which there are only some 50 or 60 in evidence, are more despicably unclean than the men. Gross immorality reigns supreme and un-checked. The lowest class of Hottentot and Kaffir woman are to be seen going in and out of these places with an air of ownership. There is not a vestige of doubt that should the Sanitary Board take an early opportunity to eradicate the whole brood and take steps to force them to comply with sanitary regulations, they would earn the heart-felt gratitude of the law-abiding community.[44]

Although unusually provocative, these sentiments were widely shared. Indeed, the filth and illegal business dealings described in the article were confirmed by "English Jew" in a letter to the *Star*. Yet another critic of the "Dirty Peruvians" equated them with the local "Coolie," adding that both groups were undeserving of the franchise.[45] Here we have the first of what was to become a frequently drawn parallel between Jews and Indians.

It was not only in Johannesburg that the Peruvian made his presence felt. As early as 1893, a Cape Town German newspaper, *Züd Afrikanische Zeitung,* exclaimed that "the dirty proletariat from the Polish and Russian borders" should "avoid our land." By the mid-1890s, Russian Jews were identified among the growing number of "continental" prostitutes. By then the question of alien Jews had become a regular subject for parliamentary debate in the Cape Colony. While most M.L.A.s reflected burgeoning rural antagonism, some commentators and certain newspapers raised the specter of eastern European Jews undercutting the mercantile establishment and threatening Cape Town's business morality. These fears were vividly illustrated in a Cape Town weekly, the *Owl,* which described the following scene on Cape Town's Grand Parade.

> Saturday by Saturday the "Grand"—Heaven save the word—parade gets worse. The rotten trash that is put upon the sales there would be a disgrace to Petticoat Lane. Not only this but the trade is now largely carried out by Polish Jews, who import—no doubt from other Polish Jews in London—the commonest off-scourings of Houndsditch goods. Then these frowzy gentry stand around and sum up things until whoever purchases is sure to be heartlessly swindled.
>
> The fact is Cape Town at the present time is full of those Polish Jew hawkers who live in dirtier style than kafirs and existing on about half a crown a week rob the tradesman of his due. They don't pay rent, rates or taxes, yet they are allowed to sell goods just the same as if they kept a store. Respectable Europeans should order these people from their doors. That is the only way to put them down. Let these people do manual work.[46]

Evidently no one could ignore the eastern European presence, especially since their arrival coincided with an increasing concern with public health as manifested in the Cape Colony's Public Health Amendment Act no. 23 of 1897. In his Public Health and Sanitation Report, Wynberg's district surgeon, Dr. H. Claude Wright, was particularly condemnatory of appalling living conditions "owing to the large influx of Russian and other Jews, who overcrowd and cohabit promiscuously. Amongst them filth and vermin abound, and they have great objection to ventilation, the crevices all being wedged up with rags in many of their rooms. Some of these people are worse than the natives in these matters."[47]

Unlike those eastern Europeans who had arrived in the 1880s and had aspired (with some success) to bourgeois standards, those arriving in the 1890s retained, by virtue of their substantial numbers, a conspicuous and unmistakably alien identity. These impoverished newcomers clearly aroused base and atavistic fears as they threatened middle-class norms, manners, and sensitivities. Indeed, among the thousands of fortune-seekers and social casualties of Europe's economic transformation, the Peruvian stood out as the most prominent intruder. In short, he consolidated the image of the knave, which had been evident in the 1880s and, in this sense, reinforced the arguments of those who associated Jews with illicit diamond buying and "boerverneuking." Two contemporary novels, J. R. Couper's *Mixed Humanity* and G. Griffith's, *Knaves of Diamonds,* for instance, dealt with the former theme, depicting the Jew in most unsavory terms. Dishonesty was increasingly perceived as the Jewish path to riches.[48]

By the turn of the century the eastern European, or Peruvian, Jew was thus a sharply defined outsider, set apart by language and accent. Merriman succinctly captured his alien status when commenting on the behavior of the Reverend Tobias, a Jewish minister in O'Kiep, who had allegedly deprecated patriotic sentiment. This had not surprised Merriman "because the Jewish race with all its marvellous gifts never had a country." It was, he lamented, "a cosmopolitan race and would not understand the feeling." Having been accused by the *Cape Times* (in a bid to gain electioneering capital) of antisemitism, Merriman reaffirmed his stand. Accepting the "excellent qualities of the Jews as citizens," he nevertheless argued that "the fact remains that for good or evil, they elect to remain a race apart who do not, with few exceptions, merge in the population of the land they dwell in." The Jew, he repeated, "has no country, he is a cosmopolitan."[49]

Merriman's remarks explicitly reflect the eastern European Jews' impact on popular perceptions. They are also indicative of the marginal and shifting position of the Jew in South African society. Initially defined purely in terms of religion, eastern European Jews now affirmed a "racial" Jewish identity. Undoubtedly these perceptions were influenced by the current eugenicist ideas in which mental, moral, and physical traits were attributed to immutable and inherent racial differences.

Eastern European Jews, after all, had not acculturated into bourgeois society as their English and German coreligionists had a generation before. They had failed to fulfill the "emancipation contract." More importantly, in maintaining a distinctive and alien identity they conjured up images of the traditional Jew, derived from the preemancipation or medieval Jewish model. As Aschheim puts it when discussing eastern European Jews in the German context at this time, the newcomer was perceived as the "real" Jew, the "living model" of Jewishness.[50]

Religious Deviants

The question of the "real" Jew, of course, raises the issue of religious belief as a formative influence on perceptions of the Jew. With regard to late nineteenth-century South Africa, it is fair to argue that religious differences reinforced the alien or outsider status of the Jew. To what extent this was the case, however, is difficult to assess. Nonetheless, in certain quarters at least there is evidence that Jews were perceived through a theological prism. That is to say, sermons and religiously inspired literature and comment—especially, although not only, that emanating from the pietist Dutch-speaking sector—related to Jewry's biblical roots and historical experience. Jews were very often portrayed as a people who had deviated from their roots or had lost their way by failing to accept the Truth as revealed in Christianity. The Jew, in other words, was perceived as the archetypical deviant. In this sense theologically based views confirmed the racist Peruvian stereotype. As "G" maintained in a letter to *De Kerkbode,* the official organ of the Dutch Reformed Church, the Jews had deviated from their ethical foundations and in the process had been transformed. Although secularization had made them susceptible to atheism and Christianity, they still, argued "G," harbored a deep-seated hatred for the latter. Indeed, the call to crucifixion heard nineteen hundred years ago had been taken over by the modern day "Jewish Press." Having abandoned their hope for the Messiah, Jews still wanted to rule the world. Moreover, in their search for money and power they were undermining good morals. "G's" letter provides a classic illustration of how theologically based conspiratorial views could be secularized and transformed to suit a modern age.[51]

The notion of deviance was similarly captured by another correspondent to *De Kerkbode* who questioned the so-called historical mission of the Jews. He was confounded by the fact that Jews, supposedly a light unto the heathens, always lived among monotheistic peoples. This apparent contradiction was reconciled by the notion of Christianity superseding Judaism, a result of Jews rejecting God at the time he wanted to build his Kingdom in Israel. The dispersion of the Jews was a means of enabling them to see the advantage of the Kingdom of Christ. Unlike "G," who identified Jews as a subversive threat, this correspondent viewed them as a spent force. However, both letters illuminate the power of religion as a formative influence on perceptions in late nineteenth-century South Africa. That power is further illustrated in responses to a speech by Rabbi Hertz (to a Jewish audience) in which he reportedly diminished Jesus by describing him as an ordinary Jew rather than as a perfect person. In addition, the rabbi contended that Jesus was a rebel and had been crucified as such. Because the world was still divided and without peace, Hertz maintained that Judaism's challenges remained and would indeed be ultimately fulfilled.[52]

Hertz's view that the world had to be made free, united, and peaceful through the righteousness of the Jew proved abhorrent to *Land en Volk*, which, as already shown, had for some time adopted an anti-Jewish stance. Jewish ideals, the newspaper reminded its readers, were not always noble. Their idol was money, with 99 percent of Jews being indifferent as to how they acquired it. Could such a people, asked *Land en Volk*, produce right and righteousness? In light of the facts about international and local Jewry, Hertz's statements were ridiculous. Rather than furthering righteousness, Jews were polluting society and creating evil. This, the newspaper contended, was evident to all informed people in Pretoria and Johannesburg. Indeed, the so-called virtuous Jew played an important part in unsettling things in the republics. Once again *Land en Volk* had introduced Jews into the domestic political arena. "Een Christen" (A Christian) supported this newspaper's sentiments, claiming that his earlier sympathy for Jews had disappeared following the rabbi's libelous statement. Those propagating Jewish rights were commended to read *De Joodsche wet onthuld: Talmud studien* (The Jewish law unveiled: Talmud studies). This, he suggested, would enable them to appreciate Jewish opposition to Christianity. Having once tortured Jesus on the cross, they now continued to slander him. If, after 1,900 years, the Jewish spirit had not changed, Jews were not worthy of citizenship in a Christian country.[53]

Theologically inspired hostility was not unique to the Dutch Reformed Church. The Reverend James Gray of Pretoria, a Presbyterian, also responded to Hertz's speech. He criticized the rabbi's understanding of the historical record, arguing that since the dispersion, Jews had not "been the pilot that . . . steered the world." All "higher things," he contended, had been the church's work. In addition to Gray, the Anglican dean of Cape Town warned his flock on Good Friday of 1899 that Jews were gathered in their synagogues at Passover to curse and anathemize the Gentiles. The Jews, he said, "were reviling us and praying against us, for they could not countervail the truth that their forefathers crucified Christ on that day. Much as they might admire them as fellow-citizens and public spirited men, they could not forget that. It was Caiaphas and his false friends who accepted bribes and bribed as at election time earning their money by the Jewish system of 'shent per shent.' "[54]

Here was theology blended with crass racism. Consequently, the *Cape Times* berated the dean for speaking "however unintentionally in the very accents of the Judenhetze that disgraces the Continent of Europe, and the anti-Dreyfus fury that degrades France." It was ridiculous, it said, to "throw up" the crucifixion at the modern Jew, "the cultivated ones at any rate," who "far from reviling profess a high respect for the ethical teachings of Jesus."[55]

The *Cape Times* response and the rather hasty apology from the dean at the behest of the Reverend Alfred Philipp Bender of the Cape Town Hebrew Congregation suggest that such irrationally inspired condemnation of the Jew was, at least for some, unacceptable. Indeed, the dean's retraction, in which he claimed to have "heard and read" of such Jewish attacks but was satisfied that this was not the case in Cape Town, did not entirely satisfy the *Cape Times*. Nonetheless, the newspaper published two letters supporting the dean, one, from J. Samuels, on racist grounds, and another from J. Asteup, of the Lutheran Parsonage in Cape Town, on theological grounds. Asteup was unable to forget "that the Jews of today practically join their forefathers in their malice, because they hate and persecute those of their own members who become converts to the Christian faith."[56]

Thus theologically based ideas were not without influence in turn-of-the-century South Africa. They certainly hardened existing divisions between Jew and Gentile and of course reinforced the outsider status of the Jew.[57] By and large, however, Jews in late nineteenth-century South Africa were characterized in essentially secular terms. "Thrifty," "cunning," "enterprising," and other such appellations were attributed to them rather than religiously inspired labels, such as "Christ-killers," "anti-Christs," and so forth. This is hardly surprising in an age that was becoming increasingly secularized (albeit at a much slower pace in South Africa) and in which the religious idiom was less influential.

Philosemitism

Despite the negative impact made by Peruvians and the divisive consequences of religious differences, the liberal ideals of religious tolerance and full political rights for all whites remained an important goal. These ideals certainly motivated the Uitlanders in their campaign for franchise reforms in the South African Republic during the 1890s. Jews and Catholics were prominent within that campaign and they were not without support. Even *Land en Volk*—as we know, notoriously opposed to Jewish influence in the Republic—supported this struggle: "If a Jew becomes a burger of the Transvaal," argued the newspaper, "there ought to be no bar to prevent him from becoming a member of the Volksraad or filling any other position. Why should men who are in all probability atheists, be allowed to fill positions while the same privilege is denied to the Jew who believes in Jehovah?" A Cape Town Dutch newspaper, *Het Dagblat,* similarly condemned legislation in the South African Republic which oppressed Jews, noting that Jews had proved able politicians as evidenced by Lord Beaconsfield.[58]

In such comments we see how insignificant religion was as the arbiter of citizenship. More important, we see a powerful ambiguity and ambivalence in perceptions of the Jew. Clearly, Jews were not all branded with the negative racial attributes of the Peruvian. The onetime prime minister of the Cape Colony, J. G. Sprigg, for instance, championed the rights of destitute Jews, while the British parliamentarian James Bryce claimed that many of Johannesburg's best citizens were Jewish.[59]

German Jews also impressed Stuart Cumberland, another visitor to the Witwatersrand:

> The trail of the Teuton especially of the Hebraic Teuton—is distinctly visible—on the Bourse, in trade, in society, in fact everywhere. Indeed, it would be no exaggeration to say that the greatest wealth and enterprise are to be found in the German-Hebrew community. Your Johannesburg German-Hebrew is, as a rule, in almost everything an Englishman and a Londoner, but his *Sprache* frequently persists in giving him away, although it is little short of marvellous

how readily, and in some measures naturally, he changes the skin of the bear for that of the lion.

I don't know how, in point of numbers the Jews compare with the rest of the inhabitants of Johannesburg, but I should imagine it is the one town in the world where they, in the upper grades of social and financial life are a distinct majority. Indeed, is not Johannesburg frequently called Jewhannesburg?[60]

Chief Justice Kotze of the South African Republic also spoke of Jewish warmth, intelligence, and influence which were "used to promote the material and intellectual advancement of the country." An Irishman from the Witwatersrand even attributed the good behavior of the Uitlanders to the "great preponderance of Jews." Obviously positive attitudes toward the Jew still existed, but it was the acculturated Jew as distinguished from the Peruvian Jew who found favor. For some, class and class aspirations mattered most—hence the repeated references to "cultivated" and "better class" Jews. As an editorial in the *Johannesburg Times* noted, "Higher class Jews" were "law-abiding citizens and faithful supporters of the flag under which they dwelt." They were doing excellent work in the field of education, and in many other areas they were an example to non-Jews. Such commentators were confident that with freedom and opportunity, eastern European Jews would emulate their acculturated coreligionists. This view was put most effectively by Olive Schreiner, the renowned author, who illustrated her case in the most vivid terms: "That scorned and oppressed Russian Jew, landing here today, unified by our fresh South African breezes may yet be the progenitor of the Spinoza and Maimonides of the great future South Africa, who shall lead the world in philosophy and thought."[61]

Cosmopolitan Financiers

Emerging at the same time as the Peruvian stereotype, but far more sinister, was the image of the South African Jew as part of a network of international finance. This association had already taken root in Europe and found fertile ground in South Africa where mining magnates, among whom Jews were disproportionately represented, were such a prominent feature of society.[62] It made little difference that these Jewish financiers had largely assimilated and were Jews in name only. Their presence ensured that the negative stereotype would be accentuated in the mounting struggle between mining magnates, with their international connections, and "intransigent" Boer leaders in the 1890s.

The first taste of the power of foreign finance had been evident in Kimberley during the 1880s when powerful mining houses had rapidly engulfed weak and scattered smallholders. The process was accelerated on the Witwatersrand where, three years after the first gold discoveries, a mere six mining houses dominated the industry. Jewish industrialists were prominent in the process. Some had important business and banking connections that would, as Hirschfield puts it, "be utilised to maximum effect in a world where fortunes were clearly waiting to be made."[63]

The abortive attempt to overthrow the Kruger regime in 1895 was attributed to the much-feared role of international finance. This Jameson Raid, named after its leader, one of Rhodes's right-hand men, evoked enormous condemnation in Britain, where labor leaders and the left-wing press relentlessly attacked allegedly unscrupulous financiers bent only on larger profits. Short of revolution, exhorted the British Labour parliamentarian John Burns, it illustrated how South African capitalists did practically what they liked.[64] And for Britain's radical Left, the raid clearly revealed the connection between Jewish finance and British imperialism.[65] Although these views were not systematically articulated in South Africa, their penetration can be assumed, if only because of the circulation in South Africa of British labor-oriented newspapers such as the *Clarion*. Despite the fact that British expatriates were probably the greatest consumers of this literature, one should not underestimate the number of Afrikaners (particularly in the Cape) who read English journals and magazines. Educated Afrikaners in fact used English for correspondence.

While the involvement of Jews specifically in the raid was not commented upon in South Africa, the role of international finance certainly came under fire. The raid was perceived by the English and Afrikaners alike as an indication of the depths to which financiers would purportedly sink in order to attain their objectives. For one visitor to South Africa, A. Mitchie, the raid was "a means to enthrone a select group of capitalists, in whose justice, purity and philanthropy the general community of Johannesburg felt less confidence than in the corrupt circumstances of the Hollander ridden Boer." Numerous commentators at the time of the raid made it clear that financiers posed a threat to order and stability. The labor leader J. T. Bain, for instance, referred to Eckstein, Beit, Rhodes, and Phillips "ruling affairs," while W. R. McNab, addressing a gathering in Krugersdorp at the height of the crisis, identified Beit, Lippert, and others as seeking imperial expansion and territorial aggrandizement. Even a local Jewish correspondent for the eastern European weekly *Hameliz* recognized the role of magnates in the struggle between Uitlanders and Hollanders, on the one hand, and the rulers of the country on the other.[66]

Within a few months of the raid, the caricature of a bloated and opulent financier entered South African iconography.[67] The involvement of the international financier in political events was firmly established, particularly in labor circles. From the time of the Jameson Raid, an economic interpretation of political events was inescapably added to existing analyses of the South African situation. As "Two British Working Men" put it in a letter to the *Press,* "Johannesburg [was] forced to fight the battle [the Jameson Raid] for a few bloated capitalists."[68]

One acute observer of the power of capital was Frank Reginald Statham, author and onetime editor of the *Natal Witness* and a Kimberley newspaper, the *Independent.* His early experiences as a journalist in Kimberley informed his views of big business and provided him with the background for his first novel, *Mr Magnus,* published in 1896. While the plot rested on an attempt to ruin a young man by falsely charging him with illicit diamond buying, the backdrop to the story exposed the enormous power wielded by De Beers. Many well-known Kimberley personages were depicted, in the words of the bibliographer Sydney Mendelssohn, with "the flimsiest veil of disguise."[69]

In *South Africa As It Is,* Statham's second book, published in 1897, the writer attacked the imperial power and the influence of financiers or "the spirit of Mammon" in South African politics. Statham argued that these sorts of people would stop at nothing in their attempt to attain their objectives. He referred bluntly to the political tyranny of De Beers which, helped by the Rothschilds, showed how the influence of millionaires was felt in every corner of the social and political structure.[70]

Statham's observation that Rothschild had a dominant interest in De Beers during the early years of the company had been commented on by numerous contemporary observers.[71] This belief no doubt enhanced Statham's conspiratorial view of international capital, a view doubtlessly shared by others.[72] For Statham, the Uitlanders' struggle for the franchise was a mere ruse used by the capitalists to gain power. He believed this was well known to the Volksraad which, according to Statham, knew very well that by giving political rights to all foreigners resident in Johannesburg, the city would fall under the control of financiers as had been the case in Kimberley where De Beers held effective power.[73]

Although making no allusions to specifically "Jewish finance," Statham's conspiratorial view of big business needs to be noted. It reflects the massive impact made upon contemporaries by the Kimberley mining magnates, an impact reinforced by the Jameson Raid and the burgeoning power of Johannesburg's mining magnates, popularly known as "Randlords." By the time Statham's *South Africa As It Is* was published, all were aware of Kruger's struggle against the might of international capital and British imperialism in tandem. The prominent Transvaler Percy Fitzpatrick captured the somber mood when he wrote to mining magnate Julius Wernher of "the bitterness of feeling and the distrust of capitalists which obtain here."[74]

As tensions mounted between the South African Republic and Britain over the franchise question in the years before the outbreak of war in 1899, the role of financiers moved to center stage. Republicans in both the Transvaal and Free State recognized the power of international finance and its connections with British imperialism. Boer leaders had not forgotten the lessons of the Jameson Raid. Free State's President Steyn, for instance, characterized Cecil John Rhodes as an archcapitalist who, under the guise of imperialism, had viciously exploited the working man. His words were greeted with approbation by Johannesburg's satirical weekly the *Mail and Skeptic*. Lippert, Lewis and Marks, and Netherlanders, it exclaimed, "are the curse of the country."[75]

English-speaking labor spokesmen and anti-imperialists voiced similar apprehensions about what they considered to be the malevolent intentions of Johannesburg's Randlords. Speaking to an audience of pro-Boers shortly before the outbreak of war, H. D. Stiglingh reminded them that at the time of the Jameson Raid, "a certain book of Lionel Phillips [a prominent Jewish Randlord] was found in which it was stated that the franchise was not wanted, but the MINERAL RIGHTS in the shape of a monopoly which would have made the country a second Kimberley." The "so-called imperialists," he claimed, "were getting a better franchise deal than they received in their own country." This was patently an allusion to Jews being the key conspirators, for he added that before 1870 "no Jew could have the franchise in England."[76]

The conspiratorial view of international finance was most clearly enunciated by J. A. Hobson, the *Manchester Guardian*'s correspondent in Johannesburg. Hobson, whose writings influenced the pro-Boers in England and the views of Lenin on imperialism, went beyond a mere condemnation of financiers. In his view, it was specifically Johannesburg's Jews who wielded inordinate power: "The entire mining industry with the partial exception of Consolidated Gold Fields," he informed his editor, "is in their hands, the Dynamite Monopoly, the illicit liquor traffic are theirs, they and Rhodes own or control the press, manipulate the share market, and run the chief commercial business in Johannesburg and Pretoria. These men will rig the politics when they have the franchise. Many of them have taken English names and the extent of Jew power is thus partially concealed. I am not exaggerating one bit. I think I can prove it."[77]

On the eve of war Hobson was even more strident, attempting at all costs to expose the preponderance and power of Johannesburg's Jews:

> If one takes recent figures from the census, there appears to be no less than seven thousand Jews in Johannesburg, but the experience of the street repeatedly exposes the fallacy of figures. The shop fronts and business houses are sufficient to convince one of the large presence of the chosen people. If any doubt remains, a walk outside the Exchange, where in the street "between the chains," the financial side of the gold business is transacted, will dispel it. Most of these Jews figure as British subjects, though many are in fact, German and Russian Jews, who have come to Africa after a brief sojourn in England. The rich, vigorous and energetic financial and commercial families are chiefly German Jews.
>
> I lay stress upon this fact because, while everyone knows the Jews are strong, their real strength is much underestimated. Though figures are so misleading, it is worthwhile to mention that the directory of Johannesburg shows sixty-eight Cohens against twenty-eight Jones and fifty-three Browns. The Jews mostly took little part in the Uitlander agitation, they let others do that sort of work. But since half of the land and nine-tenths of the wealth of the Transvaal claimed for the Uitlanders are chiefly theirs, they will be chief gainers by any settlement advantageous to the Uitlanders.[78]

Even a supporter of the imperial connection such as Merriman recognized the congruence between international finance and British motives. "War to you," Merriman informed the British parliamentarian Lord Bryce, "would be an incident of what you call 'Empire'; to us it would mean absolute ruin, financially and socially, undertaken at the bidding of a subsidised press in order that those who are bursting with riches may grow richer."[79] Once war began, Merriman was even more condemnatory, describing the conflict as "a scandalous plot of money-seekers using the British Government as a catspaw backed by the pure Jingo practical spirit."[80]

Merriman was merely echoing what would become a veritable flood of anticapitalist propaganda by Britain's radical pro-Boers. Labor weeklies such as Robert Blachford's *Clarion,* Keir Hardie's *Labour Leader,* and W. M. Thompson's *Reynolds Newspaper* condemned the war at every opportunity. Britain's Fabian society too was critical of imperial motives. No less than Hobson or the *Clarion,* it condemned "the influence exerted over imperial councils by the passions of the newspaper correspondents, and the cosmopolitan capitalists of the Rand." Cosmopolitan, of course, referred to Jewish capitalists. These sentiments were, as we saw, best captured by J. A. Hobson in his book, *The War in South Africa.* Put crisply, the book postulated the notion of a war fought in the interests of a "small group of international financiers, chiefly German in origin and Jewish in race."[81]

The Anglo-Boer War thus popularized the concept of war-mongering international—and often specifically Jewish—financiers. As noted, this critique had been most vociferously articulated by England's pro-Boer lobby, and its paradigm was well received in South Africa.[82] In Cape Town, for instance, noncombatant Uitlanders began to assert that imperial officials were unduly influenced by capitalists, and caricatures of corpulent and semitic-looking capitalists, relishing the spoils of war, began to adorn the pages of popular journals.[83]

The most vivid indication that anti-Jewish rhetoric in Britain had penetrated South Africa and been extended in the process was evident in letters written by Jews to newspapers denying charges of a "Jewish conspiracy" behind the war. When, for example, one of Hobson's articles was quoted with approbation in the *South African News,* Manfred Nathan, a journalist and advocate, rose to his coreligionists defense. He could not accept Hobson's suggestion that Jewish power ought to be restricted in a future dispensation for the Transvaal. Nathan similarly attacked "Australian MLA" who informed the *Cape Times* that he would be most upset if the Transvaal or Orange Free State were granted responsible government in the near future as this would enable Jewish capitalists to gain too much power. In a letter to the *Johannesburg Gazette,* one Dr. B. Liknaitsky complained that anonymous anti-Jewish letters had appeared in a range of Natal and Orange Free State newspapers. He pointed out that Jewish refugees from the gold fields were suffering no less than Christian refugees and that those who remained on the Rand had behaved in a most correct manner. He contended, moreover, that "some crimes have been committed but the overwhelming majority of Jews were law abiding [and] would be the first to hail with the utmost joy the advent of a regime that would put an end to those multi-malpractices that were rampant in this part of the world."[84]

It required little effort, of course, for Boers to accept the view that Britain's war motives were inspired by economic greed. These motives were relentlessly and compellingly unveiled in the anti-imperialist tract *A Century of Wrong.* The book vigorously denounced the "greed of capitalist speculators" and the "sterile, empty, soulless" chauvinism of British jingoism. While no specific mention was made of Jews, a case can be made that their purported influence was inferred by the readership. As Lord Kitchener reported during the war, many Afrikaners were "absurdly afraid of getting into the hands of certain Jews who no doubt wield great influence in this country."[85]

War: Consolidating the Image

The war had resulted in a huge exodus of refugees, including Jews, from the Transvaal to the coastal ports. Within months of the outbreak of hostilities, Cape Town's Jewish population swelled from five or six to ten thousand. The newcomers, many of them impecunious, aroused concern and even resentment, and the British high commissioner, Alfred Milner, was quick to inform the secretary of state, Joseph Chamberlain, of the situation. "Many of the refugees," he reported, "are not only penniless but belong to a very undesirable class. They include the loafers and hangers on of society, and those who made a precarious living by mean and in some cases illegal trades—such as the buying of stolen goods and the sale of liquor to natives. A great number of them are the low class of Jews known as Peruvians."[86]

Milner's wife, then Lady Cecil, was similarly unimpressed with the quality of refugees. The worst of these, she recalled, "were the Jews who had come to South Africa from the ghettos of Eastern Europe (they were known as Peruvians), and had taken British nationality and proposed to live on this and on their wits. They remained a heavy burden for as long as the war lasted, a curious people, in rags, with their belongings in untidy bundles and yet it was often found that they were quite well off, and the possessors of valuables." As Van Heyningen points out, Lady Cecil's remarks contained "all the blend of dislike, resentment, prejudice and ignorance which the Jewish refugees generally aroused."[87]

Van Heyningen might have added "untruths," for despite selfless benevolence from Jewish individuals and institutions, the refugees remained conspicuously poverty stricken.[88] Their arrival furthermore aggravated an already serious housing shortage, and in a city acutely sensitive to the dangers of overcrowding and poor sanitation, these newcomers posed a potential health hazard.[89] Indeed the appalling living and health standards of the Jews once again featured in the Public Health Report for 1901 of Wynberg's district surgeon, Dr. H. Claude Wright: "Their houses are filthy in the extreme" and the children of "80 per cent of that persuasion bathed once a month," he noted. Wright recommended a "very rigid supervision" over their health standards when dealing with the dairy products they vendored.[90] One year later his medical report reiterated the same concerns:

> Dwellings of the Jewish community are much overcrowded and ill-ventilated. These people herd together and overcrowd to an alarming extent. They are exceedingly afraid of fresh air and ventilation, and close every aperture in their rooms, notably when they have any illness. Their mode of living is objectionable and dirty in the extreme. They seldom or ever bath and their bodies are covered with vermin. They therefore remain a sickly crowd, entirely oblivious to decency and sanitation. Many of their habitations are unfit to be used as such, and as they are large vendors of food, some serious notice should be taken of their mode of life and preparation and storage of articles of food. Some time ago I came across a manufacturer of casein or cream cheese at a Jewish milk vendors place. It would baffle description to depict the filth of that place in which the trade was carried on. I cannot too strongly denounce the state of affairs, and express my emphatic opinion that strict supervision should be given this very undesirable class, look at him from any point of political or sanitary economy you like.[91]

Dr. Wright's revulsion was widely shared. A medical expert, Professor W. J. Simpson, went so far as to identify Jewish living conditions as a contributory factor to a major plague epidemic in 1901. Nevertheless, despite these suspicions, Jews did not receive differential treatment during the plague. That they did not can be attributed to respect for the Jewish establishment and to the fact that, as whites, eastern European Jews could be regenerated. There was certainly no consensus that they were beyond improvement; the problem was essentially one of time. Significantly, this was not the case for Indians—a primary focus of antialien activity and action. Indeed, as South Africa's racial order solidified, these unfortunate people were perceived as inherently corrupt and beyond improvement. Behavioral characteristics ascribed to them—although similar to those ascribed to eastern European Jews— were allegedly immutable and thus beyond correction, a product of undoubted racial difference.[92]

Besides associating Jews with insanitary living conditions, caricatures linked the Jew to a range of Cape Town's social evils. The *Owl* was particularly malicious, its journalistic invective comparing favorably with anti-Jewish journalism in Europe at this time.[93] Especially crude in his depictions of the Jew was the *Owl*'s German-born cartoonist, Heinrich Egersdörfer. "The Evil of the Hour" and "Curses of Cape Town" were just two of his many cartoons which reflected his violently anti-Jewish sentiments (see figs. 1 and 2). But the *Owl* was not alone in its coarse stereotyping. Another periodical, the *Telephone,* claimed that the Jew was prepared to "do his own brudder."[94] Even a respectable daily such as the *Cape Times* had few qualms about vulgar ethnic stereotyping as evident in the following outburst against Yiddish-speaking fish merchants in the Cape Town seaside suburb of Kalk Bay:

> A disreputable-looking coterie of the parasites of the social fabric, standing a little apart, conversing in a gibberish of mid-Europe, bare-legged, frowzy headed, shifty eyed, and nervously sharp, ready to pounce upon the rough handed sons of the seas as they come to land. . . . The keen-witted specimen of the lower species of the immigrant Hebrew race in unvarnished guise and unreserved demeanour. . . . Rapacious foreign Hebrew who never risks his own life or safety . . . indignantly asks in pig-English "Call that a fish? Vy, I will haf to give it away." . . . The Peruvian soon pockets his profit, and so he prospers from day to day.[95]

Hostility toward the Peruvian Jew that had existed in Cape Town before the Anglo-Boer War had obviously been exacerbated by the arrival of so many eastern European refugees. "A most undesirable crowd," was the way P. Ashendon, Cape Town's city engineer in charge of relief, described them. In his view they were appalling laborers, filthy, and with a negative attitude toward physical work. One of Ashendon's overseers considered them "more like wild beasts in a tent than human beings." These people, concluded the engineer, "are legitimately the pariahs of society and should by right be under police protection, not the public works."[96]

Similar attitudes toward eastern European Jews were evident in the Transvaal, where British administrators placed "eastern European and Russian Jews" well up on their unwanted list when considering the question of returning refugees. Colonial officials, however, were instructed by General Roberts not to mention the word *Jew* in their policy formulations and focused instead upon class. But there is no doubt that Peruvian Jews were their target. As Milner's political secretary, G. V. Fiddes, put it, "The Peruvians are a wholly objectionable element, and the more of them that can be sent down the better."[97]

The refugee influx had clearly consolidated the negative dimension of the Jewish stereotype. As pedlars, shopkeepers, and impecunious drifters, they augmented the knave image crafted on the diamond fields, the Witwatersrand, and in the rural areas of the northern, southern, and eastern Cape. In addition, the image of the cosmopolitan financier introduced a new dimension to the stereotype, that of Jewish power. This idea would gain momentum in the twentieth century. And yet notwithstanding the Peruvian and cosmopolitan financier stereotypes, the image of the gentleman Jew was not obliterated. The reader will recall the many instances of support for Jews and distinctions made between the acculturated Jew and the Peruvian Jew. Substantial goodwill certainly remained, and Jewish contributions to cultural and socioeconomic life were respected in at least some quarters. When the *South African Jewish Chronicle* was established in February 1902, for instance, numerous Cape newspapers praised the "influential role" played by South African Jews and their "abnormally developed faculty for business." Like "the Chosen People everywhere," noted the *Fort Beaufort Advocate,* South Africa's Jews were "enterprising, energetic and a business-like race . . . supreme in finance and great commerce." They were also, noted the newspaper, prominent in law, medicine, philosophy, history and had indeed "produced great soldiers."[98]

Notwithstanding such comments, the earlier more favorable image of the Jew that prevailed in the 1880s had been substantially eroded. Increasingly the popular view embraced only the seemingly dishonest eastern European Jew and ignored his bourgeois and acculturated counterpart. Dr. M. J. Farrelly, author of *The Settlement after the War,* was certainly correct when he expressed concern about the way in which a few Jewish criminals had influenced perceptions of all Jews. He pointed out that there were criminals in every community. This did not mean that all Jews ought to be identified with illicit liquor dealing any more than the tricks a few Jewish pedlars had played in the old days on the Boer were a legitimate excuse to besmirch them.[99]

Farrelly's concerns were evidently shared by Rabbi Joseph Hertz. A year after the conclusion of the Anglo-Boer War, in an address inaugurating a new representative Jewish institution—the Jewish Board of Deputies for Transvaal and Natal—he lamented that "no community in recent years has been slandered as the Johannesburg Jew has. A few journalists as clever as they were unscrupulous, broadcast the misinformation that as a class, the Jews of this town were illicit liquor dealers, and that they and they alone were given to this form of law breaking. By dint of constant repetition everyone in and out of South Africa came to believe it."[100]

CHAPTER THREE

From Pariah to Parvenu: The Making of a Stereotype, 1902–14

Antialienism

RABBI HERTZ'S unease about negative stereotyping and its potential dangers for the Jewish community was well founded. In the postwar period, antialien rhetoric and especially the debate and legislation surrounding Yiddish-speaking immigration into the Cape Colony confirmed a widely shared unfavorable image of the eastern European Jew.[1] Jewish vulnerability was further exposed by the impact of socioeconomic changes generated by mining and capitalist growth. Local merchants now found themselves marginalized, unprotected, and certainly in no mood to compete with "undercutting" and "dishonest" eastern European and Indian traders. In the countryside, sustained drought (1903–8) slowed down rural recovery and exacerbated the poor white problem. In these conditions, the visibly alien Jew—often perceived as successful and upwardly mobile—was an easily identifiable target upon whom to vent anger and frustrations. The "anti-Semitic microbes penetrated here too," lamented N. D. Hoffmann, a Lithuanian-born Yiddish journalist who, having anticipated a free society, was not sanguine about the future: "The local press is already worrying its head off as to whether they [the Jews] are suited to the country! . . . Here our hygiene is found wanting—there our economy is not to their liking. They cannot bear it that we buy properties, that we found wholesale business undertakings. . . . In brief even in the country where we thought we would be able to live peaceably we are disillusioned, as we are still being looked upon with disdain, hatred and mockery."[2]

Such prejudice was exacerbated as economic recession in the Cape Colony (1902–4) and Transvaal (1906–8) generated an acute xenophobia. Peruvians Jews, however, were not the only targets of scurrilous and crude stereotyping. Continentals (southern Europeans), and more especially, Indians or Asiatics were now disparaged. To some extent this deflected attention away from the eastern European Jew, but for many the latter remained unwelcome and beyond redemption, albeit the victims of historical circumstance and misfortune. This view was succinctly explained by the *South African Review:*

> The Russian Jew, small blame to him, has been debased by centuries of tyranny to such an extent that it will take generations to work off the brand of slave. Look at the hang-dog faces, the bowed shoulders, and the shambling walk of specimens of the race who are landing here, and ask whether they are "men". Of course they are not. They are hopelessly demoralised and to make self respecting citizens out of the great bulk of them (there are of course rare exceptions) is impossible. . . . Now it must be clearly understood that the Jew is not objected to because he is a Jew. As a matter of fact his religion makes him a better product of his circumstances than he otherwise would be. But from no fault of his own he has, in certain countries, been shamefully persecuted, and the iron has ground out of his soul all his manliness and every quality which goes to make a good citizen.[3]

It seems ironic that this effete and emasculated import was perceived as a threat to South African society.

While antialienism was strongest in the Cape Colony, opposition to the newcomers permeated beyond the colony's borders. Johannesburg's *Transvaal Leader,* for instance, echoed the *South African Review* when it recommended a quarantine for the newcomers: "Broken by centuries of espionage and oppression, with every fibre of manhood beaten out of them, ignorant of how to obtain justice, save by bribes, it is indubitable that they stand in need of a certain quarenteen ere they become valuable citizens of a free community. An Englishman of the middle ages, with his turbulent and lawless instincts were he suddenly sat down in our midst, could not assimilate."[4]

The unassimilability of the newcomers was confirmed on a daily basis as thousands of eastern Europeans entered the country.[5] Their disheveled appearance, exotic language, and alien manner rudely threatened bourgeois sensibilities and standards. A "large proportion of the immigrants," according to Dr. A. J. Gregory, medical officer of Health for the Cape Colony, "were unsatisfactory in important respects." They were, he noted, "ill-provided, indifferently educated, unable to speak or understand any language but Yiddish, of inferior physique, often dirty in their habits, persons and clothing and most unreliable in their statements."[6] The Cape Colony's agent-general in London, T. E. Fuller, was similarly unimpressed with the quality of the newcomers whom he described as being of a very low class and offensively dirty.[7] He warned that such immigrants would hardly prove an acquisition to the colony.[8] These were certainly not the sort of immigrants envisaged by Milner in his efforts to ensure British cultural and political dominance in South Africa.[9]

At the height of Cape Town's economic recession, it was not uncommon for alien Jews to be described as "the scum of Europe." The "lowest class of Russian, Polish and German Jews, filthy and evil smelling," was the way one H. S. Smith (in a letter to the *Cape Times*) described the newcomers entering the country. Such sentiments were corroborated and further inflamed by a vicious brand of journalism that included grotesque caricaturing (see fig. 3). Henry Farmer's description of "Fagin," whom he identified at the Southampton quayside, encapsulates the sort of emotion and venom aroused by the eastern European Jew: "I saw him from the quay. He might have been a somewhat younger edition of Charles Dickens' Fagin. . . . His nose was hooked most semitically. His unkempt beard was red. His bowler hat with a generations dust upon it was dented in. His frock coat was undesirably greasy. The bottoms of his trousers were frayed. He looked worth no more than the clothes in which he stood. He was bound for South Africa." Farmer's prejudices were confirmed by a ship steward who informed him that when the immigrants underclothes were worn out they simply threw them out of the porthole. Little wonder, then, that Farmer was appalled by "Fagin," "still muttering in Yiddish, but grinning and showing unwashed teeth."[10]

Jewish distinctiveness—both physical and cultural—was reinforced by ghettolike neighborhoods, in which Jews, like all immigrants, congregated. The alien ambience of one particular neighborhood of Cape Town—District Six—made an enormous impact:

> The impression that will prevail in my mind is rows of shabby and unclean shops whose walls and signboards are sprinkled with Yiddish characters, sloping streets crowded with coloured people, Indians, Russians and Poles; narrow lanes where little black and brown babies tumble amidst the discarded rags and the empty canisters flung out of the houses. . . . I remember the shuffling gait, the hunted crafty look

and the greasy dress of the Jewish refugee. I recall the glimpses of indescribable dirt and squalor that I had through open doors and windows. I recollect the dark and heavy smelling shops of the Indians at the corners of the lanes and streets; the group of men that stand around the counters of the tailors and the jewelers holding debates in Yiddish, the lean and ragged little children that rush from miserable and secret lanes into the crowded streets, or crawl out of the doors of the mean houses to stretch their bare brown limbs in the dry gutters, the hard white faces of the wives and the daughters of the hunted Russians, sitting on shabby balconies or lounging against the shop doors.

The writer went on to describe Caledon Street "with its innumerable shops, all of them small and shabby." Yiddish-script characters abounded, while in a "dying and cleaning shop several gents are chattering in Yiddish whilst waiting for their finery. . . . And there are loungers—it is Saturday afternoon and also the Jewish sabbath. In a nameless lane, there is Tolstoi leaning against a water shoot, looking up at the balcony in Constitution Street. I am shattered by the very image of Fagin. Heaven knows but that he may be the most gentle of men; that nameless persecution may have brought that look of the hunted beast in his eye."[11]

For many, then, the alien Jew—different in dress, manner, language, and physiognomy—evoked a range of images varying from devious to pious and even to outright debasing.

The picture was much the same in Johannesburg where by 1904 Jews numbered 10,800, or approximately 12 percent of its entire white population. Most of the newcomers congregated in the poorer sections of the city, keeping alive the prewar association of Peruvians with filth and vice. Even the *SAJC* noted that it would be no loss to the town if the Jewish quarter in Marshall Street were removed. In a *Sunday Times* article on the squalor of Johannesburg, Peruvian Jews were prominent: "In the early morning, even before sunrise you may see the Peruvian milkman starting on his morning rounds. Some of the milkcarts also carry sacks of laden bottles. Probably these contain an inferior sort of milk intended for Kaffir consumption."[12]

At a purely physical level, then, eastern European Jewish immigrants, pouring into South Africa after the war, reinforced and confirmed the negative characteristics espoused in the 1890s. Outsiders in the classical sense, the impact of these new arrivals on the social landscape could not be ignored. For many, their external appearance reflected a lack of respectability and consequently a moral depravity. This was not surprising, given notions popularized at this time by the Italian criminologist Cesare Lombroso. In his view, physical characteristics mirrored behavioral predilections—a thesis confirmed for many by the alleged record of the Peruvian in South Africa.[13]

Postwar iconography and journalism continued the attack. By way of illustration, a poem, "The Devil," published in the *Owl*, viciously attacked the probity of "a lean little Kimberley Jew" who, quite predictably, was welcomed by the mining conglomerate, De Beers. In similar vein, an Egersdörfer cartoon, "Pauper Peruvians or the whitening of South Africa," focused on the depravity and dishonesty of the Peruvian Jew (see fig. 4). He clearly left his mark on the popular consciousness. Indeed, his notoriety spread to Natal, where parliamentarians, discussing the question of immigration, noted the corrupting influence eastern European Jews had had upon local affairs on the Witwatersrand. For instance, Natal's secretary for native affairs, F. R. Moor, declared that they had only to go to places like Johannesburg and other large cities where substantial numbers of Jews had settled to appreciate the harmful influence they had on the native population through their illegal liquor dealings. His sentiments were corroborated by the colonial secretary and minister of education, C. J. Smythe, who complained that the newcomers were inclined to work "in ways and under conditions that are not in accordance with our ideas of what is right and proper." These immigrants, added K. H. Hathorn (Pietermaritzburg), had demoralized natives on the Witwatersrand. Such concerns were particularly acute in Natal, where racial harmony was finely poised and labor shortages linked to liquor consumption went back to the 1870s. By the early 1900s legislators understandably shunned the prospect of Durban rivaling the Witwatersrand for vice, crime, and labor instability.[14]

The eastern European Jew had manifestly become a countrywide symbol for corruption and vice. He would allegedly balk at nothing in the process of self-aggrandizement and was shrewd, crafty, and dishonest. It is not surprising that the *South African Review* considered the arrival of these newcomers as perhaps the most important problem facing the country. Even the local rabbi of Paarl, according to a Standard Bank inspector, did not hold a "high opinion" of the alien Jew.[15]

The clearest indication of the lowly status of the Peruvian is evident in comparisons with the Indian, an even greater focus of concern in the

postwar years. "Linguist," for example, informed the *Natal Mercury*
that eastern European Jews were as undesirable as the lowest class of
"coolies" and far more dangerous. For the author of "The Real Peril, of
the Rand, from a Woman's Point of View," the "swarthy alien Jew" was
an even greater menace than the "coolie":

> As jerry builders, workers in stop-shops etc., they oust the white
> artisan. As purveyors of produce or small storekeepers they cut prices
> and undersell in every department. Servile to a degree so long as
> poverty prevails, with the first glimmer of opulence, they assume
> British names, demand British rights, and display despotic ruthless-
> ness savouring of the cent per cent tyrant. Of such are the British
> colonies being filled, and of such should the white artisan beware.
> The genus "Peruvian" is far more of a rival than any indentured
> fellow-labourer.

The writer went on to assert that low-class Jews had instigated blacks to
murder persons publicly opposed to the traffic in drink. Even the liberal
Merriman associated the two groups when he warned Smuts, in a letter
regarding the expulsion of Indians, that "the place of these people,
unsavoury as they are, will be taken by the lower class Jew who is
scarcely a more wholesome element in the population."[16]

Merriman's assessment, and indeed the general comparison of Indians with Jews, was shared by the *Transvaal Critic* which, in a cartoon,
depicted a policeman removing an Indian while three gloating Peruvian
Jews wearing hats with the inscriptions IGB, ILB, and IDB looked on.
The legend beneath the cartoon confirmed the association of the Peruvian Jew with the Indian while the acronyms on the hats also told a story
(see fig. 5). As the *SAJC* complained, no one could doubt what was
implied. But the *Transvaal Critic* was even more blatant. Once the
government had its hands free, suggested the newspaper,

> it might with profit turn its attention to the gentry and the situation
> depicted in the cartoon. We have in our midst a class of degraded
> Europeans who plot in the dark, encourage crime by providing a
> refuge for the criminal and depot for his plunder, and debase the
> native by supplying him with that which destroys body and soul.
> There are hundreds of vagabonds of this sort, compared with whom
> even the Indian is a polished gentleman. They are or should be well
> known to the police. We have a law full of terrors for such evildoers,
> yet they wax fat under the very shadow of the Temple of Justice.
> When the asiatic controversy is done with, let the Attorney-General

and his subordinates root out these pestilent knaves who thrive on illicit liquor-selling, illicit gold and diamond buying, prostitution and every crime on the calendar. If necessary, all South Africa could co-operate in the effort. Political opinion is good. The removal of this scum would be better for our future.[17]

Quite clearly, the press both reflected and inflamed antialien senti-ment. Indeed, its use of the epithet "Jew," when identifying wayward individuals who happened to be of that faith exacerbated antagonism. Although the latter custom was not the case for all newspapers, its practice by some served to reinforce the anti-Jewish stereotype. That stereotype was further harmed by the trial and conviction of Abraham Cohen—alias "Jewey Cook"—and Jack Silverstein for rape. "Crowds of the lowest type thronging the court during the trial" were noted by the *Transvaal Leader,* while a *Sunday Times* cartoon depicting the scene left no doubt as to which sector of the community was most involved and concerned.[18] Moreover, according to the cartoon, Peruvians continued to be associated with illicit liquor dealing.

The *Sunday Times* was not alone in its view. Commissionaires inves-tigating the Transvaal liquor problem in 1909 were told that it was mainly poor Dutchmen from Vrededorp or low-class Europeans and Peruvians who ran the illicit trade. The association of Jews with illicit liquor dealing was further reinforced by the "Trapping System" in which Jews appear to have been the primary target. Africans in the employ of the police would purchase liquor illegally and then report the transaction to their employers. The system, as the *SAJC* noted, was open to abuse.[19]

Obviously the postwar influx of alien Jews had consolidated the negative Jewish image already evident before the Anglo-Boer War. The newcomers, by virtue of their numbers, accelerated the erosion of the favorable image of the "law-abiding" and "respectable" Jew—a process well understood by the Jewish elite, who did all they could to encourage their coreligionists to behave appropriately.[20] Understandably, the Jew-ish establishment feared being tarred with the Peruvian brush.

Rural Antipathy

Although postwar antipathy toward aliens was most marked in the urban areas, negative sentiments continued to flourish in the country districts. Prejudice of the crudest sort, for instance, was displayed in a letter to the *Cape Times* from "A Farmer Pure and Simple." His complaints about the unfair methods used by Russian Jews in the rural areas convey the sorts of concerns and perceptions among sectors of the country population:

> These men obtain at the start of their careers a small credit from certain merchants, mostly without any references, upon which they stalk the country with a bundle on their back, soliciting custom in a very humble way from the poorer farmer on their beats, and as they never pay for food and shelter, and sell inferior articles at enhanced prices, the very fair profit they make is clear gain which is immediately invested in a donkey, with a consequent increase in carrying power involving additional trading facilities. . . . Up to this stage there is not much harm done, but now the man becomes dangerous. He soon sets up a permanent shop at or near some of the farms he has been frequenting in a humble capacity, and now begins the steady plotting and planning for the expropriation of his poorer Dutch neighbours and customers, for he rarely succeeds with the more wealthy farmer of standing, who in general has no dealings with this class. His prey at first consists of the poor *Bijwoner* [tenant farmer] who owns a few sheep, ostriches or cattle, from which a very precarious income is derived. This man is inveigled into buying and purchasing far above his legitimate income by the insidious and ingratiating manner the Jew knows so well how to adopt.

In this way, argued the writer, thousands of Jews all over the country emerged from pauperism. The state had to control their entry into the country.[21]

Crass prejudice was also obvious in Middelburg (Cape Colony) where, according to the *Middelburg Echo,* P. J. Hannon, the Cape government's expert on agricultural cooperation, had at a meeting of farmers advocated protecting people from the hands of moneylenders and Jews. An association of farmers (based on the Irish experience) could, Hannon argued, provide its members with money in a more economical way and on more attractive lines than that of the Jew. Hannon also alluded to scheming "Jew speculators" in the feather industry planning the downfall of the farmer. That this statement reflected popular perceptions was shown by the acclamation with which it was greeted.[22]

Hannon's statements were vigorously challenged by the Cape Jewish Board of Deputies, a representative Jewish institution established in

1904 to safeguard Jewish rights. The board was particularly upset that the Cape's secretary for agriculture, A. J. Fuller, had shared the platform with Hannon. In response to the board's request for an explanation, Fuller claimed Hannon had used the words "feather speculators" and not "Jew speculators." In any event, he continued, hundreds of farmers had complained about speculative transactions.[23]

Alleged Jewish "speculation" (and success) was especially irksome given the background of burgeoning poor-whiteism, exacerbated by the Anglo-Boer conflict, drought, and the capitalization of agriculture. In these conditions observers were quick to project legitimate tensions and insecurities onto the Jew, a visible symbol of change. The M.L.A. for Oudtshoorn, H. J. Mulder, for instance, in his evidence before a Select Committee on Indigent Whites, stressed that many Jews were profiting at the expense of the Afrikaner. The credit they received from the Jew soon landed them in debt and eventually forced them to sell their land to the Jew. Sometimes, argued Mulder, they even ended up working for him.[24]

Very similar views were articulated by the Reverend J. H. van Wyk of the Dutch Reformed Church in Adelaide, Cape Colony, in his evidence to the Transvaal Indigency Commission of 1908. Van Wyk drew attention to the evil credit system that resulted in moneylenders enchaining the ordinary man. However, he contended that an even greater problem was a "certain kind of unscrupulous trader." To illustrate his argument, Van Wyk related a story told by a "reliable man" about a farm shop that had failed under three successive owners but which succeeded under Jewish management. Two Jews, explained Van Wyk, "gave the farmers unlimited credit, and today that property is in their hands and he is a poor man." "You will find," he continued, "numberless examples of that in almost every district." A question put by the commission to J. B. Skirving, the resident magistrate for Potchefstroom, suggests that the commission shared Van Wyk's views: "We have heard in other parts of South Africa," noted a commissioner, "that the Jew storekeeper gets control of all the land about." Skirving confirmed the statement and then went on to inform the commission that natives were also exploited by the Jews who dominated the mealie market.[25]

The Jewish trader was thus perceived to be exploiting the population through his allegedly powerful and ubiquitous position in the rural economy. As one correspondent, "Piquetberg," informed *Ons Land:* "Sir—from whence do all these Israelites come? The ninety who were here before have everyone of them got ten brothers now. They have all the butchers businesses and all the hotels in the village. Besides all the small shops they own in the district, one finds them on almost every farm, either on foot or leading a horse and cart."[26]

Commenting on the foregoing letter (which it reprinted), the *Owl* reminded readers that "Piquetberg isn't the only town where nearly all the stores are in the hands of the Jacobs and Moseses who are running this Christian country."[27]

The notion of Jewish domination and exploitation in the rural areas is again evident in the qualified support given by Cape parliamentarians (representing rural districts) to a motion in the Cape Legislative Council condemning anti-Jewish massacres in Russia. Discussion revealed an empathy for the Russian administrators and a feeling that Jews themselves were responsible for their own misfortune.[28] These sentiments were clearly indicative of a widespread rejection of the "stranger within the gates." In postwar South Africa, the Afrikaner's own misery was preeminent.

Enter Hoggenheimer

In addition to widespread antagonism toward the competitive and omnipresent alien Jewish trader, the postwar years witnessed further reinforcement of that other stereotypical Jew, the cosmopolitan financier. The consolidation of this image must be seen against the background of postwar reconstruction. These were years in which the Milner administration in the Transvaal, ably abetted by mining capital, vigorously displayed its power and influence. In short, the prewar and wartime fears about the power of mining magnates rapidly materialized. This became apparent shortly after hostilities ceased in 1902 when mineowners began to advocate that Chinese laborers be imported to replace dwindling reserves of African labor.[29] This was an issue of great concern and disturbed important sectors of the white population.

In the struggle against the proposal the cosmopolitan financier figured prominently. As G. H. Maasdorp (Midlands) put it in the Cape Legislative Council, the "Yellow Peril" was the result of a few people wanting to make money and wanting to get rich even faster than at present. Mining interests, he argued, undermined South Africa's real interests and were to be resisted. Some months prior to Maasdorp's condemnation, Merriman, who, as we saw earlier, was a man of xenophobic tendencies, had warned that if action were not taken, the country would very rapidly be dominated by the Chinese. This, he warned, would mean the end of South Africa as a European country.[30]

Opponents of the Chinese-labor scheme saw the plan as complicating the country's already fragile racial and labor problems. Smuts, for one, warned that the importation would exacerbate the "racial tangle." According to his official biographer, W. K. Hancock, Smuts was furious with the imputation that the Boers-Afrikaners had consented or even acquiesced in Milner's plans. In a major address, he claimed the Boers were indignant "against the sacrilege of Chinese importation—this spoliation of the heritage for which the generations of the people have sacrificed their all." Because 80 percent of the gold mines were unproductive, there was, in Smuts's opinion, enough labor for the needs of the country. He was particularly upset with the mineowners and foreign administrators who looked upon South Africa as a black man's country, "good enough to make money or a name in but not good enough to be born or die in." International financiers were once again in the dock. By bemoaning their sinister influence, however, the Boers placed themselves, as Denoon puts it, "in a flattering light as the only realistic salvation for a magnate-dominated society."[31]

Boer interests were supported by the *Transvaal Critic,* which argued that importing Chinese labor would result in conflict between the mining industry and the vast majority of the population who wielded political power. This, explained the newspaper, would have deplorable consequences for the country. The same newspaper argued that the "capitalist press" minimized or ignored public opinion in this "money-ridden country." Mining companies, it noted, were offering Johannesburg a stark choice between accepting Chinese labor or being ruined.[32] Once again the Randlord, or "Goldbug," had captured center stage of South African politics.

Talented cartoonists and vitriolic satirists relentlessly "exposed" the allegedly malicious and malevolent designs of the mining magnates. The *Owl* was again particularly prominent in its critique of mining power. This weekly continued to conflate capitalist and Jew, with its cartoonist, Egersdörfer, excelling in his vicious depictions of financiers, devoid of scruples and bent only on self-aggrandizement. His message was simple: Only the magnates would benefit from the importation of Chinese labor. African and Afrikaner labor was now dispensable. Egersdörfer's cartoons were replete with sarcasm and crude insinuation, and the semitic appearance of his Goldbugs left no doubt as to which sector of the population was responsible for the state of affairs (see fig. 6). Indeed a typically contemptuous comment beneath one of his Goldbug cartoons made the implication abundantly clear: "A thumbnail sketch of a well-known Rand Magnate who believes in Chinese labor, in forcing the black man to work on the mines, in no taxation of mineral products, in the IDB Act and in fact in all things but truth, justice, charity and God."[33]

The reference to truth, justice and charity—the cornerstone of an ethical life according to the Hebrew prophet Micah—was an obvious jibe at Jews and their association with the interests of capital. For the Jewish reader, the blatant abuse of the prophet's teachings must have been particularly offensive.[34]

Clearly the Goldbugs were under assault and Egersdörfer depicted them having to escape a Johannesburg crowd that had protested against the importation of Chinese labor.[35] Another Egersdörfer cartoon portrayed a Jewish taskmaster, "Moses," in conversation with Milner, capturing all the nuances of the cosmopolitan financier: the exploitative capitalist allied to the state (Milner) and advocating the importation of Chinese labor. In the cartoon, Moses is asked by the high commissioner whether all magnates consider Chinese labor necessary. The Jew replies: "Vy yeth, of courth they do." The passive observers witnessing Milner's interaction with Moses respond: "We have had Milner and Moses; the other fellow will be no worse" (see fig. 7). Significantly, the accents are those originally associated with Jewish traders and Peruvians. Here was a crude way of ensuring that the financier was recognized as a Jew and an indication that the Peruvian and cosmopolitan financier were the same—a harbinger of future perceptions.

The Jewish financier, then, was portrayed by the *Owl* as the villain behind the importation of Chinese labor. While one commentator suggested that the Chinese might outwit the Jew, it was seen as more likely that Jew and Chinese would form an alliance. In that case, explained a futuristic account, "Roughing it up in Joburg," only whites of "the Jewish persuasion" would be allowed to walk the pavements of the "golden city."[36]

While the *Owl* was most vociferous in associating specifically Jewish financiers with the Chinese-labor issue, its opinions were shared by others. Labor politicians in Cape Town, for instance, very often identified Jews as the villains behind the scheme. As labor spokesman J. Carver claimed, the idea of importing Chinese workmen originated with men bearing names such as Beit, Solomon, and Moses, and not Englishmen. In his opinion, aliens "were parasites and from parasites they became usurers and then capitalists."[37]

Mining power was thus popularly perceived as malevolent and subversive. As H. C. van Zyl (North Western Province) told the Cape Legislative Council, the Transvaal was "in the power of money magnates to the detriment of the people of the country." Van Zyl went on to paint a picture of mineowners exploiting the country at the expense of all and then behaving like vultures "who having devoured the carrion, left." His views were shared by J. A. C. Graaff (North Western Province) and expanded by a left-wing orator, J. W. Kelly, at an antialien rally in Cape Town: "Where were these people to be found in case of emergency?" asked Kelly. "Whenever England was engaged with the enemy in battle, were the people found on the side of England? No, they were always on the side of the enemy and they came in and reaped the harvest for which Britain's sons had shed their blood"[38] (see fig. 8).

The "Yellow Peril" had obviously rekindled conspiracy theories and issues of Jewish loyalty that went back to the Jameson Raid and Anglo-Boer War. As "Jewchina" complained to the *Natal Mercury,* New Zealand troops had fought "for the benefit of the grasping Jewish capitalist whilst those men who did the fighting are denied employment." The writer wondered why white labor on the mines had been economical in other parts of the world but could allegedly not be in Africa. It was, he pointed out, the Jew who "is not satisfied with 10, 20 or even 100 per cent on his money, but must have it increased, at the expense of the Britishers, many of whom would be glad of the proverbial half loaf today."[39]

This sort of attack provoked a Jewish response. An indignant correspondent, "Israel," stated in a letter to the *South African News* that it was "time the current nonsense indulged in by thoughtless, ill-informed people about Jews being responsible for the coming of Chinese had its quietness." Some weeks earlier a Jewish communal leader, David Goldblatt, had similarly taken exception to Carver's accusation that specifically Jewish mining magnates were behind the Chinese-labor proposals. Goldblatt correctly perceived Carver's charges as examples of blatant antisemitism hidden under the convenient "Yellow blanket."[40]

Both "Israel's" and Goldblatt's retorts had little impact. By the time they responded, "Jew" and "capitalist" were securely and comfortably conflated in the popular mind—a bond exemplified in the emergence of a popular cartoon character, Hoggenheimer, the quintessential Jewish parvenu. Although D. C. Boonzaier was responsible for this cartoon representation, Hoggenheimer was not his creation. This distinction belongs to the English playwright Owen Hall, who created the avuncular millionaire Max Hoggenheimer, in his West End musical comedy *The Girl from Kays*. This story of an alluring show dancer who enthralled a South African millionaire opened at London's Apollo Theatre in 1902, playing for 432 performances before being brought to South Africa by the London Gaiety Club under the auspices of Messrs. Wheeler and Edwardes.[41]

The loud-mouthed Hoggenheimer became an instant favorite with South African theatergoers.[42] By all accounts the English comedian W. W. Walton delighted audiences with his portrayal of the wealthy Jewish financier of Park Lane.[43] It was ten days after *The Girl from Kays* opened at the Good Hope Theatre in Cape Town that Boonzaier published his first Hoggenheimer cartoon, acknowledging Owen Hall's creation by appending the caption "with apologies to 'The Girl from Kays.'"[44] Thereafter Hoggenheimer became a regular feature in the *South African News,*[45] following the cartoonist for close on four decades as he worked for the *Cape,* the *Observer,* the *Cape Argus, De Voorloper, New Nation,* and *Die Burger.*[46]

Hoggenheimer manifestly struck a responsive chord in the popular consciousness. Only in this way can we explain the delight expressed by audiences at Walton's portrayal of the Park Lane millionaire and the enduring popularity of Boonzaier's Hoggenheimer cartoons. The ostensible power of the Randlords, the imperialist nature of the Anglo-Boer conflict, the infiltration of pro-Boer ideology from Britain's radical Left, which associated the Anglo-Boer War with Jewish financiers, and the controversial issue of Chinese labor ensured Hoggenheimer's transition from stage character to popular culture. It is no wonder that, within two years, he became in the words of Merriman, "a classical character." More important, however, was the fact that Hoggenheimer was a specifically Jewish symbol, following in the tradition of cartoons that appeared in Europe toward the end of the nineteenth century. In the South African context Hoggenheimer was closely associated with Milner, the man accused of siding with the mineowners to enable, in the words of the *South African News,* "an alien plutocracy to crush a much larger section of the British people."[47]

Boonzaier significantly contested the "Hebraic" nature of his cartoon creation in a "pictorial evolution" of the caricature which argued that the Hoggenheimer character was an amalgam of European types. It is difficult to gauge how convincing Boonzaier's explanation was. Suffice it to say that the *SAJC* reprinted his explanatory "evolution" without comment. The uncanny similarity between the cartoon character and the onetime Cape Town mayor, Hyman Liberman, suggests that the latter—a rather squat and corpulent gentleman—may well have served as Boonzaier's inspiration. Certainly Liberman was well known to the artist. This, however, remains conjecture.[48]

Far clearer was the popular postwar perception (and one that would be a leitmotif of South African antisemitism throughout the first half of the twentieth century) that Jews or "foreigners" threatened to dominate South African society. This fear was lucidly illustrated in the Reverend A. I. Steytler's reminder to the Dutch Reformed Synod that during his youth the only known photograph of a Jew had been in his possession. Today, he warned, "there were over 12,000 Jews in Cape Town," and "if they did not convert the Jews the Jews would convert them." While Steytler was driven by religious imperatives, others viewed Jewish ubiquity in a more fundamental way. "We are beginning to realize," noted the *Natal Witness* in 1906, "that there is no value in the prosperity of enormous industries, protected by elaborate laws, owned and managed by a dozen men, principally foreigners, and from whom the racial owners of the land are excluded." It was this sort of sentiment that had provoked the *SAJC* to deny charges that Jews monopolized commerce in Johannesburg and that the city was "entirely dependent" on them.[49] Evidently the purported power of "Hoggenheimer" and the unabated influx of alien Jews together provided a sense of Jewish domination as well as a threat to English control of trade and commerce.

The notion of Jewish domination, coupled with the conflation of all dimensions of the negative stereotype discussed hitherto, was concisely illustrated in a letter to the *Owl* from "Rondebosch Britisher." Having visited Johannesburg, the writer was struck "with considerable force at the presence of representatives of the chosen people." "Jewburg," he maintained, was certainly an appropriate appellation for the city. The Jews had, after all, "spread in all directions, they permeate every phase of life; they are ubiquitous." Their "connections," he maintained, "extend to the remotest point of the country," and their influence was felt "everywhere." For "Rondebosch Britisher," that influence was unquestionably pernicious. A mining magnate had in fact told him that the Jews were unhappy with British rule, a view confirmed for him by "a rather well known Johannesburg Jew." The latter had quite blatantly informed him that he had "no time" for "de Pritish Government!" According to "Rondebosch Britisher," such disloyalty was "common knowledge" and hardly surprising since Jewish "loyalty resting as it always did, on a materialistic and cash basis, could not well be expected to stand the strain that had made itself felt in their pockets since the war came to an end." The Jews, he argued, "did not bargain for adversity and disappointment and, possibly work." As his friend had put it, "they would probably have another war tomorrow to change the state of things and I'm not sure whether some of them are not using their influence in this direction."[50]

Philosemitism, Culture, and Race

Given the pervasiveness of such anti-Jewish sentiments as manifested in the negative stereotype, it strikes the historian as something of an anomaly that so many Jews attained prominent positions in South African public and civic life during the early twentieth century. Consider, for example, the following Jewish mayors in office around the turn of the century: D. Wasserberg (Barberton); F. Ginsberg (Kingwilliamstown); Landau (Standerton); H. Liberman (Cape Town); W. Sagar (Kimberley). Without a reservoir of goodwill and respect toward the Jew, this would surely have been impossible. One may indeed argue that the stereotype was merely a "dislike of the unlike," a low-keyed antipathy toward the outsider, be he Jew, Indian, or any other ethnic minority. It was, in other words, the sort of "vague" and "often mild" antipathy referred to by Marrus in his concentric-rings model of antisemitism, which will be discussed in the concluding chapter. Such antipathy could manifest itself in negative stereotyping, snobbishness, and even social exclusion. Krut has shown some evidence of the questionable status of the Jew in private clubs at this time, although it must be noted that this sort of exclusion was far less pervasive than in the United States.[51] But it is not to be confused with strident European antisemitism at this time, the sort of hatred that enters public life or the political agenda. This would have to await the 1930s. In early twentieth-century South Africa the Jews' alleged thrift, enterprise, energy, and intellectual prowess continued to be respected. Despite a vicious and fast-growing anti-Jewish stereotype, ambivalences and ambiguities evident in the 1880s and 1890s survived the onslaught of itinerant pedlars and Peruvians.

The positive dimension of the stereotype was captured most eloquently in Olive Schreiner's "A Letter on the Jew," read publicly at a Cape Town meeting in 1906, which protested against Russian pogroms. Besides requesting international assistance for Russia's Jews, she reminded the audience of the enormous contribution made by Jews to "the European peoples since they emerged from barbarism." Wherever the Jew "has been given even a limited measure of protection and liberty," she argued, he "has blossomed out into the noblest forms, as poet, thinker, musician, ethical teacher, and social reformer." Schreiner was astounded by those who wanted to keep the Jew out "because he has nothing today to offer the world but unholy financial methods, and that he is incapable of any other aim than making wealth for himself." The Jew, she argued:

> has been driven to finance and dealing in money as the one path open to him, and he was bound to bend all his energies to the acquiring of wealth; not only because no other paths for expanding his intellectual powers were open to him, but because, only by the possession of wealth could he hope to buy breathing space for himself or for his people. Today the Jew excels in finance, as with his perseverance, concentration and intellectual force, he is bound to do in almost every line of life to which he devotes himself. But when it is asserted that the Jew should be excluded because he corrupts our excellent financial and commercial methods, I am astonished at the temerity of the assertion.

Schreiner condemned those who castigated the hapless Russian Jew, separating him from the respectable Jewish establishment. She had lived among poor Jews in the East End of London and had witnessed their standards and values: "Therefore I say that I would welcome the exiled Russian Jew to South Africa, not merely with pity, but with a feeling of pride that any member of that great much suffering people, to whom the world owes so great a debt, should find a refuge and a home among us; and with the certainty, that however broken, crushed and dwarfed he might appear to be by the long ages of suffering and wrong which have passed over him, he would recuperate and rise."[52]

Schreiner's liberal sentiments reflected the worldview of the late nineteenth century. Her comments were certainly a far cry from her initial reactions to Jewish fortune-seekers in the early 1870s. In the ensuing decades she had obviously developed an overwhelming sympathy for the downtrodden and persecuted Russian Jew. Of course, her feelings were underpinned by a general sympathy for the underdog and an enormous respect for the individual, coupled with religious tolerance and a broad-based humanism. Liberty and equality would in her view "regenerate" the Jew, a victim of historical injustice. They reveal too, the pervasiveness of the anti-Jewish stereotype and the inclination of some commentators still to separate "knave" from "gentleman" Jews.

Nevertheless, nineteenth-century Whiggish assumptions of progress and improvement had evidently survived and were by no means limited to Schreiner. Even Merriman, despite his disdain for the Peruvian, looked forward to second-generation Jews becoming good citizens. He commended the Jews' emphasis on education, noting how these immigrants sent their "children to school to learn the way of the country, in order that they might prove good citizens in the future." Russian-Jewish immigrants were also praised by Johannesburg's mayor, J. W. Quinn, who claimed that Jews were "always foremost in all that went into the making of good citizens." On another occasion he spoke of the magnificent way in which the "Jewish people . . . bound together by kith and kin . . . ran to help each other." This, he contended, was a lesson "for the whole world."[53]

Substantial sympathy for Jews obviously existed, frequently fueled by the excesses of anti-Jewish journalism. Hence the *Peninsula Herald* expressed disquiet at the treatment of Jews in the local press and reminded its readers that these people had stood "side by side with Britain's sons" in the South African War. Jews, in other words, were not simply exploiting the country without giving anything in return. This popular myth was similarly challenged by Paarl's mayor, Septimus de Villiers, who maintained that Jews did not "come to a country to make as much money as they could and then return to their homes." In his estimation, the fact that Jews were building a new synagogue in Paarl was indicative of their confidence in the country. This pleased him because Jews were, as he put it, a race "who by their keen business instincts and general traits so peculiar to themselves, had always their eyes open to eventualities."[54]

It should be noted that in both philosemitic and antisemitic discourse, Jews were perceived as a race. This was the point Merriman had made in 1898 when he criticized the Reverend Tobias of O'Kiep, and was of course consonant with Jewish self-definition at this time. In the early twentieth century race and culture were conflated with cultural predilections being ascribed to inherent and ineradicable racial traits.

Thus Judge J. G. Kotze could praise Jews for their thrift and sound business qualities, and the Boer General Louis Botha could allude to the keen "business insight" of Jews. It was similarly this conflation of race and culture that enabled the educationist M. C. Bruce, to generalize about Jewish racial identity when describing Jewish life in Johannesburg. The community, she claimed, indulged in concerts, dances, "and gaieties of various descriptions," while the children were, on the whole, "intelligent, very musical and able to make the best of their advantage." Despite very austere conditions for many of the immigrants, claimed Bruce, "there are no paupers and there are no beggars." Jews, moreover, were not "bigoted." "Hospitable and kind, hardworking and thrifty" was her summation of Johannesburg's Jewish community. "If they succeed where other people fail," she argued, "it is because they deserve success." That view was in line with Johannesburg's mayor, G. H. Goch, who argued that it was to the credit of Jews that they dominated financial and commercial pursuits.[55]

In many ways, then, the Jew was appropriated as the exemplar of bourgeois values that were considered necessary for a society undergoing economic and political reconstruction. More significant, however, was the previously noted racial definition of Jewish identity, a product, at least in part, of the hugely conspicuous eastern European presence. By the early twentieth century, the latter vastly outnumbered Jews of Anglo-German origin, consolidating a distinctively racial image of the Jew.[56] As a result, in the postwar years commentators were less inclined to distinguish between acculturated and alien Jews.

By way of example, a series of articles on "Ways to Wealth," in the *Sunday Times* maligned Jews (without qualification) and Portuguese for illicit gold buying. "The Kaffir," noted the article, "sells to the Jew or Portuguese illicits in exchange for liquor at a price which represents nothing like the gold contents of the slime." A Standard Bank inspector in the Johannesburg suburb of Fordsburg (considered to be South Africa's Whitechapel) similarly reported that "opportunities for doing any sound business seem limited, the trade of the place being largely in the hands of branches of Johannesburg houses or of Jewish traders whose commercial morality is often of a low order." The absence of class or regional distinction is important—an omen of the future. When Mofi, a black man, complained to the police about a transaction with one J. Rostovsky, the policeman responded that "had he gone to some decent firm . . . not to the Jewish dealers, he would have experienced no

trouble." The wording of an advertisement placed by a Mr. Walton in a
Krugersdorp newspaper went even further by introducing the notion of
exclusion—an idea that would gain greater adherence in the 1920s and
1930s: "All work done by British workmen—no Jews employed here." A
new discourse in which perceptions of eastern European Jews defined
all Jews was patently in the making. It was now even necessary for
a Standard Bank inspector to include the word *respectable* when referring to particular Jewish businessmen whose accounts were considered
satisfactory.[57]

Another factor consolidating a Jewish racial identity inhered in the
incipient Zionist movement. Zionism reinforced the idea that Jews
were a people or a nation apart and not simply a religious group. This
premise was accepted by a range of Christians sympathetic to the
Zionist ideal. One such sympathizer, W. P. Schreiner, told a Zionist
meeting in Cape Town that Jews

> had throughout the whole years of history provided . . . [the] seers,
> the poets, statesmen and the workers, and the makers of the world. . . .
> They possessed in their leading thinkers and men, men whom hu-
> manity at large was proud to own. . . . That people with their great
> history . . . was ever seeking an answer to one great question . . .
> "Wither go ye?" . . . There was the noble ideal which once realized
> that the highest ideal of the free brotherhood of man but they were
> still far away from that ideal. In the meantime there was an ideal
> which was not so lofty, but eminently more practical and that ideal
> was embodied in the term Zionism.[58]

Another prominent liberal, Sir James Rose Innes, chief justice of the
Transvaal, was even more trenchant in his supporting claims for "Ter-
ritorialism," a Jewish national movement not specifically centered on
Palestine:

> No one could think unmoved and unconcerned of the history of that
> wonderful people who had exercised an influence on human kind out
> of all proportion to their numbers, a people without a territory of
> their own, sojourners and strangers on the face of the earth, retaining
> their individuality and their national characteristics, who after 2000
> years of difficulty, oppressors and persecution, still stood as a nation
> and still held their own amongst the people of the world. They had
> supplied men of letters, statesmen, peers, poets, artists. In all depart-
> ments of human activity the Jews were not far from the top.[59]

Thus Zionism, in the words of C. L. Botha, was for the Jews an "emblem of nationality, the pride of their race." Canon H. W. Orford also observed that despite being scattered throughout the world, Jews had maintained their nationality. Going even further, Councillor C. A. Lane of Johannesburg referred to the Jews' "purity" of race which, he argued, was an essential part of "Jewish patriotism." Their "distinguishing physiognomy," he noted, "proclaims the care with which they have preserved Isaac's tradition. Exceptions to the rule are condemned."[60] Of course, the antisemite had much the same to say but with malice aforethought.

Preserving their "nationality" did not necessarily pose problems for the Jew in South African society. In other words, "racial" loyalty was not perceived as being irreconcilable with a broader loyalty to the country. This notion was best articulated by Lord Milner at the inauguration of the Jewish Board of Deputies for Transvaal and Natal in 1903. The new organization, he noted, was "natural and above board." "This great community has its own religion, it has its own race traditions, its own loyalty. There is absolutely nothing incompatible in this with the most thorough-going British patriotism." In Milner's view it was quite acceptable that there should be "an organisation intended to protect special Jewish interests and to voice Jewish opinion."[61]

Milner's comments reveal an erosion of the classic emancipation bargain—the notion of total assimilation. Jews were encouraged to acculturate, but this did not mean jettisoning their own identity. His comments were also in line with a wider discourse vis-à-vis the African at this time. Whereas classic nineteenth-century South African liberals had wanted to "civilize" the African and amalgamate Africans into the body politic, a new ideology had begun to challenge "amalgamationist" politics. In short, a new ideology of segregation had gained ascendancy in which Africans were rather to develop along their own lines.[62] A new sense of cultural difference (in today's parlance "multiculturalism") was emerging in which ethnic or, in the case of Jews, religious differences were fully accepted. This idea was succinctly summed up by the mayor of Kingwilliamstown, J. B. Byrnes, when he pointed out that "while they might not see eye to eye" with the Jew "in regard to spiritual truth or interpretation of prophecy," "they recognised that those who composed the fellowship of that synagogue, though distinct in certain respects . . . formed a corporate part of the whole community, and whose influence would ever be with those who sought the best interests of the whole." Forming a corporate part of the community was hence quite legitimate and an understandable product of history. As the *Transvaal Leader* put it: "In Lands where Jews are harassed and persecuted, the instinct of self preservation draws them together until they become a class apart. But it is remarkable how, under free institutions, they merge into the political life of the country, without abandoning their own racial loyalty."[63]

Jews therefore had no reason to share the Reverend D. P. Faure's fears that the Draft Union Act of 1909 might discriminate against them because of stipulations that parliamentarians had to be of European descent.[64] By that time, despite their racial image, Jews were accepted as a part and parcel of the white population and, in line with liberal principles, were not to be politically differentiated. Thus, when it was rumored that Jews would have special representation in the new Union Senate, the *Transvaal Leader* asked why they should have any more claim to representation than Roman Catholics or Christian Scientists? There was, argued the newspaper, no need "to leaven the Senate with the influence of religion and culture." Special senatorial appointments would, in its opinion, be seen by the Jews "as a reflection of a sub-nationality, as indicating that it is in some way different from the members of the British Empire in South Africa."[65]

In many ways the comments of the *Transvaal Leader* reaffirmed nineteenth-century assumptions that Jews were merely a religious group and as such were fully accepted into the body politic, which was founded upon notions of common liberty, welfare, and rights. Popular perceptions of the eastern European Jew, and many other formal statements, belie these assumptions and demonstrate clearly that Jews were perceived as ineradicably different, unmistakably alien, and set apart by specific cultural predilections, underpinned by a racial essence. This image, which was not necessarily negative, would ultimately define all Jews with obvious implications for those who anticipated total assimilation.

Upward Mobility and Metamorphosis

Despite contradictory images of the Jew and the ambiguities of culture and race, observers all shared a common perception that the newcomers were upwardly mobile. This was explained in different ways, but the Jews' apparent rise from rags to riches was always commented on. It was evident in the *Johannesburg Times* description of the Peruvian, in the diatribe of "A Farmer Pure and Simple," and in many other commentaries. Even Wynberg's district surgeon, Dr. Wright, who had had so much to say about unhygienic Jewish practices in his 1902 medical report, could not ignore the transformation two years later:

> They arrived in this colony very poor, and therefore huddled together considerably. They are now all of them well-to-do. They can, therefore, afford all the luxuries of civilization. I use the word civilization with pride, for when many of them arrive they are certainly not more civilized than the Indians, an intermarried and enfeebled race. The freedom and climate have done much to invigorate them. Like Jeshurus of old, they have "waxed fat and kicked", certainly kicked off the trammels of serfdom. I also think they have kicked off the vermin and filth in which they formally lived, and to which I alluded in my previous report. They have waxed fat, rich and are good citizens, law abiding and laying good store for themselves.[66]

Besides reaffirming notions of Jewish endogamy, Wright's comments convey vividly the perceived metamorphosis of the newcomer. For some, success was seen to be a product of thrift, enterprise, and even sacrifice. For example, when judging a plaintiff accused by the deputy sheriff of being unable to afford goods because he was "a mere hawker of vegetables," Judge Kotze reminded the court of "the thrift and perseverance of the Hebrew." Not infrequently, noted the judge "the [Hebrew] commenced business by coming to one's door with a basket hawking his goods, and next he would appear with a wheelbarrow or cart, and later he would possess a shop of his own and eventually he might rise to be Mayor of the place." That the plaintiff possessed certain goods, despite his lowly position, posed no contradiction for this judge.[67]

It was similarly no contradiction for Merriman, who argued that it was the emphasis placed by Jews upon education that had enabled them in every free country to attain "the very highest positions in the land." He went even further by suggesting that everyone owed their moral sense to the Jewish race. Like Bruce (the Johannesburg educationist referred to earlier) Merriman was also impressed with Jewish benevolence and charitable endeavors.[68]

The transformation or upward mobility of the Jew was, of course, not always perceived as the outcome of toil or valuable service. For instance, when considering a Jewish immigrant's application for a hawkers license in 1907, Councillor Van Zyl of Graaff-Reinet commented that such applicants "started today with a bundle behind their back" and "drove around a few months later with a cart and flashy pair of horses such as . . . he and his fellow farmers could not afford." Because there were too many of these sorts of men, Van Zyl was opposed to issuing a license. "Hardly any produce," he pointed out, "was being brought to town nowadays, and the class of man as the one whose application was now under consideration was responsible for the deplorable state of affairs. All products etc. were being brought by the people in the country and in many cases in an undesirable manner." While the chairman of the Aberdeen Divisional Council admitted to "a great deal" of truth in what Van Zyl said, he felt the committee could not withhold a license when the "party brought satisfactory witnesses as to his good character." Moreover, noted the chairman, "the grievances in small places were not as acute as in the larger centres. In places like Oudtshoorn, and other places the Jewish element was deplorable, and the time was not far on when these people would be their bosses." The committee, he explained, could not, according to the law, withhold their consent for the applicant's license. Van Zyl remained dissatisfied, retorting indignantly that "the people who had signed the certificate as to the applicant's good character are nearly all Jews, and we all know that Jews stick to each other like a leech." Van Zyl's motion attracted laughter but was not seconded. Clearly his talk was no more than rhetoric.[69] With Indians the question of granting licenses was far more problematic. Nevertheless, the exchange was not unimportant. Obviously philosemite and antisemite shared perceptions (but obviously not explanations) of Jewish social ascent and success.

The notion of metamorphosis was forcefully illustrated in Stephen Black's *Helena's Hope Ltd,* which played for sixty-five consecutive nights in Johannesburg when first produced. The play centers around the dishonest dealings of two Jews, Abraham Goldenstein and Samuel Shearer, who persuade a naive Afrikaans girl, Helena Joubert, to part with her inherited farm. Unknown to her, but known to them, the farm contains deposits of gold. The plot revolves around attempts at retribution, and it is ultimately only Shearer who manages to outwit Goldenstein. The interesting feature of the play is Goldenstein's ascent from bearded smous in the opening scene to opulent Parktown financier at the close, the result of sharp and dishonest dealings. Shearer too is an unsavory character. To add to the already virulent anti-Jewish characterizations, the play includes Goldenstein's wife, an ostentatious and vulgar woman who had, according to a review in the *SAJC,* "peregrinated from Petticoat Lane to Parktown."[70]

Significantly, Goldenstein's accent is thick and guttural, an indication of the impact made by eastern European Jews upon the author. Of greater import, however, was the fact that the play's billing—"A Mirror of Rand Life"—was fully believed. Both Jewish and Gentile reviewers agreed that the portrayal of the Jews was not exaggerated and the production certainly struck a responsive chord in the popular consciousness. This might be at least part of the explanation for the overwhelming critical acclaim of *Helena's Hope Ltd.* The only apparent indication of opposition came from a group of Ferreirastown (a suburb of Johannesburg) Jews who threatened to disrupt the opening night.[71] It is possible that they had been forewarned by kinsmen who had seen the production in Cape Town, where it had been performed without incident some three months earlier.

The threatened disruption did not go unchallenged. In a letter published in the front page of the *Rand Daily Mail,* Stephen Black denied accusations of antisemitism, arguing that the play contained no villain and no Jew "of the accepted stage type." After all, he pointed out, the Polish Jew, Abraham Goldenstein, "invariably came out on top," in spite of having to compete with people "of a more cultured class," and this was "due to his shrewdness and wit."[72]

In many ways, Black's defense affirms the prevalence of a widely shared anti-Jewish stereotype. By that time, the *Northern Post and Border News* could, for instance, comfortably state that Jews committed most of the frauds in the country. Certainly it was obvious that the Peruvian Jew was uppermost in Smuts's mind when, as minister of the interior in the new Union government, he introduced a clause in an Immigration Restriction Bill "to expel from the country certain classes of persons who were not born British subjects, or who have been naturalized in the Union, and who had been sentenced for certain crimes which included diamond stealing, illicit diamond or gold dealing, and illicit liquor selling." The association with Peruvians was so apparent that a leading Unionist, Percy Fitzpatrick, warned against supposing "that those people [the target of the Bill] were associated with any religious denomination." The image of the Jewish knave had obviously not disappeared and was demonstrated once again in *A Girl from Springfontein,* produced in 1912. In this play, Solomon Shine, the mayor of Springfontein, is portrayed as "a hybrid cross between a Petticoat Lane fruit or fish vendor and a flash Fagin."[73]

The eastern European Jew was patently still an unwelcome addition to society. Old associations of the Jew with uncleanliness and dishonesty were still rampant. As late as 1913, the medical officer of health for Johannesburg, Dr. C. Porter, referred to a substantial production of milk in the city being in the hands of "low class eastern Europeans who presumably by reason of their early environment and want of education have absolutely no idea of the word cleanliness." In Rustenburg, E. Alta, the secretary of the Magaliesberg Tobacco Growers Association, warned "that if certain contingencies did not take place the Dutch tobacco growers would fall into the hands of Jews." When challenged on his comments by the *SAJC,* Alta pointed out that the word *Jew* was an adjective even "used by Israelites when they wish to indicate that a certain person cannot be trusted in business matters."[74]

Alta's defense was surely of little consolation to the Jewish editor. It demonstrated just how tarnished the Jewish image had become following the influx of eastern European Jews.[75] These newcomers indeed defined the nature of Jewishness. Moreover, they were symbolic of change and social upheaval and, most importantly, the power of grasping materialism. To the "present day" claimed Jac van Belkom, a Dutch Reformed clergyman from Bloemfontein, the Jew "still worshipped the golden calf and forsook God. . . . he lived only for gold. They forget God and live for this world." Van Belkom did, however, accept "Israel" as the chosen race which would still be saved but "would have to go through the wilderness again." Thus it is hardly surprising that early in 1914 the *SAJC* arrived at the following laconic assessment: "South Africa as a whole—contrary to the expectations of the would be immigrant—does not accord a very hearty welcome and apparently is already regretting that she made it possible for them to come."[76]

Constructing a Stereotype

The Jewish stereotype that had emerged in South Africa by the outbreak of the Great War was intimately bound up with the local stresses and upheavals engendered by the "mineral revolution." Although it confirmed and, in a way, reinforced the widely shared European Jewish stereotype, the South African image was not simply its reflection. The caricatures of Hoggenheimer and Goldenstein were indeed deeply embedded in a South African reality. The Jew, in other words, was not invented in the Sartrean sense.[77] Nor was he a mythical figure.

No one could ignore the approximately 40,000 Jews (the vast majority from eastern Europe) who had entered South Africa in the four decades before Union. On the one hand, many admired Jewish enterprise, initiative, and thrift as well as their wide-ranging contributions to society. Furthermore, their communal values were considered exemplary. On the other hand, the distinctive dress, exotic language, and strange manner of the eastern European defined the Jew as a classic alien or outsider. These newcomers conjured up images of the ghetto, of the medieval. More importantly, eastern European Jews increasingly defined "Jewishness" in the South African context. Distinctions between them and the acculturated Anglo-German Jewish establishment were increasingly blurred.[78]

The overwhelming presence of eastern European Jews also ensured the definition of Jews as a racial group—a notion, as mentioned before, shared by Jew and Gentile alike. Race and culture were, as we have seen, conflated in the early twentieth century. Moreover, acquired characteristics were believed, in neo-Lamarckian fashion, to be inherited and, in eugenicist terms, ineradicable. Even criminality was associated, in the Lombrosian view, with physical appearance.[79]

While many Jews eked out an appalling and poverty-ridden existence, others achieved great heights in mining and business. The emergence of the latter from their poverty stricken Peruvian status was, for the antisemite at least, ascribable to endemic dishonesty. Guile had enabled the Peruvian to achieve plutocratic eminence. Hoggenheimer, allegedly the eminence grise of South Africa, merely symbolized on a higher plane the machinations of the Jewish pedlar and the illicit diamond dealer. The upstart in *Helena's Hope Ltd,* Abraham Goldenstein, similarly embodied all the dimensions of the stereotype: in the opening scene of the play he straddles the stage as an unkempt, bearded pedlar, only to become transformed through his cunning intrigues into a wealthy financier. His metamorphosis was that of the classic parvenu. For the philosemite, the metamorphosis was differently attributed— to thrift, enterprise, and business acumen. Ultimately, for both philo- and antisemite, upward mobility presupposed a potential for Jewish domination.

It was indeed the threat of competition and the fear of domination that fueled much anti-Jewish sentiment. This was evident in both the rural areas and urban centers. As one correspondent to the *Cape Times* put it during the height of Cape Town's postwar economic depression: "Can one wonder that there are so many British workmen unemployed in this town when these Jews, who by their mode of living, or rather existence, are able to compete with them at lower wages." "Petty trade," noted the *Cape Times* at this time, was "gradually being absorbed by a MOST UNDESIRABLE class of people. The large number of unsavory looking fruit shops, fifth rate grocery stores and similar places of business, which have been opened in recent months, furnish unpleasant proof that the undesirable alien has established himself pretty firmly in Cape Town."[80] Similar sentiments were evident in a Standard Bank inspector's report for Paarl:

> There are about 1 000 competing in storekeeping, hawking, shoe-making, tailoring and other small industries, while the amount of small shops is quite out of proportion to the needs of the community. The competition is detrimental to the needs of the larger and more expensively conducted stores, and any great increase must lead to the depreciation of store and shop property of the better class.
>
> Recent insolvencies have been confined chiefly to this class of traders, and the Manager is to be congratulated in keeping his books free from their names. The local manager of the Bank of Africa has pursued a similar policy and discouraged dealings with the small Jewish trader, with the result that this class of business is mainly restricted to the African Banking Corporation.[81]

Thus at a time of great stress and upheaval the Jew appeared for many to be the main beneficiary of change. For the impoverished farmer, he was a symbol of greed, living by his wits and alien to all that was valued; he was rootless, scheming, and not given to manual work. These negative characteristics were also evident in the urban context where Jews, allegedly adept on the Stock Exchange and supposedly comfortable with finance, stood out as "an urban people par excellence."[82] While religious differences may have sharpened perceptions, it was the actual encounter between Jew and Gentile that determined the stereotype.[83] For the antisemite the Jew symbolized all that was evil in the modern world, a world nostalgically contrasted with an idealized past age of order and harmony.

Thus, notwithstanding the influence of deep-seated European traditions and late nineteenth-century nationalist discourse, anti-Jewish prejudice in South Africa was discernibly rooted in specific local conditions. In other words, Pinsker's celebrated notion that Judeophobia was a "form of demonopathy . . . a psychic aberration" lacks sophistication. Nor is antisemitism, as he contends, "hereditary" and "as a disease transmitted over two thousand years incurable." In the South African situation Schermerhorn's assessment is more acceptable: Prejudice is "a product of situations, historical situations, political situations, it is not a little demon that emerges in people simply because they are depraved."[84]

To accept Schermerhorn's view does not mean that one may ignore the Western legacy of antisemitism. Nor does it mean that one can attribute blame almost solely to the victim as some exponents of interaction analysis, a genre of recent British scholarship on antisemitism, are inclined to do.[85] It is simply to argue that prejudice—as manifest in the Jewish stereotype—must be understood in the broader social, historical, and cognitive context. For many categories of the social spectrum—the impoverished farmer, the unemployed worker, the competing merchant, and the frustrated businessman or financier—the stereotype served as a psychological cushion. It furnished a convenient scapegoat in an age of turmoil.

Fig. 1. From the *Owl*, 1.1.1901

THE EVIL OF THE HOUR.

Fig. 2. From the *Owl*, 17.10.1902

Fig. 3. From the *Owl*, 6.5.1904

PAUPER "PERUVIANS" OR THE WHITENING OF SOUTH AFRICA

The Roumanians & Russians turn out the poor Jews wholesale.

They are shipped by philanthropic societies to London, where passes are given them to South Africa.

On the steamers they are anything but popular

One enterprising Schnorrer utilised the sheets supplied him by the C.U.S.S. to make himself a suit of clothes

At Capetown they are dumped on shore with the greatest expedition.

The Harbour Board are considering the advisability of disinfecting them immediately after landing

Fig. 4. From the *Owl*, 13.2.1903

The Law: "When I've done with this job, I shall see what can be done with these others!"   (See Special Article opposite.)

Fig. 5. From the *Transvaal Critic*, 10.1.1908

Fig. 6. From the *Owl*, 14.2.1902

Fig. 7. From the *Owl*, 18.3.1904

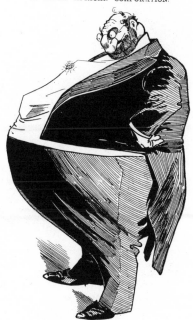

Fig. 8. From the *Owl*, 20.12.1901

Fig. 9. "Choose the right road today." From *Die Burger,* 18.5.1938

DIE OORWINNAAR

DIE MAN WAT IN WERKLIKHEID DIE VERKIESING GEWEN HET.

Fig. 10. "The winner." From *Die Burger*, 23.5.1938

CHAPTER FOUR

Shirkers and Subversives: Embellishing the Jewish Stereotype, 1914–21

War and Recruitment

DURING THE Great War and in the immediate postwar years all dimensions of the Jewish stereotype were consolidated and even embellished.[1] One elaboration introduced during the war was the accusation of Jewish "shirking" or "slacking"—a variation on earlier charges of disloyalty and parasitism, relating in addition to conceptions of the Jew as an outsider. Following the overthrow of the Russian tsar in 1917, the war years also witnessed the emergence of a powerful anti-Bolshevist ideology that incorporated anti-Jewish sentiment due to the part Jews had allegedly played in the destruction of the Romanov dynasty. The ramifications of the Russian revolution in South Africa were not inconsiderable, particularly in the immediate postwar years of economic recession and labor unrest.

The notion of Jewish disloyalty that had been hinted at before the war was ignited by the sensitive question of military recruitment. According to the Labour party politician Morris Kentridge, Jewish involvement in the war effort was regularly questioned at the hustings during the general election campaign of 1915 and the matter was also raised in parliament. By late 1915 the *Rand Daily Mail* and *Sunday Times* charged Jewish youth "with not responding to the call to arms in proportion to [their] ratio in the general population." In an apologetic and defensive tone, the *SAJC* suggested that people incorrectly assumed all Jews in Johannesburg were eligible to take up arms. In fact, argued the Jewish weekly, only four or five thousand of the eighteen to twenty thousand Jews in Johannesburg were British subjects "and consequently entitled to offer their services to the crown."[2]

That the *SAJC* deemed it necessary to respond to charges of disloyalty is indicative of extensive concern and unease. This weekly's rationalizations, together with those of the South African Jewish Board of Deputies, suggest that charges of shirking or slacking went beyond the rantings of insignificant individuals or newspapers.[3] Toward the end of 1916, a series of letters appeared in the *Natal Advertiser* accusing Russian Jews of taking advantage "of the absence of the boys to grow fat."[4]

With a major recruitment drive in early 1917, the enlistment issue assumed more serious proportions. "It is now the duty of every eligible young man to come to a final decision," noted an editorial in the *Rand Daily Mail*. Every able-bodied man, argued the newspaper, "should be made to realize what 'slacking' means when the last solemn appeal is rejected. The eligible man who refuses to help the Empire in this regard will live to regret very bitterly the selfishness which inclined him to shirk his duty."[5] Predictably, attention was focused upon the Jew. As the *Standerton Advertiser* noted: "Very few Jews have yet risked loss of life or property by leaving their homes to assist the Empire of their adoption in her hour of agony and need."[6] In the heat of the recruitment drive, the question of Jewish enlistment occupied the correspondence pages of major newspapers. "Twelve Pounder" was particularly harsh in his observations:

> Look around Mr Editor, any place of amusement in any town you like in South Africa, everywhere you will see hundreds of strong, healthy, eligible young Jews, who should be in khaki fighting. Look in the stores, there you will find them in soft, easy, comfortable cribs. Go to the seaside now, Muizenberg as a start, any evening or Sundays, see how many recruits could be picked up there. I am quite aware that many Jews have enlisted, good luck to them; they knew their duty. Slackers we hear mentioned every day, and taking a look around on Sunday last, it is the Jews that are the biggest slackers of any as far as I could count. . . . We have drawn and drained off our best from every quarter, and I really think the time has come when the Jews can make some sort of sacrifice in Britain's cause.[7]

"Twelve Pounder's" recriminations were shared by "Returned British East African Soldier," who suggested that "Jews ought to be ashamed of themselves. They are doing the American trick here—filling their pockets and doing nothing in return for the protection they enjoy under the British flag." It mattered little that "A British Soldier and a Jew" attacked the Cape Town press for allowing "slanderous letters and reports of calumnious speeches" against Jews to "continually appear . . . without even an editorial note in contradiction."[8]

In Johannesburg, R. H. Henderson, in a letter to the *Rand Daily Mail,* claimed that many businesses were falling "exclusively into the hands of aliens, chiefly Greeks and Russians [i.e., Jews]". Henderson advocated conscription, including the formation of Greek and Russian battalions. He was confident that "influential citizens of these nationalities are ready to volunteer for the work of organisation." Henderson's call for conscription was supported by "A Veteran," who argued that thousands of people of foreign origin "should either join the forces under the British flag or be compelled to return to their respective countries."[9]

The recruitment drive quite obviously kindled passions and in the process raised old charges of Jewish exploitation and disloyalty. These allegations upset "M R" (a regular but unidentified Jewish correspondent to the Cape Town press), who warned of "a revival of old hatreds and Jew baiting" in the press. These "virulent attacks" could, he asserted, "lead to an explosion of passion such as Cape Town had experienced in the anti-German riots." In defense of the Jewish community, "M R" highlighted the Jewish contribution to South African industry. He argued, moreover, that, relative to British forces in active service, Jews were serving in proportion to their numbers. His letter provoked heated responses from "T B B" and "R M." The former accused "M R" of "decrying the country that shelters him and his race" and sneering "at the English as being slackers more than his own people." "R M," in turn, quoted a viciously antisemitic letter (from Petrograd's *Novoe Vremya*) which identified every Russian revolutionary as Jewish. In his opinion this proved that Jews were slackers and internationalists. "M R's" Jewish industrialists were dismissed simply as exploiters of the "poorer classes," unlike "the Rhodeses, Hofmeyrs and Merrimans." While admitting that some Jews were good and dutiful, "R M" warned that his statements reflected "the thoughts of very many well wishers of the land, who are not out for profiteering etc."[10]

One of the complications facing the Russian Jew in South Africa and the question of recruitment was of course his enormous antipathy toward the country of his birth. Joining the allied war effort meant, in effect, supporting the very regime that oppressed and persecuted him. This issue was appreciated in some quarters. "Ex-Soldier," for instance, noted that the Russians "have a reason probably for not wanting to fight." W. H. Harrison, a prominent socialist, went further, arguing that Russian Jews looked favorably upon Germany, a country that had supplied them with forbidden literature. In addition, claimed Harrison, Jews were "essentially pacifists, and of a philosophical trend of mind rather than adventurers daring and sport characteristic of warlike communities. . . . Their religion also is a theocratic socialism unadorned by any military display so conspicuous in other creeds."[11]

These arguments naturally lost their forcefulness with the overthrow of the tsarist regime in February of 1917, a fact noted by the *Rand Daily Mail*. Consequently the question of Jewish recruitment remained alive as the war moved into its final stages. The surest evidence of widespread disquiet emerged in the proceedings of a legal wrangle between the editor of the *SAJC,* Lionel Goldsmid, and S. Vogelson, editor of the *African Jewish World*. The dispute centered on Vogelson's charge that Goldsmid was antisemitic because he had urged Jewish recruitment (and thus encouraged antisemites in their campaign) through the columns of his newspaper. Goldsmid considered the charge libelous. In his evidence he explained how Johannesburg's mayor and chairman of the Recruiting Committee, J. W. O'Hare, had urged him to push for Jewish recruitment because complaints "from all parts of the country" about Russian Jews not enlisting had reached him. O'Hare shared these sentiments, warning Goldsmid that there "was and is a certain amount of feeling against the Russian Jew which may break out at any moment!" He had asked Goldsmid to exercise whatever "influence he might possess to endeavor to induce these people to see their duty in the proper light." O'Hare's views were supported by Henry Filmer, an attorney and member of the Johannesburg Recruiting Committee. Filmer maintained that the Russian Jew as distinct from the British Jew "was very conspicuous in Johannesburg and on the Reef." To illustrate his argument, Filmer referred to a store on the Nourse Mines where, out of eight Russian Jewish employees, an anticipated two recruits could not be enlisted. According to Filmer, less than 1 percent of Russian Jews had come forward for service. That Filmer singled out specifically Russian Jews demonstrates that the old nineteenth-century divisions between Anglo-German (or acculturated Jews) and Russian Jews had not entirely disappeared.[12]

Jewish leaders appear to have heeded the warnings emerging from the Goldsmid-Vogelson case. In Cape Town the Reverend Alfred Bender, Morris Alexander, and Hyman Liberman established a Jewish Statistical Bureau to ascertain the number of Jews serving in the Union, Colonial, and Imperial Defense forces. Alexander, moreover, told congregants during a synagogue service in Cape Town "that all young men able and fit to go should join the fighting forces." His call was fully supported by the *SAJC*.[13]

When the Goldsmid-Vogelson case resumed in March 1918 after an adjournment, the evidence of Bernard Alexander, chairman of the Jewish Board of Deputies, confirmed once again widely shared negative perceptions of the Russian Jew, if not all Jews. When asked if Jews were castigated for not registering, Alexander responded in the affirmative. In mitigation he asserted that "it seems quite a common thing to make a football of the Jew, to kick him!" Alexander also drew attention to Major Bass, who had criticized Jews during a speech at a local theater and in addition noted that Jews were often slandered at meetings on the Market Square. In Durban a raging debate engulfed the columns of the *Natal Advertiser* following a letter from "True Russian" in which he claimed all Jews were Bolsheviks and recommended that Durban be the site of a pogrom. While some non-Jews defended the Jewish contribution and the ethical ideals of Judaism, the majority of correspondents shared "True Russian's" animus and used the occasion to vent their anger on South African Jews in general and Russian Jews in particular. In the main, Jews were accused of shirking, dishonesty, parasitism, and exploitation while one correspondent, "Uncle," accused them of financing the overthrow of the tsarist regime. However, the anti-Jewish message was best encapsulated in "Cataract's" letter: "The Jews are a distinct race of people with a somewhat different mind to anyone else's, it is the mind that causes the trouble, and to alter or remove that—you may as well try to alter the spots on the leopard."[14]

Debates surrounding the Jewish war effort underline the marginal and vulnerable status of the Jew in the public consciousness. The alien and conspicuous Russian Jew was especially susceptible; he continued to be perceived as an outsider and a disloyal one at that. Animus toward these "foreigners" was, moreover, clearly related to the well established Peruvian image and all its negative connotations. Of course, notions of war profiteering also reinforced in a most telling way earlier accusations of exploitation and dishonesty. Consequently the Russian Jew undermined the "emancipation contract" and raised important questions about the ultimate acculturation and assimilability of Jews in general.

The Bolshevik Threat

Fears of assimilability and questions of loyalty assumed even greater force after the war when thousands of new Jewish immigrants from Russia and its former dependencies were alleged to threaten to undermine South African order and stability. Coming from Bolshevist Russia, these immigrants were tarnished with the excesses of the new regime, depicted in South African newspapers as anarchistic, lawless, and violent.[15] "Bolshevist Culture," warned an editorial in the *Cape Times,* would inevitably result in "political, social and educational chaos and next a swing round to untempered despotism in the hands of an intolerant oligarchy."[16]

The anti-Bolshevist crusade characterizing South African newspapers was not unrelated to local tensions and problems. In fact, events in Russia resonated in South Africa precisely because of rising worker consciousness and socialist rhetoric. Wartime industrialization had generated a restive and increasingly radicalized black proletariat on the Witwatersrand. As prices spiraled upward and black wages remained relatively unchanged, the political atmosphere in South African urban centers became, in the words of Bonner, "correspondingly charged." But it was above all the fear of white labor radicalization and its influence on blacks that permeated the Rand. Militant left-wing socialists had broken away from the essentially racist South African Labour party during the war to form the International Socialist League in 1915. The league's internationalist and color-blind socialist policies confronted a wave of conservatism and xenophobia.[17]

Both the National party, which had set itself up as a "bulwark against Bolshevism," and the South African party manipulated the Bolshevist bogey in an attempt to tarnish labor politicians and trade unionists of all political persuasions.[18] The Cape Town press in particular raised the bogey following the formation of the Industrial Socialist League—a left-wing offshoot of Cape Town's Socialist Democratic Federation—in Cape Town after the war.[19] For the *Cape Times* this radical socialist movement was evidence of a rising tide of Bolshevism in the city. The substantial number of eastern European Jews in the movement, moreover, did not go unnoticed.[20] When Morris Alexander complained

about an antisemitic letter in the *Cape Times,* the editor responded that
it was quite pertinent to discuss the large number of Russian Jews who
were mischievous Bolshevist agitators. The *Cape* also kept a watchful
eye over developments, referring to the circle of Jewish left-wing agitator A. Z. Berman as Berman's Cape Town "Soviet."[21]

The conspicuous presence of Russian Jews among socialist agitators
therefore reinforced conservative fears of international Bolshevism and
its challenge to the established order. This was, of course, a worldwide
phenomenon in which the alien Jew was a primary target. Certainly it
was no coincidence that the minister of railways, Henry Burton, referred to "substantial elements of Bolshevism in this country" when
addressing a Zionist conference early in 1919. He indeed "looked con-
fidently to the Jewish community to stand firmly by law and order."
Commenting editorially on Burton's speech, the *Cape Times* noted that
the government was "keeping a very careful eye on Bolshevist pro-
pagandism. . . . All over the world experience is proving that Bolshevism
possesses highly infective characteristics. . . . It was found impossible to
keep the Influenza Epidemic from invading our territories but we have
now to be on our guard against an epidemic more infectious, more
destructive and vastly more costly in life and in treasure than the
influenza." The editorial went on to recommend that the government
closely scrutinize immigrants and Bolshevist literature that was finding
its way into South Africa.[22]

Both Burton's speech and the recommendations of the *Cape Times*
demonstrated the popular association of Russian Jewish immigrants
with the alleged Bolshevist threat. Indeed, in depicting the Russian Jew
as subversive, the *Cape Times* had drawn upon those notions of archetypical deviance established before the Great War. Associating worker
agitation with Bolshevism was also a convenient way of discrediting the
labor movement, and, in particular, its more radical wing. Not surprisingly, Morris Alexander took umbrage at the association of Jews with all
radical activity. In addition he condemned the use of religion when Jews
committed an offense or indiscretion.[23] No doubt Alexander, always an
energetic defendant of Jewish causes, sensed a rising tide of antisemitism emerging from turn-of-the-century antialienism.

The arrival in South Africa early in 1919 of two Russian Jews,
L. Lapitsky and I. Sosnovic, who had come to lecture on the Russian
revolution, aroused predictable hysteria in the press.[24] Sir Thomas
Smartt raised the matter in parliament, asking the minister of justice, Sir

Thomas Watt, how the two visitors had gained entry into the country and how the government intended to deal with them. According to Watt, the movements of the two Russians were to be watched despite their being rather innocuous Kerenskyites and thus ameliorist by inclination, and not Bolshevists.[25] Such ideological distinctions mattered little with the public and the local press. Their fears were confirmed by the Russians' opening lecture at the Johannesburg Town Hall where the two visitors told a very large and enthusiastic audience that the Bolsheviks were "destined to lead the proletariat of the world."[26] Not surprisingly, the lecture was described by the minister of the interior, Patrick Duncan, as "from end to end a panegyric of Bolshevism."[27]

Consequently the press articulated a number of questions which the public was patently asking. For example, the *Cape Times* remonstrated against "the scope given to aliens to use, for their sinister ends, a time of grave political and industrial unrest, when four years of world war have left people excited and prone to act without due consideration and sense of obligation." Alien agitation was clearly not acceptable to the *Cape Times* at a "time when there was a current of labour unrest on the Rand which was apt to unbalance mens minds and make them lend an ear to the specious plausibilities of Leninism." The *Star* was similarly concerned, wondering how the two Russian propagandists had come to hire the Town Hall. After all, exclaimed the editor, "Bolshevism . . . is the very antithesis of democracy and liberalism." The *Rand Daily Mail* in turn expressed fears that the Bolshevist emissaries could have a "bad effect upon the small section of activists on the Rand."[28]

The outcry against these two Russians must be seen against the upsurge of local socialist activism, including a major municipal strike in Johannesburg, and increasing economic hardship. It is therefore hardly surprising that the two "Bolshevist Emissaries" were given little opportunity for further propaganda. After a series of hysterical editorials in the *Cape Argus* and *Cape Times,* the two gentlemen were given a free trip to Russia by the government.[29]

The visit of Lapitsky and Sosnovic set in motion an anti-Bolshevist crusade that was particularly evident in Cape Town.[30] The *Cape Times* warned of a "very strong" feeling in regard to Bolshevists. The *Cape* was indeed amazed at the "seditious, poisonous and inflammatory" utterances being printed by the Industrial Socialist League, "a mere stone's throw" from parliament. An anti-Bolshevist resolution protesting against the introduction of Bolshevism was passed by the Cape

Town branch of the Comrades of the Great War, and in the Transvaal a unanimous motion was passed by farmers asking the government not to allow Bolshevism to take root in South Africa. The meeting also appealed to Afrikaners to stand against "Bolshevism, Kaferism and Mohamedanism, thus making South Africa into a Christian white mans country instead of a rotting place of disorder and violence."[31]

In this climate the considerable number of Russian Jews active in this League did little to enhance the image of the Jew.[32] The association of Jews with Bolshevism was popularly accepted and was spelled out by numerous letter writers to the press.[33] "S.O.E." best captured the anti-Russian Jewish mood in a letter, "The Bolsheviks in our midst":

> I unfortunately am engaged where the sole topic is Bolshevism, discussed by certain Russian Jews who have sheltered themselves beneath the Union Jack. Now the war is over, and having their skins fairly safe, they openly yelp disgusting epithets which are an insult to our constitution. How many of them want to go back? Not one, all they want is a 70 or 80 hour week. I say a single ticket to their adorable Russia would relieve us of an unwelcome presence, and so give a better chance to soldiers who have a right to obtain work after years of hardship and peril.[34]

Anti-Bolshevist Legislation

Although Jews had good reason to worry about anti-Jewish charges, of more practical concern was the introduction of a parliamentary bill that demanded the registration of aliens and the curtailment of propaganda.[35] The Public Welfare and Moratorium Acts Extension and Further Amendments Bill—known in labor circles as the "anti-Bolshevik Bill"—was patently a response to the combined effects of postwar Russian Jewish immigration, alleged incitement, press hysteria, and above all, the anxiety occasioned by the Russian revolution.[36]

Despite the minister of justice's denial that the registration of aliens was directed against any particular section of the community, Jewish leaders felt the need to take action. The South African Jewish Board of Deputies involved itself behind the scenes and the clause requiring the registration of aliens was easily removed with very few parliamentarians objecting. In fact the Members of Parliament for Vrededorp (L. Geldenhuys) and Bethal (H.S. Grobler), praised Jews for their peace-loving qualities.[37]

That the registration clause was so easily removed should not, however, be seen as lack of intent to control Russian Jewish aliens who were perceived in government circles as a threat to public order and were certainly the target of the bill. This was evident in press responses to the bill and its passage through parliament. The *Star,* for instance, focused on Russian Jews when discussing the bill in its early stages. It had even defended Jews by suggesting that they were inclined to conservatism when free of persecution, but those with Bolshevik tendencies were accused of breaching the conditions under which they were permitted to settle in South Africa. Such persons, the newspaper maintained, placed themselves beyond the pale. An editorial in the *Sunday Times* similarly accused aliens of being responsible for inciting the indigenous population, despite having no real knowledge of South African history, nor an understanding of South African conditions. They were, noted the editorial, "carrying on a despicable agitation which is a menace to every white man and woman in this country, and it is the duty of the Government to pay very serious attention to it." That Russian Jews were in fact the target of the bill was also evident in the *Cape Times* comments following the controversial clause's removal. Indeed, the newspaper argued that by dropping the clause at the behest of one section of the community, the government was more likely to arouse anti-Jewish prejudice.[38]

In practice the government had little to fear by removing the registration clause as it was able to apply controls through the census (which identified religious affiliation) and thus did not depend on it. The state, moreover, could monitor Jewish aliens through its own administrative apparatus. Immigration officers were instructed to scrutinize passports and carefully examine all foreigners and the Criminal Investigation Department (CID) requested details of undesirable aliens, "the majority of whom are low class Russian Jews."[39]

The Russian Jew thus remained, as far as contemporaries were concerned, a questionable addition to South African society. The prewar Peruvian image was now embellished with the Bolshevik bogey. Like other capitalist societies at the time, South Africa was seemingly obsessed with Bolshevism. This was a serious handicap for the Peruvian and certainly militated against his incorporation into the body politic. In reality much of the hatred directed toward the Russian alien was simply a manifestation of antisemitism, with Jews in the traditional scapegoat role. When, for instance, a Unitarian minister, Ramsden

Balmforth, defended Bolshevism, the *Cape* leapt to the attack, using as part of its arsenal a vicious and antisemitic diatribe that had appeared in the Rondebosch Boys High School magazine. The line between anti-alienism and antisemitism was again blurred, as it had been in the Cape Colony during the early years of the century and Jewish communal leaders reacted in much the same way as they had done at that earlier time.[40]

Their anger was expressed at the 1919 Congress of the South African Jewish Board of Deputies in Johannesburg. Bernard Alexander, the chairman of the Executive Council, was particularly hard hitting:

> I wish it to be clearly understood that every Jew is not a Bolshevist and every Bolshevist is not a Jew. . . . Because there are some Jews (perhaps a handful in Johannesburg, but I do not think there can be more) who are Bolshevists, is it right for the public of South Africa to say that the Jews are Bolshevists? Is it right because one Jew perhaps amongst the thousands is selling liquor to say that every Jew is a liquor seller? Why should the Jew be singled out? I deny the accusation that the Jews of South Africa are Bolshevists. The Jews are not Bolshevists and I say there are none more loyal than the Jews. It is a scurrilous anti-Semitic attack to describe us a Bolshevist.[41]

The public's emotional anti-Bolshevism at the time ensured that Alexander's protestations had little impact. Indeed, following the publication of naturalization figures that revealed a preponderance (55 out of 59) of Russians, the *Cape* published a viciously antialien letter, filled with generalizations, well-worn anti-Jewish imagery, and once again an association of Jews with Indians:

> It seems to me an anomaly that, in view of the present chaotic state of affairs in Russia, applications for naturalization should be considered from her nationals. How many of these applicants, one would like to know, shouldered the rifle for democracy's cause in the great war? I have no hesitation in saying, not a single one! . . . What a legacy for our children!—this fair land, won from barbarism and the wilderness by the blood and sweat of our Dutch, Anglo-Saxon and French forbears, now the happy hunting ground of hordes of "Russians" and Asiatics! . . . While we Nationalists, Labourites, Unionists and S A Partyites are oblivious to all else but the particular brand of Government which we severally imagine is vital to our continued existence, the off-scourings of Europe and Asia are steadily acquiring a control, economically, industrially and socially, which will leave us as impotent and futile as a crashed Zeppelin.[42]

Strikes and an election campaign kept the Bolshevik threat and the issue of undesirable immigration in the news. The charge of Bolshevism was a useful label, used by South African party spokesmen and government supporting newspapers to tarnish the Labour and National parties. The latter party in fact suffered an unfortunate handicap when its leader, J. B. M. Hertzog, allegedly referred to Bolshevism as "simply the desire of the people to rule themselves and not be ruled by others."[43]

Public persistence in associating Jews with Bolshevism ensured that the image of the Jew in general deteriorated. Morris Kentridge's victory for the Labour party over Patrick Duncan in the densely Jewish populated constituency, Fordsburg, did not help matters. The *Cape* was particularly incensed by Duncan's defeat and the Labour party leader W. Madeley's praise for the Russian-born victor:

> We see that . . . Mr Madeley . . . expressed his intense delight that Mr Pat Duncan was defeated in Fordsburg by "one of the finest men who ever stepped into shoe leather." The high-stepper in the leather is none other than Mr Kentridge who was, we believe, formerly known as Mr Kantorowich, and the suggestion that this "international" gentlemen is a better friend of the South African wage earner than Mr Pat Duncan, who has lived all his life in South Africa and who belongs to the country, is enough to draw tears from the eyes of the statue of Cecil Rhodes and from the new one of Onze Jan on Church Square.[44]

Significantly, the Jew, Kentridge, was depicted as an outsider despite his arrival in the country in 1901 and his valuable public service. Dredging up Kentridge's original surname, identifying him as "international" and inaccurately comparing him to the "rooted" Duncan says much about the status of the eastern European Jew in South African society at that time. At any moment of tension he could become marginalized. The *Cape*'s comments say much too about English-speaking South Africans and their strong ties with English culture and society. Balliol-educated Duncan, an immigrant Scot, was immediately accepted as a true South African patriot.

Social, economic, and labor tensions ensured the survival of Bolshevism as a threat. Certainly left-wing groups had taken a radical position. For example, the Industrial Socialist League published the *Bolshevist* from September 1919, in which it advocated no participation in political institutions of the "capitalist state" and a socialist revolution through the trade unions. Trade union membership and the number of strikes had increased through 1919 and 1920. Together with Afrikaner republican extremism, Bolshevism was thus classified by the government as the greatest threat to the country. At the opening of the South African party election campaign, Smuts actually warned of the moderate Labour party rapidly "drifting to an extreme socialist position and preaching a crusade for the nationalization of all land, mines, factories and industry, and behind this advanced socialism is the menacing growing spectre of international socialism." "The outlook all over the world," noted the *Star*, in obvious agreement with Smuts, "is full of menace, there is danger even in South Africa of a great financial and industrial breakdown."[45]

The fear of Bolshevism was thus manipulated by the government to deflect attention from serious labor and economic problems. Similarly, opponents of the government depicted these problems as a product of the government's alliance with the mining houses. It was around this alleged alliance that the opposition mobilized, using in the process the well-entrenched image of Hoggenheimer, the incarnation of cosmopolitan finance. Bloemfontein's *Volksblad*, for instance, railed against the political influence of "a special race" with "international interests, large hook noses and a peculiar pronunciation of English."[46] The specter of Hoggenheimer certainly evoked powerful emotions, particularly among "poor white" Afrikaners, who had flocked in great numbers to the larger centers, especially the Witwatersrand. However, the Hoggenheimer bogey was also appropriated by government-supporting newspapers who blamed economic hardship on avaricious mining magnates of clearly Jewish origin rather than on government mismanagement and the capitalist system itself. These newspapers frequently ridiculed mining magnates, exploiting in the process negative images associated with the cosmopolitan financier.[47]

This exploiting of visceral fears of Bolshevism and international finance severely harmed the image of the Jew. Increasingly strident calls to curtail Russian immigration (which in fact meant Jewish immigration) were now articulated. In parliament, J. S. Marwick, the South African party member for Illovo and "expert" on "Native labor" hammered home the subversive threat of "International Socialists," while a range of newspapers warned that South Africa was getting the wrong sort of immigrant. "The ragtag and bobtail of Europe or America would do us more harm than good," commented the *Graaff-Reinet Advertiser*. "International Socialists, Bolshevists, Revolutionists, Communists and all the elements of the conglomeration of 'workers' who do not work and only stir up agitations and turmoil and ill feeling are not wanted." Some months later the same newspaper warned that whites were sowing "the seeds of Communism and Bolshevism in the receptive native mind." The *Cape Times* in a particularly xenophobic phase under its new editor, public-school-educated Englishman B. K. Long, was insistent in calling for curbs on undesirable immigration from countries where democratic ideals were unknown and "western concepts of morality are quite unappreciated." "The articulation of these sentiments," as Bradlow puts it, "opened a flood of correspondence which revolved around the 'exclusiveness' of the Jews, their increasing numbers in relation to the total population, and the threat their low living standards posed to born South Africans."[48]

Evidently perceptions of the Russian Jew increasingly defined the image of all Jews. That image, moreover, was the South African expression of what constituted a worldwide xenophobia at that time. In this hostile climate very little was said about the potential "regeneration" or acculturation of the newcomers. Such optimism belonged to the late nineteenth and early twentieth centuries. By the 1920s "respectable" Jews of Anglo-German origin were a diminishing minority. It is noteworthy that in marshaling opposition to Russian immigration, all dimensions of the negative stereotype were employed as is well illustrated in the *Cape*'s call for closer supervision

> over the alien and Bolshevist passengers (mostly of the third class) who by devious means, as yet unknown to Western civilization, contrive to dodge immigration laws and to enter the country through some subtle forms of alien brotherhood by which they jump from pauperism to capitalism. The whole face of South Africa is scrawled over with Russian and Polish and German names—in all the devious ways of commerce and business. . . . These aliens are slowly getting a grip on the buildings of the towns, on the farms of the veld. They do no manual work; they simply speculate and barter and accumulate bank balances at the expense of South Africans, English and Dutch, who sit content in the pathetic delusion that the union's immigration laws assure the exclusion of alien adventurers.[49]

In the cauldron of postwar depression and xenophobia, the negative dimensions of the stereotype nurtured at the turn of the century—exploitation, parasitism, deviousness, and upward mobility—survived. To these perceptions were added the Bolshevik threat that would be manipulated and entrenched during the heightened struggle between labor and capital in the early months of 1922.

CHAPTER FIVE

The Rand Rebellion: Consolidating the Jewish Stereotype, 1922–24

A Bolshevik Plot

BY THE TIME mineworkers squared up for battle against the mining houses early in 1922, the government was able to arouse a vicious and visceral blend of anti-Bolshevism and antialienism that in the process further damaged the image of the Jew. All dimensions of the anti-Jewish stereotype were consolidated as opponents of the government sought convenient symbols with which to characterize and legitimize their struggle, chastise their opponents, and further their agenda. In short, the Jew—appropriated by both the ruling party and its opponents— became a helpless victim of South African ideological struggles.

The struggle between the Chamber of Mines and organized labor was precipitated by an attempt by the Chamber of Mines to reduce production costs in response to a severe downturn in the price of gold. Low-grade mines had to be made more profitable and it was proposed that this be done by removing the conventional color bar in the mining industry and thus employing more blacks, at the expense of whites, at reduced wages. The exercise involved approximately 2,000 "white" jobs and aroused fierce resistance from the exclusively white mining unions. A conglomeration of these unions, the South African Industrial Federation, braced itself for a classic confrontation and general strike. In the struggle the negative image of the Jew was reinforced as both the Hoggenheimer stereotype and Bolshevik bogey were manipulated for political purposes.

From the outset of the conflict and resultant strike, the Nationalist opposition's mouthpiece, *Die Burger,* accused Smuts of being a lackey of mining capital. Boonzaier's Hoggenheimer cartoons became a feature of this Afrikaans daily. Big capital, noted the newspaper, has no nationality, no faith, no tradition and no principles. Mobilizing opposition against the Chamber of Mines meant appealing to the historical memory, particularly the Afrikaner's traumatic experiences. As Dr. T. C. Visser, the Nationalist MP for Vrededorp explained, many of South Africa's problems, including the Jameson Raid, the Anglo-Boer War, and industrial disputes could be blamed on the Chamber of Mines. These views were shared by the Transvaal leader of the National party, Tielman Roos, while *Die Burger* defined the Chamber of Mines as foreign capitalists who had been responsible for the Anglo-Boer War. A fund-raising appeal from the Strike Support Committee exhorted every Afrikaner to prevent a takeover by parasitic, overseas capitalists.[1]

It was not, however, only Afrikaner nationalists who mobilized public antagonism against the powerful captains of the mining industry. The postwar economic recession had radicalized important sectors of the working class, and the South African Labour party now found itself well placed to further its agenda by appealing also to the Afrikaners' view of South African history. An untenable situation was blamed on foreign mineowners. Consequently the prospects of reconciling frustrated republicans with aggrieved workers had never been better. As Labour leader Walter Madeley argued, "International" finance was involved in a worldwide conspiracy "to depreciate humanity—to depreciate the flesh and blood of the worker." He concluded that it was "a crying shame that its mean, narrow, despicable outlook should be imposed on the world." Madeley's sentiments were reiterated by union leaders and spokesmen such as E. S. Hendrikz, secretary general of the Mine Workers' Union, who bluntly asserted that "Solly Joel and his men overseas" were the villains of the conflict. "A Shareholder and Worker" similarly blamed financiers for perpetuating "an immoral and iniquitous economic system which always places the ultimate burden on the world's workers." "Who were going to rule South Africa, the selected representatives of the people in Parliament or international financiers?" was the question posed by George Crisp of the Amalgamated Engineering Union.[2]

Negative memories of foreign capitalists manifestly resonated in the South African psyche and were opportune for the mobilization of workers. And when the strike which had officially begun on 28 Decem-

ber 1921 assumed more serious dimensions in 1922, Boonzaier's Hoggenheimer became increasingly Semitic in appearance. Smuts—identified in *Die Burger* as a representative of "Hoggenheimer and Co" after
his South African party had merged with the pro-imperial Unionist
party in 1920—was accused by Madeley of allying himself "with the
Chamber of Mines or rather the executive body of the international
financiers who pose as the Chamber of Mines, in their determined effort
to depreciate the whole of the South African community."[3]

The conflict between capital and labor also helped to dissipate historical differences between the Afrikaner and English worker; as whites,
both groups were allegedly threatened by the rapacious power of the
mining magnates who were accused of having no respect for white
workers. The strikers, as Duncan explained, "appealed to the public on
the ground that the 'colour bar' was being broken down and the white
man's status was being sacrificed by the greed of foreign capitalists."[4]
Herein lay the basis for a Labour–National party alliance.

In response to Labour and Nationalist rhetoric, the government
mounted its own propaganda campaign, drawing upon the Bolshevik
bogey. Across the country, government-supporting newspapers, taking
aim at the strikers, focused upon their "Russian methods," "Bolshevism," and "extremism." Such charges received welcome ammunition
when the Labour party parliamentarian R. B. Waterston sponsored a
resolution, passed by a mass meeting in the Johannesburg Town Hall,
for a South African republic to be formed by a provisional government.[5]

"From a purely industrial dispute which the strike appeared to be in
its initial phase," observed the *Graaff-Reinet Advertiser,* "the thing is
assuming a revolutionary nature." An editorial in the *Cape Argus* was
even more trenchant, noting that Waterston and his friends wanted a
"dictatorship of the proletariat—and the consequent destruction of
parliamentary government." The *Eastern Province Herald,* in turn, was
pleased that "the extremists of the Rand had come out into the open and
gnashed their teeth in public," thus ensuring that the real motives of the
strikers were becoming clearer. Thereafter the newspaper attributed a
specifically Jewish cast to events by noting "the suggestive patronym-
ics of certain of the plainer spoken of the leaders of the Communist
Party—such as, for instance, Morris Kentridge (formerly Kantoro-
wich), Kreschmar and Buirski. The source of this inspiration should
require little seeking and if we translate Councils into District Soviets
and Provincial Government into its Russian equivalent, the Central

Committee, we do not get a by any means overdrawn idea of the real position."[6]

Action by radicals who previously had been associated with the Council of Action, a grouping within the Mine Workers' Union, generated further tension. Organized street gangs now threatened policemen and black workers, thus enhancing the case of those wishing to exaggerate the Bolshevik menace. Even *Die Burger,* generally sympathetic toward the workers' demands, expressed concern about the "unruly section" when discussing the Council of Action.[7]

By late February 1922 violence was commonplace on the Rand, with Boksburg in particular witnessing worker militance and savage police repression. The radicalization of strike rhetoric and action played into the hands of government and its supporting press. The South African party was now easily able to attribute all violence associated with the strike to Bolshevism, mobilizing deeply entrenched fears. Boers and mineowners, argued one small-town newspaper, would lose out to the Bolsheviks and the proletariat would rule the land. An editorial in the *Star* noted that the Rand "has more 'Red' to the square mile than any other community in the British Empire." Meanwhile the South African party's Brigadier General J. J. Byron (Border) told parliament of the state's resolve to put down the growing tendency to Bolshevism in the country. In the *Rand Daily Mail*'s view, industrious and law-abiding mineworkers had been captured by the extremist or Bolshevik element. It was essential, warned the *Diamond Fields Advertiser,* "that the extremist elements in a great industrial and cosmopolitan community . . . bent on exploiting the situation for frankly revolutionary or purely criminal purposes, shall not be permitted to gain the upper hand."[8]

By early March the government and those newspapers supporting it were defining the conflict as an attack on civilized values by a Bolshevik revolutionary force. A violent escalation of events played into Prime Minister Smuts's hands, and on 11 March he declared martial law, sending in police and citizen force units to break the strike and to maintain order. The fierce battles across the Reef (costing approximately 200 lives) and the subsequent crushing of the last workers' stronghold in Fordsburg enabled the government to build upon the Bolshevik scare in a most dramatic way. The media equated this violence with the "horrors of Bolshevik Russia," and law and order now became a primary concern. Even *Die Burger,* despite its disdain for Smuts and his handling of affairs, expressed disquiet at the radicalization of worker rhetoric and action which, it argued, was due to Bolshevist influence. Nevertheless, this Nationalist mouthpiece did not lose the opportunity to make political capital out of the turmoil and Smuts's handling of it. The prime minister, argued the newspaper, had declared war on virtually all workers and in this way avoided culpability for poor government.[9]

Responses to the Witwatersrand upheavals demonstrated vividly the countrywide anxiety about Bolshevism. Labor turmoil, coupled with worker radicalization, certainly raised fears of social revolution. Within this climate the *Rand Daily Mail*'s conception of "a Bolshevist plot, aimed at the overthrow of the present Government, and the establishment of a Soviet control" was quite plausible. This conspiracy theory was apparently confirmed with the alleged capture of documents which proved, according to the *Graaff-Reinet Advertiser*, "that money for the Red Revolution comes from abroad." "The Jacobin element in Johannesburg," reported the *Cape Argus*, had simply wanted "to exploit the quarrel as a pretext for civil war and anarchy." The idea of a "Red" or (in Dutch-Afrikaans) "Rooi" revolution was now solidly entrenched. The popular mood was best captured in the *Star*'s editorial "The Plot Revealed," which explained just how damaging the radicalization of the movement had been for the workers' interests. In this newspaper's opinion, the "tragic" events of "the last few days" had aroused people to the fact that revolution was being planned under "the guise of a labour grievance." Indeed, the Council of Action had inveigled naive workers into revolt as a means of furthering their plans to establish Bolshevik rule. Fortunately the workers now realized they had been "led into a trap." The *Star*'s view was shared by a range of newspapers including those in the anti-Smuts camp. Also *De Kerkbode*, articulating the Dutch Reformed Church's viewpoint and reflecting the Nationalist position, expressed anguish at the turn of events and the manipulation of Afrikaner workers by radical agitators who used the "Day of the Lord" to propagate destructive teachings.[10]

The government and its supporting newspapers had obviously generated the idea of a well-orchestrated plot; the radical direction taken by the strikers was blamed on outside agents. In the opinion of the *Natal Mercury*, violence was not the creation of ordinary workers: "Such deeds are the work either of habitual criminals or of mental degenerates whose moral sense has been utterly submerged by the backing of alien Bolsheviks or anarchists, whatever they may call themselves." Defense headquarters confirmed this view with official statements attributing events to international communism. Six weeks after the "Rebellion," *Die Burger,* despite ridiculing the notion of an international conspiracy, felt quite comfortable in its assumption that a small group of Bolshevists had radicalized Afrikaner workers. These sentiments were echoed by the *Queenstown Daily,* which bemoaned the fact that Afrikaners were being "poisoned by the teaching of Bolshevists and other propaganda agents from overseas."[11]

The heady days of March had thus generated wide support for the international conspiracy thesis—that those orchestrating events were dedicated to the establishment of a Bolshevist republic. Certainly popular opinion saw events in terms of a Red Revolution. G. R. Baldwin, son of the English politician Stanley Baldwin, affirmed this view when he told the *Natal Mercury* that, in official and other quarters, South Africa was seen to have put down a Russian- or Bolshevik-inspired overthrow. *Die Burger* similarly acknowledged that a certain section of the voting public believed in the *Bolshewistiese gogga* (Bolshevik insect).[12]

It hardly needs to be emphasized that the driving force underpinning and fueling the conflict was the prospect of white workers losing their privileged status, a truth not lost on Duncan, who explained this reality in a letter to Lady Selborne: "The papers are making our flesh creep by stories of widespread Bolshevik assassination and revolution but I shall believe that when I see some evidence of it. There was no doubt a small group of men who wanted a communist revolution and a much larger number of men not revolutionist by conviction who became desperate at the thought of losing their work on the mines which they think has happened through the desire of the Chamber of Mines to replace white men by natives so as to swell their already monstrous profits."[13]

A Russian-Jewish Conspiracy

Attributing a conspiratorial explanation for events on the Rand predictably focused on the Russian and, more specifically, the Russian-Jewish immigrant. Sometimes, as previously noted, allusions were made simply to alien or Jewish names although in other instances accusations of Jewish involvement were quite explicit. A Dr. Fehrsen of Benoni, for instance, placed "the Russian Jew invasion" under the spotlight when commenting on a number of prisoners detained during the strike. He found them "a mentally deficient, repulsive-looking lot of ruffians, amongst them a Russian Jew, just three weeks in South Africa from Kovno. He could not understand a word of English. I addressed him in German and found out that 30 others had landed from the Arundel Castle. . . . How long is South Africa to tolerate the Russian Jew invasion?"[14]

Fehrsen's views were given wide coverage and his sentiments were reiterated in a range of newspapers. In an editorial, "Who Are the Criminals?" the *Eastern Province Herald* was critical of the growing foreign element who avidly sought British citizenship and who frequently changed their names. It questioned to what extent these people were responsible for recent events especially since they were associated with the interests of the Labour-Communist-International Socialist movement.[15]

The association of Russian Jews with the rebellion, together with the notion of a powerful Bolshevik element financed from abroad and bent on destroying the established government, unveiled a flood of calls to curtail eastern European immigration. The constant influx of Bolshevik-oriented immigrants from eastern Europe had to be stopped in the opinion of the *East London Daily Dispatch*. These people, argued the *Natal Advertiser,* undermined liberty and threatened to overthrow an "easy going" state that had "given them too much latitude." This newspaper recommended that "the sternest measures" be meted out to "the low down alien" and "the propagandists of Communism."[16]

It comes as little surprise that government-supporting newspapers welcomed the opportunity to divert blame away from government mismanagement to Bolshevik or Jewish agitators. Indeed, the *Oudtshoorn Courant,* after the arrest of Morris Kentridge, reminded readers that his real name was Kantorowitz and that he was born in Russia. With memories of the Bolshevik revolution and its aftermath still vivid, allusions such as these were most effective in that they tapped a powerful strand of antialienism, embodied in antagonism toward the Peruvian. Thus the *Cape Times* could advocate limiting the influx of the "human dregs of the continent," which, of course, meant the Russian Jew who was characterized as being inherently nonproductive and subversive. Correspondence in other newspapers made it abundantly clear that these newcomers were the architects of disorder. Editorial after editorial now called upon the government to tighten its immigration laws. Sharing these sentiments, the Chairman of the Worcester

Chamber of Commerce, with a fine disregard for accuracy, referred to a certain section of the population first ruining their own country and then wanting to spoil their new country.[17] In short, alien Jews were identified with Bolshevism and international revolution.

Unassimilability

In addition to associating Jews with Bolshevism, newspapers began to question the Jewish potential for integration into South African society. "Unassimilability" became the new catchword, an idea influenced directly by nativist literature from the United States, as well as by a new domestic segregationist discourse in which race and culture were conflated.[18] By introducing notions of "racial stock" and "racial quality," newspapers were able to mobilize well-established negative images of the Jew. "There is one important aspect of the Rand Rebellion," noted the *Diamond Fields Advertiser,* that

> in itself presents a damning indictment of the Government, and that is in relation to the laxity of the Union Immigration Laws which permit entry into the Union of a foreign undesirable element which inherently displays no burning desire to add to the production of the country by the sweat of its brow, but shows a readiness to sow the seeds of all the discontent which it has left behind in the country of its origin. . . . we had 1416 Russian immigrants last year, nearly all of whom will undoubtedly stay. For the most part they will be a reinforcement to the middleman class, of whom the primary producers, judging by the outcry against them have already too many on their backs. Even the co-Nationals of these redundant immigrants began to complain owing to the strain that the latter impose on charities, for they mostly arrive with very little means. The immigration law might well be tightened with general approval, provided this were done without making invidious distinctions of race or religion.[19]

Quite obviously the *Diamond Fields Advertiser* wished to avoid being charged with antisemitism and thus recommended that "invidious distinctions of race or religion" be expunged from its proposed immigration policy. Here it was voicing a tradition of religious tolerance, probably derived from a desire to set the country apart from Europe's age-old religious hatreds. Certainly tolerance was valued and, as we have seen, a persistent strain of sympathy for the Jew informed at least a part of South African culture. Nonetheless, readers of the *Diamond Fields Ad-*

vertiser would have been aware that *Russian* was synonymous with *Jew.* Indeed, by rehashing well-worn stereotypes, the new arrivals were openly and without hesitation associated with their deviant Peruvian forbears. Disentangling the Russian-Jewish immigrant of the 1920s from associations with those "undesirables" was hardly possible. The revolutionary cap was made to fit comfortably on the Peruvian head!

The concept of unassimilability was a major volte-face from earlier optimistic expectations of the "regeneration" and acculturation of the eastern European Jew. Now his future was again problematic with the radical or Communist dimension of the stereotype being simply a variation on a theme. This fusion of Bolshevism and the earlier stereotype was well captured by the *Cape Times,* a newspaper that was to be at the forefront of the call for immigration restriction during the 1920s. Its editorial comments merit extensive quotation because of the pervasiveness of the beliefs it expressed:

> Not the revelation of alien complicity in the Reef Revolution only but nearly every phase of our national life exhibits the need of a revision of the immigration laws of the Union. The habits and ideas of races who are neither capable of, nor desirous of, merging their distinctive racialism in the South African nationality they profess to acquire are leaving their mark scoured deep in the whole country. In the big towns the general debasement of our moral standards that even the most broad-minded of observers must remark is a large measure traceable to the craze for exotic pleasures which aliens have first created and then ministered to. In the rural areas, the deplorable decline in commercial morality which is now so frequently to be noted in the relations between dealers and farmers, and particularly between storekeepers and native producers, is probably due to the astonishing change which in recent years alien immigration has wrought "in the trading personnel." In our social life, too, the contacts made with newcomers from countries where anti-social customs flourish are having an effect which is neither pleasant nor encouraging to contemplate. . . .
>
> How much longer are we going to permit Bolshevist agitators to preach treason and revolution in our streets. . . . The education test needs to be made more stringent except in the case of those few races who are readily assimilable into our national life.[20]

Notions of unassimilability, inherent inferiority, and cultural determinism, all attributed to something vague called an "alien" but readily understood as "Jews," are again fundamental in the *Sunday Times* description of the newcomers:

> Some of them are out and out Bolsheviks. Others are sympathisers with Bolshevism and are ready at any moment to help overthrow authority or impede it in suppressing disorder. Such people have no knowledge of South African history or conditions. They are aliens in mind and disposition and habits. Their ideas and methods are those of Eastern Europe—generally of Bolshevist Russia. . . . We are not opposed to all immigration. . . . We are not trying to stir up feeling against immigrants who are not British or not Hollander. . . . But we do say that a land with the complicated racial problems we have here ought to inquire somewhat carefully into the records of those who wish to enter it. South Africans also do not desire to have in their midst a lot of aliens who have no respect for constitutional government and who are invariably on the side of revolution, or anarchy, or any upheaval promising the overthrow of ordered authority. . . . It is significant to our mind that at least fifteen hundred Russians entered the Union last year from overseas. We should like to know how many of them were wholeheartedly on the side of the Government during the revolutionary outbreak. What is certain is that some of them were fighting in the ranks of the Reds. . . . They joined the upheaval simply because they are Bolshevists at heart and do not care fruppence about the real welfare of the land of their adoption. Those are the kind of immigrants South Africa must keep out.[21]

Paradoxically the newcomers were defined as "unassimilable" at the very time when they were penetrating sectors of the South African economy previously controlled by the English mercantile establishment, thereby merging into the dominant structures of South African society and threatening the English mercantile elite. Herein lies a major motivation behind calls to limit immigration, with the Rand Rebellion providing the occasion for the mercantile establishment to articulate fears and prejudices rooted in prewar experiences and exacerbated in the postwar economic recession. These cathartic exercises, coupled with the manipulation of the Bolshevik and Hoggenheimer bogeys, strengthened the existing negative image of the Jew, which had reached a new low. This is indicated by the assertion of the *East London Daily Dispatch* on 21 March 1922 that antisemitic feeling in South Africa was stronger than it had been for many years. Certainly, popular attitudes toward the Peruvian encouraged the belief that the newcomers were the instigators of unrest and disorder and should therefore be limited by government policy. This was certainly the view of those sympathetic to the government. The latter, as Duncan informed Lady Selborne, "firmly believe in a Bolshevik plot being at the root of the trouble and are all clamouring loudly for the exclusion of all Russian Jews and the deportation of anyone who is suspected of being in any way unorthodox in his economic creed." As noted earlier, Duncan was aware that the wrong fish had been caught but was quite happy as a member of the government to go along with the opposition to eastern European immigration.[22]

Jewish Responses and Calls for Exclusion

Naturally the association of Jews with Bolshevism and the clamor for exclusion left the Jewish community vulnerable and uneasy, and its leaders were understandably quick to take steps to deal with the problem. A meeting of the South African Zionist Federation that was held in March 1922 at the height of anti-Jewish accusations moved that the Jewish Board of Deputies be asked to call a special meeting of its Executive Council to consider the implications of recent events for the Jews.[23] A letter to the *Rand Daily Mail* by one Nathan Levi confirmed feelings of Jewish insecurity. Levi, who was a Pretoria-based journalist and longtime friend of Smuts, had visited Johannesburg where he had observed a great deal of anxiety in the Jewish community. While admitting that a few Jews were mixed up with Bolshevist propaganda, Levi warned that it was dangerous and against the public interest "to make a whole race suspect for a few black sheep, even for several!" "Tens of thousands of loyal and law-abiding Jews," he argued, "whose self-interest alone (to put it at the lowest level) would make them condemn lawlessness are heart and soul with the Government and with the people of the Union in the crisis."[24]

Levi's realization of the potential danger in the nexus of current antisemitism and immigration policy appears to have been shared by the *Sunday Times*. Despite favoring influx curbs, the newspaper expressly stated that it had "no wish to see the movement [to curtail alien immigration] tinged with anti-Semitism." "Every sensible South African," it contended, "realises and appreciates the good work done by the Jewish community in the country both in peace and war. If we thought for a moment that the demand for stricter immigration laws was a mere excuse for an anti-Jewish campaign we would wash our hands of the whole thing at once."[25]

The *Sunday Times* may well have wished to separate Russian from Jew, and at an official level this may have been possible. At the popular level, however, the two were obviously associated. No amount of subtlety on the part of this newspaper could erode the public's adherence to the belief in an alien, and more specifically, a Jewish role in the recent violence. These perceptions were further consolidated with a popular pictorial account of the "Red Revolt" and a documentary film, *Red Revolution,* which played to packed audiences across the country.[26] Separating "Red" from eastern European Jew, and the latter from Jews in general, required a cognitive sophistication that was rarely forthcoming.

Even reports in *Die Burger,* a newspaper that was skeptical of the conspiracy thesis, reflected in its journalism a sense of alien, or "Jewish," involvement.[27] Being a Nationalist and opposed to Smuts seldom meant support for the eastern European Jew. In fact there is evidence that even "primitive" religious hostility informed a measure of anger toward the newcomers. A letter in *De Kerkbode,* for instance, went so far as to identify Lenin as a Jew and described him as the Anti-Christ. The writer noted that South Africa had welcomed the Russian Jew not knowing that he would utilize the opportunity for anti-Christian propaganda. Anti-Christian feelings, he argued, increased with the growth of Zionism.[28]

It is therefore not surprising that a government plan to curtail alien immigration (by stringent use of the educational provisions in the Immigrants Restriction Act of 1913) was greeted with approval. The *Rand Daily Mail* was particularly pleased in view of the fact that the United States had introduced legislation to exclude "undesirables" who might have chosen South Africa as the next country of opportunity and security. "No private individual," it noted, "would allow into his house a person whom he strongly suspected would soon begin to cause him trouble. Why should a Government?"[29]

The Rand Rebellion had generated a call for strong exclusionist policies in contrast to the lack of action that had accompanied the earlier expressions of dislike and contempt.[30] Apart from alterations to American policy, factors contributing toward this change included an economic recession caused by the falling gold price and other primary products, postwar urbanization with its attendant unemployment, and the labor violence on the Rand. Of course, hostility toward the newcomers was deeply embedded in the South African experience as we have seen. As South African society experienced tensions and the established forms of domination were threatened, hostility became increasingly marked. Certainly, Jewish upward mobility and the penetration of Jews into social and economic preserves previously dominated by the English-speaking establishment aggravated matters.[31] This process is well captured in a letter from "Occidens" in the *East London Daily Dispatch:*

> Johannesburg is today naturally crying out loudly against the indiscriminate admission of aliens into this country. The Rand is the first portion of South Africa which has suffered from the curse acutely and at the same time openly, though the whole country suffers from it silently and almost unknowingly as yet. But the evil has been brewing up for forty years. . . . For forty years a certain peaceful demonstration from eastern Europe has been quietly and steadily going on in this country of ours. Let any merchant turn up an old ledger index from last century, and compare it with his current one today and he will be startled to see how many healthy British and Dutch names have given place to a horde of alien surnames. If we handle any Government or commercial gazette today, the same thing is alarming in evidence. Today if a business property inland comes into the market, the chances are ten to one that an alien will acquire it.
> . . . The worst among us are attracted in some form to a code which came in near two thousand years ago—the code which the western world has to thank for all the good that it can boast of. British and Dutch, South African or nationalist, are all events at one in holding to that cult. Not so the materialistic aliens. Their ways are not as our ways, their thoughts are not as our thoughts.[32]

Invective against Jews during the Rand Rebellion must therefore be seen in the wider context. Quite simply, alien eastern European Jews seemed to threaten traditional values and norms; the "Red Revolt" provided an ideal opportunity to mobilize support against their entry. The "real" motivation behind immigration restriction is patently apparent in the following letter from Duncan to Lady Selborne. As minister of the interior he was obviously in a position to understand the factors informing government policy:

> It amused me to get your advice about keeping out the Peruvian as I have just been working a small effort in the direction. Since the US closed the door to a large extent against the immigrant from eastern Europe we are getting him here in growing numbers and I have been putting in force a clause in the Immigration Act which enables the

Minister to bar anyone he deems unsuitable on economic grounds or from standards or habits of life. The victims are of course all Jews and the result has been a revelation of the political power which the Jew has here. Many members who have been making most noise about keeping out the Russian Jew come to me privately and say that while they agree on general grounds that the Jew must be kept out an exception must be made in favour of A who has an uncle in their constituency an excellent fellow who gave them great support last election. And so it goes on all down the alphabet. There is a central Jewish Board in Johannesburg and it arranges for telegrams to be dropped on members from various quarters where they have sensitive points and it really is as good as a play to see the game being worked. I am very doubtful if much can really be done to stop the stream in the circumstances but they are really coming in much faster than we can assimilate them and the present Bolshevik scare—which is nothing but a scare—gives a good opportunity for trying a little restriction. But I fear they are too strong for us.[33]

The threat of a Bolshevik overthrow was patently a useful diversionary tactic for a piece of legislation designed to curtail the immigration of "unassimilable" and "undesirable" eastern European Jews.[34] Needless to say, Duncan's notion of Jewish power and unassimilability (a theme that would gain in prominence during the 1920s), had its roots in South Africa's earlier history. In the wake of the Rand Revolt, however, it was easier to express anti-Jewish feeling under the acceptable rubric of anti-Bolshevism. This was surely the reason why a wide range of individuals and organizations opposed further alien or Bolshevik immigration, which in reality meant Jewish immigration.[35] This was affirmed by Tielman Roos in a hard-hitting vote-catching speech in parliament that castigated the government for seeking scapegoats rather than blaming itself. Why, he asked, "did they not use the term 'Russian Jew' when they spoke of Russians and Bolshevists?"[36]

Debate surrounding further eastern European immigration and threats to limit it, coupled with aspersions cast upon their loyalty and behavior, further eroded Jewish confidence and precipitated predictable responses. In parliament the two Jewish MPs, Morris Alexander and Manfred Nathan, spoke out strongly against the popular practice of associating Jews with the rebellion. Even the small rural Jewish community of Volksrust, on the Transvaal-Natal border, protested "in the strongest possible terms against malicious accusations hurled at the heads of Jews throughout South Africa implying that they in particular were responsible for the recent regrettable occurrences on the Rand." The Volksrust community "strongly urged the authorities to investigate and contradict these basic rumours at once." Its concerns were quite understandable, and despite Smuts informing parliament that "Afrikaners were largely responsible" for the rebellion and that "the government did not hold that the Jews were in any way responsible," the association of Russian Jews with the upheavals was well entrenched.[37]

The Rand Rebellion had crystallized unspecified and unstructured attitudes toward Jews, precipitating calls for definite exclusion. In these calls, prewar and wartime images of the Jew were appropriated and embellished. This is well illustrated in a letter to Smuts from Charles H. Frude of Hillbrow, Johannesburg, in which he complained about the granting of trading licenses to Peruvians, "who do not care a toss for any suburb or any country, only for what can be made out of it." Frude deprecated the activities of low-class Jewish businessmen whom he referred to as "the scum of the world," a description he also attributed to "the fat, prosperous, well-dressed Jew who battens on the community with his dishonest, unscrupulous ways and schemes as well as the dirty half human louts from Russia and mid-Europe whom we allow to come to South Africa." Frude also raised the issue of Jews' "shirking" during the war and rhetorically asked Smuts where "our Jewish friends" are to be found when needed to defend South Africa? In conclusion, he warned that despite the presence of some "honourable Jews in Johannesburg," there was a growing bitterness "against the whole crowd and one frequently hears remarks about the coming pogrom etc. etc." Frude's letter brought together most of the historical antagonisms that had marked attitudes toward the Jew: anti-Hoggenheimer, anti-Russian, crude racism, the failure to volunteer during the Great War, and unscrupulous business practice. His imagery of the nonproductive Jew with its connotations of parasitism and exploitation also hailed back to the turn of the century. Most importantly, Frude's letter demonstrated that the eastern European Jew was perceived to be inherently beyond the pale and unworthy of entry into South Africa. As the *Cape* put it, "South Africa has suffered and is suffering from too large an influx of Russian and eastern Europeans whose peculiar standards of morality and law are rapidly tending to degrade the social and commercial life of the country." Such comments demonstrate a decisive shift away from late nineteenth- and early twentieth-century ambivalence. At that time observers were optimistic that the newcomers could be regenerated and acculturated. By the time the dust of the Rand Rebellion had settled, however, such optimism was rapidly fading.[38]

The notion of the eastern European Jew as inherently unassimilable was buttressed by an important shift toward racist assumptions. Such assumptions underpinned a revealing pamphlet by "Brutus" (Hendrik Francois Viljoen) on the origins of the Rand Rebellion that in addition reiterated a number of common stereotypes.[39] Brutus's analysis revolved around the deep-seated and more immediate cause of the revolt. Among the former he identified was "the legacy and traditions of the international financier in the control of the Rand, and the consequent widespread suspicion of the mining houses." Here Brutus consolidated the Hoggenheimer bogey, deployed in the early stages of the conflict. With regard to the immediate problems, Brutus identified (amongst others) the "undue influx of an undesirable type of European immigrant," "the spread of Socialist and Bolshevist propaganda by extremists, mostly of Scottish or Jewish extraction," and "a regrettable tradition of the doings of the big financier in the early days that tends to prejudice the case at the outset in the mind of the average man-in-the-street." Brutus, in addition, argued that "those on the spot were merely mechanically carrying out a dictated policy that was to subserve primarily interests other than those of South Africa."

Brutus's pamphlet is particularly interesting for its curious conflation of big mining capitalists and radicals plus the combined effect of these two groups on public opinion. The thrust of his argument undoubtedly reinforced a range of ideas evident at the beginning and at the conclusion of the conflict. His focus on the impecunious Jew from Central Europe, and in particular from Russia and Poland, is riddled with racist assumptions. For example, he claimed that the eastern European Jew came to South Africa without any respect for government yet quite prepared to take advantage of constitutional freedom and free education. This in itself was not serious but unfortunately the new immigrants congregated in specific cities where they applied substantial influence. Indeed, argued Brutus, these immigrants had the temerity to foment unrest and to tell those "races," long experienced in freedom, what to do. For Brutus the alien Jew was inherently unable to cope with freedom, threatening moreover to dominate society. The pamphlet also referred to "abundant evidence" that "the newer Jewish population on the Rand" had, for a number of years, been propagating Bolshevist doctrines. "The debasing moral effect of the dissemination of the plague of Bolshevism among our men—and still more among our women—

has been disclosed to an extent that could not have been believed possible."

Besides reinforcing both the Hoggenheimer and Bolshevik stereotypes simultaneously, Brutus also criticized the "more recent immigrants" for their attitudes of "aloofness or hostility during the Great War—an attitude that was in striking contrast with that of a number of older Jewish families who had fully identified themselves with the two chief elements of our people in this responsibility and service required by their citizenship, and bore their full share willingly during the perilous years." Brutus, in other words, was once again separating the "loyal and responsible" Jewish establishment from the eastern European newcomers. By doing this he was simply echoing an earlier theme which, in the 1920s, was largely academic. By then eastern European Jews dominated the community in all ways and it is quite certain that aspersions cast upon alien Jews reflected to a greater or lesser extent upon all Jews. Needless to say, there is also no hint that the "more recent immigrants" could be "regenerated." However, Brutus's separation did avoid charges of antisemitism (thus keeping his views within the bounds of respectability) and prepared the way for acclamation of his pamphlet in the general press. In short, his pamphlet gave a substantial boost to the antialien lobby's clamor for restriction. The *East London Daily Dispatch* quoted at length from the pamphlet in an editorial which expressed hope "that the Government will turn a deaf ear to those who urge any relaxation of the immigration restrictions. . . . South Africa has plenty of difficulties of its own, and there is no reason why they should be added to by the unrestrained introduction of unsuitable alien immigrants from parts of Europe where the name of Government has been synonymous with oppression."

Not surprisingly, the antialien lobby's arguments disturbed the *Zionist Record,* which blamed the deteriorating Jewish image on "a violent press agitation . . . which sought to cast blame upon Jewish Bolshevists." The Jewish weekly did, however, note that after "a time the agitation died down owing partly to the country having recovered from its momentary hysteria, and partly to intervention from the highest quarters."[40]

Restriction and Jewish Fears

Popular agitation may well have subsided but was hardly dormant. The government's release of immigration figures a few months after the rebellion, for instance, rekindled the issue in the *Cape Times*. Readers were reminded of the "Rand upheaval" and the "large proportion of low class foreigners largely Russians" among the "loafers and hooligans." The Jewish community, therefore, had every reason to feel insecure. Nor could they feel relieved when the findings of the Martial Law Commission failed to indict South African Jewry for the Rand's problems. By then the government had begun to apply Section 4(1)(a) of the 1913 Immigration Act, whereby the minister of the interior was empowered to curtail immigrants unsuited to the requirements of the Union on economic grounds or on account of their standards or habits of life. The board's attempt to persuade the minister, Patrick Duncan, that Section 4(1)(a) was originally intended to be used against Indians and not Jews failed. Duncan, in fact, denied discriminating specifically against Jewish immigrants, maintaining instead that he was motivated by purely economic interests, an argument not without foundation. Unemployment was high at this time and the economy was generally in a poor state. Duncan in fact warned the Jewish community that the National party would push for even harsher restrictions if eastern European immigration continued unabated. As it happened, the Nationalist opposition, with its eye on the Jewish vote, attacked the government for its poor handling of the immigration issue, and one of its spokesmen, P. G. W. Grobler, even went as far as accusing Duncan of being antisemitic.[41]

Despite the Jewish Board of Deputies applying further pressure upon the government to amend its immigration policy, the cabinet refused to deviate. This was a tense period for the Jewish community. For the first time it faced an active restriction policy rather than the usual rhetoric. Its sense of vulnerability is evident in the board's fear that the Class Areas Bill of 1924—which set out "to make provisions for the reservation of residential and trading areas in urban areas for persons other than natives having racial characteristics in common"—would be applied toward Jews. It was of little comfort that Smuts, who was fully aware that the bill's purpose was to curtail Indian trading, expressed surprise at Jewish concern. Nor indeed could Jews feel entirely comfortable following the removal of the word *European* from the category of persons included in the Class Areas Bill. They were clearly seen as a people apart.[42]

Shortly before the 1924 general election the Department of the Interior announced the suspension of the application of Section 4(1)(a) in the case of Europeans for a trial period of six months. This action—a blatant election ploy to gain Jewish votes—was predictably criticized. A government-supporting newspaper, the *Queenstown Daily Representative and Free Press,* deplored the change in policy "which will open the door to hundreds of people who will add to the congestion in the slums of our big towns and do nothing to enhance the progress and prosperity of South Africa."[43]

Jewish fears were further exacerbated by an election pamphlet in Swellendam that depicted the Jewish parliamentary candidate and mayor of Swellendam, Eli Buirski, as "an enemy of Christ." Christians were called upon not to support him. The pamphlet was based on a sermon delivered by Buirski's political rival, the Nationalist Reverend G. Du Toit. According to the *Cape Argus,* Du Toit would have accepted a Jew representing the constituency had Jews been in the majority. This, however, was clearly not the case in Swellendam, a rural village. Du Toit, in fact could not understand how "the Christians of such a place could think of choosing a Jew, a person who on account of his belief is an enemy of Christ, to further the holy interests of our people in the Assembly." For Du Toit a general election was "nothing else but the choice of the Government of the land, the Government, whom, according to God's word we must obey and for whom we must pray? Are we not, therefore, called upon to take care that we have a Christian Government? Do we realize the privilege which God has granted this land— that the choice of the Government of the land is in the hands of the Christian Church? . . . Does our Christian religion mean that Christ must rule in our hearts, but can or must be shut out from the State?" *De Kerkbode* expressed a similar message arguing that it was a Christian's duty to send men of Christian principles to parliament. This was repeated by the Synodal Committee of the Transvaal Church.[44]

Notwithstanding Buirski's victory in the general election (presumably a demonstration of the weakness of mobilizing support on religious grounds) and assurances to Jews from the new Labour-National party coalition government (known as the Pact and in power until 1933), that it would not use Section 4(1)(a) against Europeans, the "Jewish Question" had not been removed from the national agenda. Indeed shortly after the election the *Bloemfontein Friend* published a long editorial dealing with Jewish business morality. The article was particularly interesting for its "reasonable" tone and for the way in which it acknowledged the substantial success of Jews and other positive qualities. Nonetheless the essential message left the reader in no doubt: Jews were inclined toward dishonest and parasitic behavior. The editorial thus urged Jewish leaders to encourage their coreligionists to take up productive occupations such as farming; to cooperate with legislators in putting a stop to business malpractices (the idea of proscribing name-changing was even mooted) and to raise the standard of Jewish commercial morality.[45]

How the *Bloemfontein Friend* could explain the presence of honest Jews in terms of its racist discourse is difficult to answer.[46] What is clear, however, is the notion of upward mobility and Jewish power, which was being ascribed in large part to dishonest practices grafted onto inherent business ability. The *Bloemfontein Friend*'s sentiments would certainly have been shared by Sidney Marwick, patently a fervent anti-semite and champion of immigration legislation. He expressed great fear that South Africa would become a haven for undesirables from southern and eastern Europe because the Nationalists allowed open entry for Europeans. This policy, he argued, would bring on "its own punishment." Needless to say, in referring to southern and eastern Europeans, Marwick had Jews in mind. The use of *southern* was a convenient decoy; everyone knew what his real objective was. When challenged by Madeley, who asserted that there was no reason to curtail the influx of these "intellectually developed people," Marwick made his views quite explicit: "These people [were] here for no good [and] bent on mischief."[47]

Philosemitism Revisited

While this chapter has focused on the negative Jewish stereotype as it evolved during the Rand Rebellion and in its aftermath, it should be noted that the philosemitic image discussed in earlier chapters was not entirely obliterated. But that image too was based on racial criteria. Smuts, for instance, generalized about Jewish charitability, while *De Kerkbode* recommended that "poor white" Afrikaners emulate Jews who were perceived as a model of success.[48] Such messages when seen against the backdrop of anti-Jewish sentiment indicate the complexity of human responses rather than essential contradictions.

The notion that Jews were a race was captured most effusively by Tielman Roos in an address marking the opening of the Jewish Memorial Hall in Pretoria. "In the whole history of the world," he pointed out, "there is no greater spectacle of solidarity and cohesion than that which has been displayed by the Jewish race. Jews are sundered over the whole face of the world and they manage to remain one race." He attributed this to "religious considerations," arguing moreover that "Jewish energy and power, had done a tremendous amount in building up South Africa."[49] Racial pride, solidarity, and cohesion were admirable characteristics in the eyes of Afrikaner nationalists who, it may be added, had gained a number of Jewish voters—frustrated and angered at the South African party's inconsistent immigration policy—in the 1924 election.

Another important feature of philosemitic discourse evident in Roos's speech and noted in earlier chapters was the allusion to Jewish power. This power, conceived by philosemites as a product of enterprise, shrewdness, and business acumen, could of course for the antisemite be seen as the result of Jewish "pushiness" and dishonest business dealings.[50] There is a link between alleged Jewish power and the Bolshevik bogey; underpinning both views is an emphasis on a dynamism, in one case used subversively, in the other formatively. The notion of subversion resonated more strongly with the popular psyche in 1922 than the formative notion precisely because an anti-Jewish stereotype had been so pervasive in the prewar years. The South African party and the media, in other words, were able to manipulate well-established images of the Peruvian and combine these with postwar fears of Bolshevism. In this way they avoided culpability for mismanagement. The Bolshevik or eastern European agitator was an ideal scapegoat.

The process of manipulation and its success were illustrated in an address by Siegfried Raphaely to the Fifth Congress of the South African Jewish Board of Deputies. He explained how the board had monitored the press during the Rand upheavals and how it had observed the practice of newspapers copying from one another. In this way they misled the public and gave the impression that the disturbances were caused by Russian or alien immigrants and that the whole country was antisemitic. Even Winston Churchill had seen the upheavals as "Lenin's Last Kick," and a British newspaper had advocated curtailing the entry of aliens into South Africa. Raphaely claimed it was terribly difficult to undo the harm caused by poor reporting. Nonetheless the board had attempted to do so and, following talks with the minister of defense, all antisemitic reports had ceased.[51]

The very success of the media's campaign as outlined by Raphaely ignored a fundamental factor—that the animus directed toward Jews during the Rand Rebellion and in its aftermath was possible only because of a well-entrenched Jewish stereotype in South Africa that had the potential to be manipulated at any time.

CHAPTER SIX

Outsiders and Intruders, 1924–30

Anti-Jewish Outbursts

THE INFLUX of eastern Europeans increased considerably from the mid-1920s as a result of deteriorating conditions in Lithuania and changes to United States and Australian immigration policies.[1] In 1925, 1,353 Jewish immigrants entered South Africa, the number more than doubling by 1929 to 2,738.[2] The arrival of these newcomers, at a time of severe unemployment and escalating "poor whiteism," ensured that Jewish immigration would remain a contentious issue in South African public life. In particular, the "poor whites"—those large numbers of dislocated, recently urbanized, and unskilled Afrikaners—perceived the new arrivals as a threat to their prospects. These casualties of modernization were ill-equipped to compete in the manufacturing and commercial marketplace, dominated as it was by the English-speaking sector, within which Jews were perceived to be powerful and manipulative.[3]

A specifically Afrikaner "volk" attack against Jews was made within a few months of the Pact's electoral victory of 1924 by the Boer War general Manie Maritz. Maritz had returned to public life after serving part of a three-year sentence for his role in the 1914 Rebellion—an armed attempt by onetime Boer generals to undo the result of the Anglo-Boer War and to restore the northern republics. His early release was an obvious gesture of reconciliation on the part of the newly elected Pact Government. Perhaps it considered Maritz's eight-year postrebellion sojourn in Portugal and Germany a sufficient punishment for one who was, after all, a volk hero. Whatever their motivation, Nationalists soon regretted the decision. Indeed, they were acutely embarrassed by Maritz's anti-Jewish outburst which took place during an address to farmers in the Northern Cape town of Mcquassie. The occasion—a commemoration of seventeen men killed near the border of South West Africa at the time of the Rebellion—was used by Maritz to castigate the Jews:

> We have recently learned a great deal about the poverty of our people in the Northern Cape and Namaqualand. Who are responsible for this? Our archenemy the Jews who come to this country with a bundle on their backs and always manage to amass a large sum of money. The Afrikaners of these districts were virtually the servants of the Jews. It was similar in all other parts of South Africa, and a people who made their money here out of the suffering of the people usually left the country and spent it somewhere else.

While Maritz's prejudices may well have been sharpened during his years abroad, his animosity was deeply rooted in the South African experience. His essential message certainly echoes comments made by Thomas Upington (and many others) in the 1890s. Like his counterparts of that era, Maritz spoke on behalf of Afrikaners who had experienced acute upheaval and dislocation. Industrialization and urbanization had taken a severe toll with many Afrikaners experiencing a social crisis by the mid-1920s. Their position contrasted visibly with the success of many Jewish immigrants and first generation South African–born Jews. In the popular perception they appeared, quite correctly, to be wholly suited to city life and its commercial ethos, an alien and hostile world for the uprooted Afrikaner. Maritz was thus quite astute in contrasting the behavior of Germany's commercial class with that of South Africa's. The former, he argued, were "patriots" who had rescued Germany after "the havoc wrought by war" while South Africa's commercial men "were nothing but a lot of bloodsuckers."[4]

Maritz's outburst attracted substantial press coverage and condemnation.[5] The opposition (South African party) press regarded his attack on the Jews as unwarranted. His diatribe, moreover, presented an ideal opportunity for that press to taunt the government since Maritz was a very prominent Afrikaner nationalist. By linking the two, they probably hoped that Jewish support for the Nationalists (which, as noted above, had increased following the South African party's vacillating immigration policy) would be curbed. Maritz's excesses would also be seen as indicative of the dangers of a "republican" cast of mind and its concomitant extremism.

The Nationalists recognized the potentially negative repercussions of

Maritz's utterances. They were sensitive to the fluidity of the English-speaking vote (including the Jewish vote) and the tenuous nature of their alliance with the very largely English-speaking Labour party, several of whose prominent members were Jews. Certainly they had no desire at that juncture to introduce a Jewish Question into South African public life. It is therefore not surprising that *Die Burger* simply omitted Maritz's comments about Jews in its report of the speech. More pointedly, a card-carrying member of the Nationalists, F. J. M. van Zyl, distanced the National party from Maritz in a letter to the *Star*. Van Zyl noted how, as a member of the party, he had taken it upon himself "to get in touch with the [Transvaal] leader of the Party [Roos] in Pretoria, drawing attention to the speech as some of our Jewish friends may be under the impression that Mr Maritz was speaking as the mouthpiece of the National Party. I have, however, Mr Roos's authority, through his private secretary, when I state that Maritz is not a leader and has not the slightest influence on the counsels of the Party." In addition to distancing the National party from Maritz, Van Zyl noted that Jews had attained prominent appointments under the present government and that several of his nationalist friends had condemned Maritz's speech as malicious and beneath contempt.[6]

That Maritz was aware of the controversy surrounding his Mcquassie speech was shown in a speech commemorating the death of Boer rebel and martyr Jopie Fourie. He asserted that he did not mind Jews having businesses, but he did not want them to "take in" the land. They could have all the commerce they wanted but were not to be merciless in their business dealings. After all, he explained, they were "Israelites in a strange land." Despite his implication that Jews were in South Africa on sufferance, Maritz stated that he had no desire to persecute them. His real concern was that Afrikaners should organize themselves. This, he argued, was the only way for South Africans to attain freedom and independence.[7]

Maritz's comments provide a fascinating glimpse into the direction right-wing Afrikaner politics were taking as the crisis of modernization overtook alienated Afrikaner workers and intellectuals. It also illustrates the useful scapegoat Jews would later provide in the mobilization of Afrikaners. There was no question at this point of persecuting Jews, but there was a definite sense that the alleged Jewish role in commerce could be used as a stalking horse to exploit growing radical Afrikaner sentiments.

Maritz's revised stance did not assuage his critics and his comments drew further criticism from the *Pretoria News,* which compared his "reckless and vulgar outburst" with Roos's philosemitic attitude. Maritz had obviously embarrassed the party leadership, and the minister of agriculture, Gen. J. G. Kemp, issued a speedy statement dissociating the National party from his utterances.[8]

Kemp may well have misjudged the amount of support for, or at least ambivalence toward, Maritz's sentiments. The *Sunday Times* did not even address the issue while *De Volksstem,* despite chastising Maritz for his anti-Jewish comments, used the occasion to raise the question of Jewish assimilability. It noted moreover that Jewish immigrants, unlike Christian immigrants, took generations to integrate into society. This, it argued, had resulted in anti-Jewish prejudice. The *Cape,* in similar fashion to *De Volksstem,* expressed a double-edged message. While reveling in the Nationalist predicament, it hastened to point out that because Jews had been persecuted for many centuries they were disproportionately represented among "rogues and tricksters." While blaming "fanatical Christianity" for this state of affairs, it nevertheless made it clear that Jews were a questionable acquisition.[9]

The Maritz episode trenchantly demonstrated that while crude and vulgar antisemitism was publicly unacceptable in the mid-1920s, anti-alienism and cultural xenophobia were permissible. This was illustrated again only a few months later in the responses to yet another anti-Jewish outburst. The perpetrator this time was the Reverend H. G. White of Bloemhof. During an address to the Anglican Synod in Johannesburg, White referred to Jews (and Indians) in a most derogatory fashion when elaborating upon his opposition to the segregation of Africans as a policy. For White, segregation taken to its logical conclusion would mean dealing with "the two Oriental races among us—the Indians and the Jews." Both of these groups, he suggested, were subversive: The Indian had a lower living standard and the Jew had two moral codes— one for the Gentile and one for the Jew. White contended that the segregation idea was born of "fear and misunderstanding" and contrary to the biblical prophesy which made it clear that "the lion, lamb and cockatrice" would "lie down together." "There is no segregation in that," he explained, "and the logical outcome of segregation would be to place the lions in Johannesburg, the cockatrices in, say India, and the wolves in Palestine." The last statement drew laughter.[10]

By implication, of course, White was caricaturing popular percep-

tions of the Jew as an outsider, and a dishonest one at that, to mobilize opposition against the Pact government's segregationist policies.
Predictably, the Jewish community responded with alacrity. Manfred
Nathan criticized the minister in a lengthy letter to the press and the
South African Jewish Board of Deputies took the matter up with the
Anglican Church. The latter responded by begging Jews "to live and
conduct themselves in a way that the finger of scorn would not be
pointed at them." In other words, Jews were regarded as responsible for
animus toward themselves. Numerous non-Jews expressed disgust at
White's comments, and the *Sunday Times* devoted a long editorial
condemning his intolerance and indiscretion. It was especially disturbed by the report that White's speech was greeted with laughter. It
would appear from this that the Anglican layman and the hierarchy
were not *ad idem* on the Jewish issue. The layman, if laughter is an
indication, did not take the matter too seriously, whereas the Reverend
H. G. White and his peers, in warning Jews to improve their behavior,
did.[11]

The White episode once again revealed the unacceptability of blatant
antisemitism on a public level in South Africa at this time. South
Africans, by and large, sought to distance themselves from European
"Judenhetze." This, as has been frequently shown, did not mean the
approbation of eastern European Jewish immigration. On the contrary,
White's harsh and insensitive metaphors revealed just how entrenched
the anti-Jewish stereotype was in South Africa. The unabated influx of
more eastern European Jews thus continued to be a cause of concern
and disapproval.

Immigration Alarm

Alarm bells were initially sounded by the director of census, J. E.
Holloway. In his report on immigration for the period 1920–25, he
declared that the most salient feature of the immigration figures was
the increasing influx of poverty-stricken Lithuanians. The majority, he
noted, were involved in commerce, the very sort of category not wanted
at this stage.[12]

Holloway's sentiments were shared by a range of newspapers strad-
dling the party divide. A consensus certainly existed in which middlemen (often perceived to be dishonest) were unwanted, particularly at a
time of economic austerity and growing "poor whiteism." "Prominent

members of the commercial community," noted an editorial in the *Rand Daily Mail,* "have declared that in the present stage of South African development too many people are already engaged in trade and commerce. Indeed this has been one of the causes of the depressing record of insolvencies, and it is impossible not to feel that, until other portions of the population have grown considerably, those now concluding the trading business of this country are ample for the purpose. Unfortunately unemployment is still rife, and there is little room for immigrants with small or unspecified resources."[13]

The *Rand Daily Mail*'s comments were predicated upon one dimension of the oft-repeated negative Jewish stereotype—namely, the newcomers' inherent predisposition toward commerce, their nonproductivity, and dishonesty in business. There was, however, much more to the antialien alarm than the question of economic competition and the alleged economic predilections of the newcomers. By the mid-1920s eugenicist-based fears of "race mixing" and "mongrelization"—primarily associated with South African blacks—appeared to have influenced perceptions of the eastern European. In other words, a new "race" discourse, in which "Russians" and "Jews" joined "Orientals," "Africans," "Europeans," "Anglo-Saxons," "English," "Nordics," and "Mediterraneans" as racial groups, impacted on the question of Jewish immigration. So-called "moral degeneracy" haunted South African eugenicists while "miscegenation" or "cross-breeding" was a fear voiced even by liberal social scientists and philosophers.[14]

The antialien lobby was thus fortified with a sound intellectual rationale, reinforced by nativist assumptions (based similarly upon the eugenics paradigm), emanating from the United States. There the Johnson Act of 1924 had finally, through a rigid quota system based on racial origins of the population in 1890, erected a formidable barrier against the influx of "alien" or "non-Nordic" immigration. In South Africa, racial nativism focused on eastern European immigrants who were perceived as a special threat.[15] By way of example, the *Star,* in response to Holloway's report, referred to the fecundity (even in later life) of the eastern Europeans and the impact this would have upon the country's intellectual and physical development. It contended that eastern European immigration would profoundly modify the racial composition of the country and that it would be far better to encourage "Nordic immigrants" as the United States had done.[16] A similar argument was employed by the *Cape Times:* "We have barely 1,600,000 Europeans in

South Africa . . . in the main a population of Nordic type. If, however, we continued to lose annually a large number of South Africans of Nordic type . . . and to introduce annually a large number of Southern and Eastern Europeans—Lithuanians, Finns, Poles and what not—we may easily find that the whole character of the South African nation may be changed." This, argued the newspaper, was a matter which deserved the attention of South African statesmen.[17]

The new racial discourse was shared by the Nationalist mouthpiece, *Die Burger*. It expressed concern at the loss of Nordic *stamgenote* (kinsmen) and their replacement with southern and eastern Europeans and, in particular, Lithuanians. The matter would not have been so serious, it argued, had the newcomers been farmers and not middlemen. Once again the eastern European Jew had been racially or culturally typecast, albeit in a way more or less consonant with reality. But this reality was a product of historical circumstances and structural conditions rather than inherent predilections within the Jewish psyche. In the popular view, however, ethnology and culture were conflated and accorded primacy. Thus *Die Burger* could warn that if steps were not taken to curtail the eastern European influx (especially in view of the United States and Australian immigration policies), South Africa would have another race problem. The newspaper's rationale, which focused on the unassimilability of the eastern European Jew and his different business morality and social concepts, vividly illustrated the impact of eugenicist thought. The issue, concluded *Die Burger,* was that the government had to encourage "assimilable" immigrants and stop "unassimilable" types.[18] In fact the reverse was taking place; after 1924 there was a large outflow of English immigrants and an inflow of eastern European Jews.

"Unassimilable" had clearly become a label for Jewish, or, more specifically, eastern European Jewish, immigrants. The latter were perceived as outsiders, immutably alien and inherently devious. Most importantly, they intruded into, and threatened to overshadow, the white or European establishment. While "unassimilable" reflected the new discourse of race and culture, it conveniently dodged charges of antisemitism. Almost everyone wished to avoid that charge, for crude antisemitism remained unacceptable, running counter to a persistent strain of philosemitism in South African culture. This was once again demonstrated in responses to the formation of a sinister Ku Klux Klan–type organization, the League of Gentiles.

The League of Gentiles

The League of Gentiles came to the public's notice late in November 1925 through sensational disclosures in the *Rand Daily Mail* and the *Star*. According to the *Star* (which broke the news), the league had approximately 10,000 members, mostly from the middle classes. Its aim was to boycott Jewish traders, an action which, in the league's estimation, would cost Jewish traders approximately 3,000,000 pounds per annum. On the day the *Star*'s report appeared a large advertisement was placed in the *Rand Daily Mail* calling for "20,000 more Gentiles to complete the Scheme of Co-operation for the benefit of all true" Gentiles. Those who recognized the persistent danger of Jewish domination and who wanted to help were asked to write to a Johannesburg post-office box number.[19] This suggested that the league was an established organization rather than the work of individual crackpots. Further developments indicate that this was not the case.

The following day, under a huge headline, "Blindfold Interview with League of Gentiles," a *Rand Daily Mail* journalist described his secret blindfolded assignation with an executive member of the League of Gentiles in the woods outside Johannesburg. The league's spokesman made it clear that the organization's objectives were quite constitutional. They were, in essence, to counterpoise powerful Jewish organizations that exerted a great deal of influence with an equally powerful Gentile organization. He noted that although Jews constituted 6 percent of the population, they practically controlled 94 percent of the food supply. His organization wanted to influence the Government in the same way Jewish organizations did and to protect Gentiles and in particular Gentile women.[20]

Factors motivating the league were further elaborated in a poorly written preamble to the membership form that advocated "casting out socially, industrially and economically the Jewish element, which is too prominent today. . . . The general discontent of late years proves conclusively that there is much room for improvement on our social order. . . . Wealth among the Jews is a real danger point to the future prosperity of the Gentiles; and their power of wealth is the greatest danger we have to guard against."[21]

The melodramatic nature of the secret interview, coupled with the poor language and style evident in the membership form's preamble, suggest that the league was the work of a few disturbed individuals. Indeed, two days after the membership form's preamble was published, the *Rand Daily Mail* published an amended version that was hardly indicative of an established organization as suggested in the *Star*'s initial report. On the other hand, it is possible that someone more educated had tried to reverse the earlier poor impression. Notwithstanding the seemingly amateurish nature of the league, it attracted widespread concern both in Jewish and non-Jewish circles—this despite a Jewish Board of Deputies denial of a report in the *Rand Daily Mail* which referred to Jewish communal alarm. The board claimed to have known about the league for some time and that it had been assured by the CID chief that the matter was of little consequence.[22]

Interviews with other Jewish communal leaders suggest that the formation of the League of Gentiles was taken seriously. The president of the South African Zionist Federation, A. M. Abrahams, for one, defended the Jewish record, arguing that their enterprise had created employment for thousands. In addition, he pointed out that those Jews who had settled in South Africa were desirous of becoming "true sons of the land." The chief rabbi, Dr. J. L. Landau, similarly extolled South African Jewry's contribution to the country and reminded readers that hitherto Jews had enjoyed equal opportunities and the absence of antisemitism.[23]

The formation of the league and its objectives were also condemned by a number of non-Jews in letters to the *Rand Daily Mail*. This newspaper, in turn, ridiculed the league's "manifesto" and bitterly regretted the potential it generated for social conflict. That seems to have been the general attitude of the press to the establishment of the league, confirming once again its rejection of crude anti-Jewish prejudice. Yet prejudice of a less crude kind was becoming acceptable when used to advocate restrictions on Jewish entry into South Africa. In this contradiction we see the essential ambiguity of the Jewish image. The very newspapers that criticized the league and its crude proposals were quite happy to associate eastern European Jews with an inferior business ethic and to blame antisemitism on the inordinate influx of these newcomers. Thus could *Die Burger* argue that it was the Jew's business principles and practices rather than his race that generated anti-Jewish feeling on the Rand.[24]

In *Die Burger*'s comments the interrelationship between the economy and prejudice is evident as indeed it had been during the 1922

Rebellion. Of course we also see a burgeoning racial nativism that depicted the eastern European Jew as a threat to Western values and norms. This was undoubtedly the case for the *Cape Times,* which, while distancing itself from antisemitism, blamed the sentiments expressed by the "Gentile League," at least in part, on Jewish immigrants replacing British-born European immigrants. It was, argued the newspaper, not because they were Hebrew that they were problematic but because they hailed from central Europe and belonged to an undesirable class of immigrant. In the opinion of the *Cape Times,* South Africans would have to make up their minds whether they really wanted 70 percent of immigrants to come from Lithuania and neighboring countries. It pointed out that the United States, faced with a similar problem, had a quota system to restrict such immigration. Southern and eastern Europeans were unassimilable and in fact had no desire to assimilate.

The *Cape Times* was effectively acknowledging that the "emancipation contract" had been broken by the newcomers. Of course, in an age when the biological quality of human stock was so important, it was virtually impossible for eastern European Jews to fulfill their contract. Thus the whole argument was specious. The fact of the matter was that *eastern European* was synonymous with *Jew.* There was nothing in South Africa like the United States protest against southern Europeans. The newspaper palpably wished to harness the sympathies of those already in South Africa in its campaign against further eastern European immigration. However reasonable its comments appear to have been, beneath its rational discourse lay a strong strain of anti-Jewish prejudice.

Projecting from current immigration and emigration figures, the *Cape Times* went on to warn that they would very soon find the whole character of the country changed. Once again the newspaper stressed that its viewpoint was not informed by antisemitism: "It is simply a question of South Africanism and we believe that the great majority of the 65,000 Jews who are in South Africa to-day and are helping to build up its wealth and its prosperity would agree that the indiscriminate inpouring of so many hundreds of Southern and Eastern Europeans every year, as long as the other fountains of immigration are so dry, is not desirable and [not] in the interests of South Africa."[25]

Anti-Jewish views were similarly expressed by the *East London Daily Dispatch,* which argued in an editorial, "The Alien Invasion," that Russian immigrants could not, by and large, be compared with those of British stock.[26] The heavy preponderance of southern and eastern Europeans together with the diminishing ratio of people "of Nordic strain" also perturbed the *Eastern Province Herald:*

> Students may well ask what will be the ultimate ethnological influence of the heavy influx of this strain into the country. That it will have an effect on our manners and customs, and even on our national characteristics and outlook, few will doubt. The Nordic strain which is, of course, predominant in the country at present in the form of the old Dutch and English population, is highly resistant in some ways, but we have a curious example of the penetrative power of the type of immigrant so heavily in the majority in the figures quoted in the case of the United States of America. In that country the Nordics have preserved all their characteristics and may even be said to represent the governing class; but side by side there is in rapid growth another class of population racially distinctive, the product of the Latin, the Slav and the Semitic immigrant. That they are making an impress on at any rate the surface of the American native is very clear. The question is whether that impression is purely superficial or whether it is gradually penetrating below the surface and into the very vitals. Of course we have to remember that the influx into the United States in recent generations has been on a far more wholesale scale than even the present influx in South Africa. Yet we think that even at this early date we can trace the first shadowy markings of the impress of the new population on some parts of the surface of South Africa.[27]

The foregoing responses—reminiscent of antialien rhetoric in the old Cape Colony—demonstrate the deeply embedded nature of the eastern European stereotype as well as the deeply entrenched nature of antisemitism in South Africa at this time. The newcomers embodied decades of negative labeling. This was well captured in *Ons Vaderland's* response to the league. While distancing itself from antisemitism and expressing hope that South Africa would not experience the sort of hatred evident in Germany in the 1870s and France at the time of Dreyfus, the Afrikaans Nationalist biweekly nevertheless opposed an open immigration policy. Rather it argued that South Africa should admit only the best class of Jew. This, in effect, meant the introduction of an entry quota such as that in operation in the United States.

In defining its stance, *Ons Vaderland* dealt with a number of anti-Jewish stereotypes popular among Afrikaners. It noted that it was no longer justifiable to see Jews as industrial exploiters, nor was it reasonable to begrudge Jews their partial monopolization of industry. On the contrary, Jewish initiative had done much for the country. Workers simply had to see that white workers were employed and that wages were not at the *hongerlone* (starvation) level. Jewish shopkeepers (usually very successful) could also be dealt with by regulations and by the lengthening of the credit period. This, *Ons Vaderland* claimed, would prevent the repugnant consequences of shopkeepers' behavior. It was also confident that Jewish "pocket-patriotism" would end with the next generation, who would come to look on South Africa as a genuine fatherland.[28] The newspaper also dismissed the view that the uniquely sly nature of the Jew, honed over centuries of oppression, had made him master over those of more righteous Indo-German stock. Only occasionally was the Afrikaner squeezed and reduced to poverty and the Jew was not his master. In its final defense, *Ons Vaderland* (in an apparent allusion to English speakers) noted that Jews, being unable to return to their country of origin, did not remove their money from the country. In short, the Jew was not an unmitigated evil.[29]

Ons Vaderland's refutation of prevailing anti-Jewish images reveals much about the pervasiveness of negative Jewish stereotypes in the mid-1920s. These stereotypes were now consolidated and reinforced by the eugenicist paradigm discussed above. Thus the *Eastern Province Herald* could vilify the new arrivals in the following terms: "They are generally people whose one ideal is to deal in some commodity or another, to be a shopkeeper, a buyer and seller, very frequently a speculator. And as such and taking into consideration their pushful characteristics, they are more calculated to leave their mark ethnologically on South Africa than were they workers in an industry or agriculturalists."[30]

The focus of nativist rhetoric was thus based on culture or economics or both rather than on religion. In this way the problem was not defined as a Jewish one per se and thus the pitfalls experienced by Maritz, the Reverend H. G. White, and the League of Gentiles were avoided; the failure of the latter organization demonstrated conclusively that the time for public antisemitism had not yet arrived.[31]

Jewish Domination

By the mid-1920s the question of eastern European immigration had receded with the emergence of the more pressing issue of South Africa's status within the British Empire and the "Native Problem." In addition, during 1926 and again in 1927, the country was convulsed by the flag controversy, an issue that aroused bitter conflict over the very symbols of the nation's past and future. Despite immigration concerns being moved temporarily to the periphery of public debate, certain individuals, supported by the *Cape Times* in particular, did their utmost to keep the question alive. J. S. Marwick resuscitated the old canard that Jews were subverting the social order through their involvement in liquor merchandising. Alien liquor merchants, he told parliament, were ruining the Africans and respect for the white man in the Transvaal. The burden of Marwick's complaint was that Jewish liquor dealers were destroying the "proper" relationship between whites and blacks, merely for the sake of a little profit.[32] In this sense Marwick added a new dimension to the negative stereotype, the Jew as a subverter of existing race relations and of social stability. Of course these ideas resonated precisely because the Peruvian and cosmopolitan financier were already associated with purportedly subversive intentions and behavior. Had the Jew not engineered the Anglo-Boer War? Was he not the inspiration behind the Rand Rebellion? The ultimate force of Marwick's charge, however, rested upon burgeoning fears of African proletarianization, radicalism, and social breakdown.

What is most noteworthy is the fact that Marwick's comments went unchallenged. Rather the *Cape Times* used his speech as a springboard for yet another attack on unrestricted immigration. While acknowledging that South Africa's 65,000 Jews had contributed in the past and continued to contribute toward the development of South Africa, the newspaper made it clear that it did not welcome the prospect of more Jews. They might be (as one Jew had put it) "the salt of the earth" but, as a "'witty young poet' once remarked," "too much salt is worse than none." For this reason the *Cape Times* urged the government to consider a quota system. In classic eugenicist style the newspaper warned that non-Nordics might alter the whole character "of the future race." Here was the eastern European Jew viewed as a racial outsider, an unwholesome and unhealthy presence in South African society. This is even more apparent when one considers a *Cape Times* assertion that it was a contradiction to restrict Asiatics while "positively encouraging a class of immigrant who is in very many cases questionably superior to the Asiatic and scarcely qualified in many cases to be classed as of European stock at all."[33] What this newspaper was really arguing was that the eastern European Jew had a dubious commercial morality and was racially not European. For these reasons he ought to have been consigned where the Asiatic already was by statutory law.

One correspondent to the *Cape Times,* sensing the newspaper's anti-Jewish mood, summarized the whole spectrum of misdemeanors with which the immigrant Jew had been, and was now again being, charged:

> As traders, the role in which most of them have figured, they have succeeded in gaining for South Africa's commercial morality the reputation of being the lowest in the world. . . . By giving unlimited credit to farmers and presenting a bill of undreamed of dimensions at a time when the failure of their mealie crops, or an invasion of locusts has made it obviously impossible for them to pay, the alien trader in the country has gained possession of numerous farms. . . .
>
> A study of last year's statistics of crime in the Union reveals the illuminating fact that aliens were responsible for 60 per cent of it, as against 18 per cent, committed by English and Dutch combined, and this despite the fact that aliens form less than 10 per cent of our population.
>
> Illicit liquor selling, illicit diamond buying, fraudulent insolvency, and conflagrations of obscure origin have long been almost a monopoly of the aliens. But so cleverly does he keep in the background, that in the first two cases the responsibility more often than not falls on the comparatively innocent shoulders of his dupes of the poor white and unemployed classes.
>
> To the Eastern and Southern European we owe the majority of the Communist agitators, whose power of fomenting trouble was demonstrated in the Rand revolt of 1922, and, more recently the seamen's strike.[34]

The absence of support for eastern European Jews in the press suggests a widespread aversion to their presence and certainly to the arrival of a further influx. Marwick in fact argued that besides the two Jewish parliamentarians, Morris Alexander and Morris Kentridge, everyone regretted the eastern European influx. He believed the public would soon demand legislation to restrict the entry of undesirable aliens. However, Marwick compromised his own argument by calling upon the government to initiate propaganda which would generate antagonism toward the eastern European. When Alexander pointed out that South Africa's Jews had been praised by numerous people including farmers, Marwick became vitriolic. Once again Jews were characterized as parasitic middlemen of dubious morality as well as subverters of the social order:

We know that the majority of these people are not engaged in primary production. A very large number come to this country and take up such occupations as the middleman, trader, yeast seller, hotel-keeper, bar-keeper, canteen-keeper, eating-house keeper, and occupations of that sort which are already overstaffed. . . . We want primary producers.

In America anarchists and Bolshevists are not admitted, and there is no doubt that a large proportion of the people who came to this country are of this particular belief. We can well do without them and I know of no Europeans who are less likely to have a beneficial influence on the natives than the particular immigrants I speak of. It is within my experience that these particular people demean themselves with the natives for the sake of a little gain, and they have no idea of the relative position that should be occupied by the white man and the native in this country. . . . I am convinced and absolutely satisfied that there is a strong feeling in South Africa against this particular type of immigrant coming in.[35]

Although Marwick had undermined his own argument by advocating state-initiated agitation, it is clear that he was expressing an opinion held by many members of parliament as evidenced by the noticeable absence of challenging debate in the proceedings. In fact, Lt. Col. M. J. Pretorius, the South African party member for Witwatersberg, contended that the country wanted people who would not simply exploit the population. This, he argued, was not to be defined according to religious denomination.[36]

Notwithstanding his apparent even-handedness, Pretorius's emphasis on the parasitism of the immigrants was enough to classify his speech as antisemitic. This was obvious to all and explains the fancy footwork on the part of Pretorius to distance himself—as others had previously done—from antisemitic charges. In truth, however, rhetoric surrounding restriction was based upon racist assumptions in which all Jews were ascribed inherent attributes and immutable characteristics. These were usually but not always negative. Even when Jews were praised, the essential message was one of exaggerated Jewish power and influence. Often Jews were singled out for their intellectual ability, their charitability and their contribution to mankind. Gen. J. G. Kemp best captured the philosemitic view when addressing a Jewish audience commemorating Jewish soldiers who had fallen in the Great War:

You, as a race, have throughout the ages and in all parts of the world, produced leaders in religion, law, politics, business and war. You have

given the world the Ten Commandments, which serve as a foundation for all our laws. Even in modern times you have produced one of
the greatest lawyers in the world, namely, Lord Reading, in England.
In South Africa today you have a distinguished representative on the
South African bench, namely, Judge Greenberg. In politics you have
produced such a man as the famous Prime Minister of England,
Disraeli; in business such great captains of industry as Rothschild and
many others, in war such a man as David.[37]

An important feature of philosemitic discourse was patently the
emphasis on Jewish "excellence" and concomitant power. At the structural level the philosemitic and antisemitic views were, as noted earlier,
not dissimilar. It was essentially this fear of potential Jewish domination
that kept alive the concern surrounding Jewish immigration. Thus
could the party of Roos, Kemp, and Hertzog, all of whom had spoken
favorably about Jews, call for stricter control of undesirable immigration at its Cape Congress in 1926, and for a quota system of Jewish entry
at its Natal Congress during the same year. Afrikaners obviously feared
a loss of influence and power as they confronted the Jewish immigrant
in the urban setting.[38]

The subtle shift in National party policy had obviously been detected
by Manie Maritz, who delivered yet another anti-Jewish diatribe to
7,000 miners in Lichtenburg. Once again Jews were identified as "the
biggest blood-suckers in the world." In particular they were accused of
dominating the Afrikaner: "We have fought for a Republic and independence, but today a lot of our people are the agents of the Jews. . . . In
the meanwhile the Jews are coming into the country in thousands.
Jerusalem is already here." Maritz no doubt sensed a rising impatience
among Afrikaner blue-collar workers who feared a loss in social status
and a decline in living standards. Whereas his previous outburst had
shown some measure of restraint, he was now blatantly and viciously
antagonistic, contending that Jews did "the meanest and lowest things
in the country."[39]

In sensing the Afrikaner mood in the western Transvaal—an area
whose inhabitants were increasingly exasperated by poverty and dislocation—Maritz's sentiments were a harbinger of the 1930s, when, as
we shall see, the Afrikaner Right mobilized power around the notion of
Jewish domination. However, conditions in the late 1920s were not
felicitous for a popular anti-Jewish movement. The Pact Government
had begun to address economic problems and there was some hope that
a range of mainly segregationist legislation would improve conditions

for the white worker. Perhaps that was the reason why the League of
Gentiles had, according to Tielman Roos, decided to transfer its attention to the countryside. Roos was confident, however, that the league
would be as unsuccessful there as it had been in the urban centers. The
rural community, he argued, valued the contribution of Jewish shopkeepers who—rather than banks—kept farmers afloat during difficult
times.[40]

Some farmers may well have appreciated the Jewish contribution,
but Roos palpably misunderstood the nature of power inherent in the
encounter between debtor and creditor.[41] That relationship underpinned much animosity toward the Jew. Roos was wrong to assume
that farmers in general shared his view that it was "only right and proper
that the Jewish community should be rewarded for their enterprise,
initiative and ability." And, of course, his view that the country would
suffer enormously if Jewish enterprise was restricted merely confirmed
the alleged hold Jews had on the country's economy—yet another
example of the power attributed to Jews even by the philosemite.[42]
More importantly, his attitude confirmed that the Pact Government saw
no need for exclusionist legislation.

A far more realistic insight into rural attitudes toward the Jew is
evident in contemporary fiction and short stories. Afrikaans writing in
particular confirms the powerful impact made upon the rural community by the smous and Jewish trader. By and large, perceptions of both
were negative. If the Jewish trader was not driving a hard bargain, he
was speculating and, being sharp-witted, was easily able to outwit the
Boer. As for the smous, he was invariably ridiculed and portrayed as
being filthy.[43] It was in the 1920s too, as Afrikaners urbanized at an
increasing pace, that the *plaasroman* (farm novel) emerged as a genre of
antimodernist and romantic writing, idealizing the *platteland* (countryside) and shunning the city. More often than not, writes J. M.
Coetzee, the urban symbol of "monied townsmen" was Jewish. Jochem
van Bruggen stands out as an exemplar of this genre. In his short story
Bywoners (Tenant farmers), the Jewish butcher, Kaplan, has all the
cunning and sharp business insight associated with the negative Jewish
stereotype. Similarly, D. F. Malherbe depicts the Jewish businessman in
Die Meulenaar (The miller) as scheming and devoid of morals. These
themes blossomed in the 1930s as Afrikaners streamed to the cities. In
the words of Coetzee, the *plaasroman* at this time "comes closest to the
reactionary *Grosstadtfeindschaft,* anticapitalism, anti-Semitism, and *Blut
and Boden* ideology of the *Bauernroman*."[44]

Whether or not one accepts the argument that anxiety produces jokes and that people only joke about what is most serious, a helpful indication of Afrikaner perceptions of the Jew is manifest in the Jewish joke. Certainly the cycle of Afrikaner smous jokes, popular during the 1920s, is significant; in them the Jew is depicted as alien, obsessed with money and business, sharp-witted, miserly, and always wanting to avoid hard work.[45] Evidently these jokes projected onto the Jew the fears and tensions felt by displaced Afrikaners moving to the towns. On the other hand, English speakers did not experience the same social dislocations and therefore did not share these fears to the same extent. Popular English-language magazines in the 1920s had no Jewish jokes amongst their repertoire of regular jokes.

Distinctiveness, Upward Mobility, and Antagonism

As the 1920s drew to a close, it is obvious that Jews were perceived as yet another corporate or racial group within the complex multiethnic mix of South African society. Given the other deep and already long-standing cultural and linguistic cleavages within this society—such as the schism between Boer and Brit, not to mention color divides—it may seem surprising that certain individuals took exception to the fact that Jews had not merged fully into the broader white population. For these observers it was a disappointment and even a source of tension that Jews had not fulfilled the "emancipation contract" even though that contract was, as we know, neither formal nor tangible. It was in this vein that the onetime administrator of the Cape, Sir Frederick De Waal, encouraged Jews to become agriculturalists (and not only intellectuals), and to identify with the aims and objects of the South African people. Although De Waal's comments were expressed in good faith, they nevertheless illustrate the subtle demand for Jewish integration and assimilation.[46]

The well-known journalist Vere Stent expressed an even more explicit disappointment with the Jews' inability to assimilate into the general community when he praised those Jews who had achieved a "higher than mere tribal patriotism" and realized "their duties to the community which has treated them so much better than any other." Stent demonstrated Jewish exclusivity by drawing a comparison between the will of Sammy Marks and the Beit bequests. The latter had shown "undue tolerance and broad patriotism which many a Christian plutocrat might well emulate."[47] Stent could not have used better examples to illustrate the concept of an "emancipation contract": Marks maintained his Jewish identity whereas Beit was fully assimilated.

Quite evidently Jewish distinctiveness underpinned antagonism toward Jews at a certain level. As Dr. W. J. Viljoen, the superintendent of general education in the Cape Province warned, not everyone admired the way in which the Jews had preserved their identity. He confirmed that the following argument was most popular: "Either the Jew is, or is not a stranger and a menace. If he is not then he should become an integral part through intermarriage and racial fusion, of the people among who he lives, and not remain merely a member of a separate religious community."[48] Here again was a classic illustration of the "emancipation contract." Whereas the future was to demonstrate that loyalty to one's own religious group did not preclude loyalty to one's country, in the 1920s there were still many who took exception to a distinctively Jewish group identity as manifest in social, residential, and occupational clustering.[49] The reality, however, was that Jews perceived themselves as a distinctive group and were by and large perceived as such. These notions were reinforced by determinist assumptions of race, culture, and finally the Zionist enterprise.

By not shedding their corporate identity (or not fulfilling the "emancipation contract"), Jews reinforced the existing foundations of anti-Jewish hostility. However, far more important were the unfavorable characteristics ascribed to the Jew over decades. In other words, the Jew was more than unassimilable—he was subversive and corrupt. Furthermore, he was upwardly mobile and in this regard threatened to dominate society. The fears of those who felt themselves threatened and aggrieved by the social and economic ascent of the Jew were well captured in a sarcastic article entitled "Why I Hate Jews" by a Charles Henry Mackintosh:

> I do not like the Jews. They are too shrewd for me. They are willing to work harder than I. When they have a goal—and they always seem to have goals—they are not to be turned aside by trifles nor by obstacles which they might term insurmountable. They are not to be moved, as I am moved, by ridicule or by expressions of contempt, because the long centuries have surely taught them the lesson that words cannot alter facts. . . .
>
> They have a sense of racial homogeneity such as is unknown to any other breed of beings; because for a thousand years, the hammer of Gentile hatred has beaten them down upon each other.
>
> Jews do not like Gentiles any more than I like Jews, but even there

they have an advantage over me, because they have better reasons behind their dislike.

I do not like Jews because they outwork and outlast, outlove and outhate me.

Oppression has made his metal more firm than mine. His former helplessness drew out and developed the cruelty of my ancestors, while the cruelty of my ancestors drew out and developed the courage and endurance of his.

. . . Today in the temple of democracy erected upon the foundation that all men are created free and equal, the Gentile has lost his power to wrong, and the Jew has gained his rights. The law gives neither the advantage now, but the law gives the Jew greater advantage over the Gentile to-day than ever law gave a Gentile over the Jew in the past. For the law says that whatsoever a man sows that shall he reap.

For the Gentile has sown cruelty, rapacity, greed. The Jew has sown endurance, to bear cruelty; courage to meet rapacity; industry and cunning, to satisfy greed. And now Gentile and Jew are matched against each other without unnatural advantages on either side!

It is to take the pampered lap-dog from his cushion before the fire, to match him against the lean wolf with limbs of living steel gained in grim and long-continued grappling with granite faced necessity. It is to match the domestic chicken against the fierce falcon, the tame rabbit against the eagle of the egries. It is a battle between the alert and practical athlete and his fat and theoretical trainer, and the best man always wins.

No I do not like the Jew. They set too fast a pace.[50]

Early in 1927 a pamphlet distributed around the Cape Peninsula once again exposed the fears of those who felt their hold over commerce, trade, professional and intellectual life weakening:

CHRISTIANS

A Happy and Prosperous New Year. And may 1927 give you all that you deserve. May your Jewish Controlled Press continue to shape your political thoughts and Political Actions and Edit your Sunday Paper.

May the Jews rely on your assistance to guide the hands of your Government.

May the 75% of Jewish University Students become the Teachers of your Children.

May they continue to extract your teeth, doctor your ailments, control your food supplies and determine your living conditions.

May you continue to support Tielman Roos's gift from Heaven of

inspired Jews whose intellect, perseverance and financial ability has
built up South Africa and made it a land for you to live in.

May you continue to sacrifice your land, your name, your home,
your creed, your individuality and the right to your existence and
become more and more a dutiful servant to your kind Masters, the
Jews—Amen.[51]

The pamphlet's message, not unlike sentiments expressed in Europe
in the late nineteenth-century, resonated in the South African context
precisely because second-generation South African Jews had moved
rapidly into the professions and industry.[52] It mattered little that this
generation was more acculturated than their forbears; very often the
Jew-hater had an even greater fear of the assimilated Jew.

Jewish upward mobility therefore was in itself a phenomenon worthy of comment. Indeed, as was the case in the early twentieth century,
it also received positive comment. The Jews, in the words of Sir Abe
Bailey, "are everywhere climbing to the top of the trees where the plums
are to be found. With their capacity for hard work and their zest for
application, it will assuredly not be long before they control the professions, especially law and medicine." While Bailey viewed Jewish
achievement positively and indeed commended the Dutch and English
to be as industrious, others, as we have seen, felt threatened and en-
vious of Jewish success. That success was epitomized in the "well nigh
perfect picture of a Rand Jew attorney" as depicted by Stephen Black in
his 1928 production *Backveld Boer*.[53] Black's attorney personified the
Jewish metamorphosis from unkempt smous to powerful city professional. The outsider had become an intruder. Herein lay the emerging
consensus behind restriction.

Renewed Calls for Exclusion

Given the negative Jewish stereotype, the threat of Jewish upward
mobility, and fears of Jewish domination, it is not surprising that a sense
of urgency, exacerbated by the collapse of the New York Stock Exchange in October 1929, entered the immigration debate during the
late 1920s. The debate, cast essentially in racial terms, focused mainly on
the erosion of Western norms and values and the introduction of foreign or alien influences. At the forefront was the *Cape Times,* imbued
with an exaggerated fear that British subjects were being replaced by
aliens. The latter, it noted, were "from racial stocks which experi-

ence has shown to be unsuitable to the peculiar conditions of this country." In the *Cape Times* view, a reasonable proportion of foreigners was acceptable. However, when that proportion rose beyond a certain point, "there was a real risk of endangering the continuity of the development of those broad ideals, upon whose conservation and general acceptance throughout the British Commonwealth the health, the solidarity and the prosperity of the Empire alike depend."[54]

In parliament Marwick expressed similar concern about the quality of "stock" entering South Africa and even suggested the proscription of name-changing as a means of assessing and monitoring the alien impact. Marwick's anxieties were shared by his South African party colleague, the member for Albany, R. H. Struben. This onetime deputy chairman of the staunchly imperial 1820 Memorial Settlers Association and vice president of the Cape Agricultural Association, succinctly expressed the prevailing racial paradigm:

> The chief ingredients of our European population are of northern stock, and we should introduce people of a stock more likely to assimilate to the existing stock than we are doing to-day. I do not wish to say anything disparaging about any race, but we peoples of northern races are in the majority here among the white population and we should encourage the entry into this country of those people who will assimilate the most rapidly with us rather than encourage people, however good they may be, to come from other parts of Europe. It is time we took into very serious consideration the introduction of a quota system of immigration, as America has been driven to do if we want to preserve in the Europeans of this country the characteristics of our ancestors who settled and developed the country. It is common ground amongst all of us, whether business people or farmers, that South Africa is overstocked with traders. What we want are producers, whether by manual labor or from the fruits of the soil, rather than traders and distributors. We want people who will help to develop the country, who will make their homes in our waste places and who will not merely be.

At this point in Struben's speech, the MP for Griqualand, L. D. Gilson, exclaimed "Parasites." Struben opposed the use of that word, preferring instead the phrase "people who make their living out of the labour of others." Nevertheless, he terminated his speech with a rousing call for everyone to confront reality and encourage the right sort of people to immigrate. This meant producers and not middlemen.[55]

In the run up to the 1929 General Election—fought mainly on the question of "Swart Gevaar" (black danger)—restrictionists, probably fearful of alienating potential Jewish electoral support, were somewhat guarded in their approach to immigration. The *Cape Times,* by way of example, merely urged that the government institute a careful inquiry into immigration policy and collect data for determining a basis on which a quota system could be applied. This fear of alienating Jewish electoral support probably also explains why the National party only seriously addressed the issue after the elections. By then the economy had begun to feel the effect of declining prices for primary products and there were fears that further restrictions on eastern Europeans entering the United States would result in a large influx of eastern Europeans to South Africa. Thus the National party's Free State Congress resolved that the time had arrived to fix a quota of immigration as in the United States. The *Cape Times* acclaimed the resolution in an editorial, noting that Sir Lionel Phillips, one of the original Randlords and a Jew himself, had expressed concern that most of the "foreign" immigrants set up on arrival as small traders. His speech gave the *Cape Times* an opportunity to launch into the now frequent conflation of economic and ethnic concerns:

> He is a direct cause of the acknowledged over-trading which seems to be a chronic ailment of South Africa's. The excess means that, in all our frequent periods of depression, competition between the hucksters takes on an internecine character, and becomes responsible for the low standard of "business morality" which is so marked a feature of South African commercial life. The present tendency, in a word, is for South Africa to replace its dominant Nordic Stock of Europeans by a stock of entirely distinct characteristics, dubious quality, and undoubted suitability to the economic conditions of the country. Admittedly the process is still very gradual, but it is accelerating; and even at its present pace, it is capable of producing in a generation or so a profound effect upon the whole character of a white population which is initially well under two nations.[56]

The idea of a quota system, modeled on that of the United States, had palpably gained ground. According to Gus Saron, the general secretary of the South African Jewish Board of Deputies, this was confirmed by the minister of justice, Oswald Pirow. However, the Nationalists made no mention of impending immigration legislation during the governor general's opening speech to parliament in 1930. In retrospect it is evident that they had hoped to capture the significant Jewish vote in both the Bethal and Stellenbosch by-elections. Pirow had in fact specifically told Bethal's Jewish community during the by-election campaign that the Nationalists would oppose immigration legislation. But defeats in both by-elections demonstrated that the Jewish vote was not worth courting. Within a matter of days, on 28 January 1930, the minister of the interior, Dr. D. F. Malan, shocked South African Jewry with the introduction of a Quota Bill.[57]

The Quota Act

The Immigration Quota Bill limited to a numerical quota immigrants, of whatever race or creed, born in quota or "non-scheduled" countries. These were Greece, Latvia, Lithuania, Poland, Russia, and Palestine, the only mandated country specifically named. Obviously, Jewish immigration was directly affected. Nonquota or "scheduled" countries were free of restriction. These included countries of the British Commonwealth, Austria, Belgium, Denmark, France, Germany, Holland, Italy, Norway, Portugal, Spain, Sweden, Switzerland, and the United States.

A remarkable consensus greeted the introduction of the bill which, according to the South African party member for Cape Town (Castle), J. A. MacCallum, was absolutely and unreservedly supported by the man in the street. Thus Malan was quite accurately able to emphasize broad assent when opening the second reading debate: "The party newspapers have, with very few exceptions, greeted this Bill as one which is long overdue, and not only in principle but also as far as particular provisions are concerned, they have, to a very large extent, given it their support. I have, in the short time this Bill has become known to the country, had proof positive that it meets the desire of a very large majority of the people of this country and that in some quarters, in most, at least, it has been hailed with a sigh of relief."[58]

In motivating the need to curtail the influx of eastern Europeans, Malan explained how the bill subsumed the basic elements of antialien opinion and discourse. His explanation of the principles upon which the bill was based related essentially to the eugenicist or racial paradigm of the late 1920s:

> The first principle, I would say, is the desire of every nation in the world to maintain its development on the basis of original composi-

tion. . . . and because that is so, in our immigration Bills, we could not exclude such countries as Holland, or France or the British Common-wealth, or Germany. . . . The second principle to which I have to refer is that of unassimilability. Here we have our counterpart in the world of the individual and the home. Every home has got its own character, every home has got its own atmosphere, its own aspirations, its own outlook, its own social structure, and it is only natural for the head of every family to decide to preserve that identity, or to preserve that character and outlook. Therefore in every home by preference you would welcome not the stranger with a different outlook, but your own kith and kin. Nations desire to preserve homogeneity, because every nation has got a soul, and every nation naturally desires that its soul shall not be a divided one. Every nation considers from all points of view that it is a weakness, if in the body of that nation, there exists an undigested and unabsorbed and unabsorbable minority, because that always leads to all sorts of difficulties. . . . The third fundamental principle is what I would call the desire of every nation to maintain its own particular type of civilization. There is not only one civilization; there are several. It is not to say that one civilization is inferior to the other; one is not necessarily inferior to the other. The only thing is that these civilizations are different. Everybody will admit that the civilization of Asia is different, though more ancient, from that of western Europe. We are called upon in South Africa to maintain western civilization, and the standards of western civilization, and it is difficult enough, as it is, for us to perform our task in that respect, and I do not think that we should, as a South African nation, further complicate our difficult task by uncontrolled and indiscriminate im-migration. . . . Let me once again emphasize that the passing of the quota restrictions on some countries of the world does not in any way imply a reflection on the racial composition or on the culture of the peoples living in those countries.

The last statement of Malan's was obviously directed toward the Jewish community whom he proceeded to thank for their contribution to South Africa, making it clear that Jews from England or Holland were welcome to enter the country. The bill, in other words, was, from Malan's point of view, not antisemitic. He may well have been tech-nically correct, but his warning to Jews that the indiscriminate influx of eastern Europeans had engendered broad-based apprehension, capable of turning into outright hostility, suggests that the Quota Bill was directed at a specifically Jewish Question.[59]

This was recognized by the four Jewish parliamentarians, M. Kentridge, C. P. Robinson, E. Buirski, and E. Nathan. However, other speakers on both the Government and Opposition benches shared Malan's fears and his desire for racial homogeneity. Thus the well-known South African party segregationist Heaton Nicholls spoke in much the same spirit as Malan, arguing that if the characteristics of the "white stock" were undermined, disharmony would result. In his opinion, it was essential that the Government maintain their heritage unimpaired in the interests of the future civilization of South Africa. Nicholls's party colleague Leslie Blackwell similarly argued that a large influx of eastern Europeans would pose a very real threat if not diluted with other more acceptable European immigrant stock. Right across the parliamentary divide there was agreement on the need to maintain racial homogeneity.[60] Of course the corollary of racial homogeneity was the belief that the eastern European newcomers were, and would remain, immutable aliens or outsiders.

Where the opposition South African party did take issue with the ruling National party was on the question of the method of the bill's introduction. It ridiculed the government's subterfuge—the denial of its intentions during the governor general's opening address and the by-election campaigns in Bethal and Stellenbosch. They reminded the Nationalists that Pirow had told Bethal's Jews there would be no change in National party policy toward the Jews and immigration. The Opposition in addition argued that the bill had, in Hofmeyr's words, "cast an unmerited slur upon valued and important elements in the population of South Africa."[61] While he agreed with the principle of the bill, he was sure Jews would be able to "shake off" the "spirit of the ghetto" and assimilate fully into South African society if they were a part of other strands of immigration.[62]

Hofmeyr's arguments fell on deaf ears. Government spokesmen denied that the bill insulted Jews and instead acknowledged the important contribution made by Jews to South Africa, a sentiment emphatically and effusively endorsed by W. B. Humphreys: "I maintain that the Jews are an asset to the country. I say, further, and I do not think it is a great exaggeration, that if it were not for that section of the community, this country today would still be cattle farming on the site where Johannesburg stands." Of course, the more said about the Jewish contribution to South Africa, the more the "power" of Jewry was "exposed." However, in praising the Jew, the government (and all who shared its principles) were contradicting their policy. Nonetheless, it had no need to be self-conscious about the bill's real intentions. The South African party had been hopelessly confused about the bill—a confusion exacerbated by the absence of party leader Smuts during the first reading of the bill. And by the time he returned for the second reading and expressed his opposition in no uncertain terms, it was too late. Indeed, a number of his colleagues had fully supported the Bill and had used the debate to vilify Jews by rehashing a range of anti-Jewish images. The second reading was passed with almost unanimous Opposition support.[63]

The whole tenor of debate surrounding the Quota Bill reveals unquestionably that the issue of immigration revolved around the Jewish problem. As Kentridge explained, Malan knew that virtually all those people coming from nonscheduled countries were Jewish. In support, he quoted the *Bloemfontein Friend,* which had argued that the real object of the bill was to "keep out an unlimited influx of the Jewish people." Robinson made a similar observation: "Do not tell me this is merely a Bill for the exclusion of Lithuanian Jews. It sounds the death knell of any more Jews coming to South Africa. At present it is the poor Lithuanian, to-morrow it may be the Jew from Germany or France that will not be allowed to come in."[64]

By 1937 Robinson's fears had proved to be well founded and he was absolutely correct to stress that the divide between eastern European and other Jews was academic at best. Significantly, Hofmeyr also recognized the potential for antisemitism if immigration was allowed to continue unabated:

There is less anti-semitism in this country than prevails anywhere else. That is something that should give great satisfaction both to Jews and to non-Jews, and on both sides we should do all in our power to maintain that happy state of affairs. But do not let us deceive ourselves. It is true that there is very little active anti-semitism in South Africa today. But it is true also that as a result of recent immigration tendencies a state of tension is rapidly developing, and that if the present tendencies are allowed to develop we shall not continue in that happy position to which I have referred. Those of us who have visited many parts of this country have noted in recent years a change of feeling on the part of our non-Jewish population towards our Jewish population. We may deplore that change of feeling—we cannot but deplore it—but you do not remove a sentiment by deploring it, no more than you remove it by arguing against it. There is therefore in South Africa today the possibility of disharmony and strife between Jews and non-Jews, and if the present tendencies of immigration prevail unchecked, then I am very much afraid of that possibility becoming a fact.[65]

Hofmeyr had correctly gauged a rising tide of antisemitism although it is far from true that anti-Jewish prejudice was a product of "recent years." Nor was it true that there was less antisemitism in South Africa than "anywhere else." As this study has shown, antisemitism of a passive kind had a long tradition in South Africa and the migration "tendencies" referred to by Hofmeyr provided the opportunity and not the cause for a more active antisemitism. An essential problem was the outflow of English men and women after 1924 and a concomitant inflow of Jews with all the inherent and immutable characteristics ascribed to them over decades. These characteristics were reinforced by eugenicist assumptions that were particularly resonant in a changing South Africa beset with racial, ethnic, and segregationist phobias. Within these circumstances the eastern European Jew was yet another threatening source of tension and concern, and it was now necessary to take action.[66] Despite some bickering over details in the Report Stage, the Quota Bill was assented to on 11 March 1930. Thereafter, writes Bradlow, "a camel could have gone through the eye of a needle more easily than a poor Lithuanian immigrant could have entered South Africa for the first time."[67]

CHAPTER SEVEN

Reappraisals and Reflections

Programmatic Antisemitism

MALAN's warnings, Hofmeyr's forebodings, and the general tenor of debate and discussion surrounding the introduction of immigration quotas demonstrated clearly the intensification of anti-Jewish sentiment in South Africa by 1930.[1] These sentiments, it must be noted, predated Hitler's ascent to power as well as South Africa's major economic problems following the collapse of the New York stock market and the political upheavals that saw the coalition and subsequent fusion in 1934 of South Africa's two major white political parties, Jan Smuts's South African party and J. B. M. Hertzog's National party.[2]

Therefore anti-Jewish manifestations during the 1930s and early 1940s cannot be seen purely in terms of the contingencies specific to the early 1930s. While the latter were important in transforming the nature and magnitude of antisemitism in South Africa, they do not provide anything like a full explanation for its rise after 1930. It was the preexisting widely shared negative Jewish stereotype that prepared the way for popular outbursts and programmatic antisemitism in the 1930s and 1940s. What emerges during these years is an intensification of accumulated anti-Jewish sentiment.

That sentiment, as we have seen, had its roots in the late nineteenth century when a decidedly ambivalent image of the Jew was constructed on the diamond fields and in the northern, southern, and eastern Cape. On the one hand, Anglo-German Jews were praised for their loyalty, initiative, and enterprise; on the other hand, Jewish fortune-seekers and traders were depicted as exploitative and dishonest. The influx of Peruvians in the early 1890s and the emergence of the cosmopolitan financier at the turn of the century contributed further toward the evolution of an anti-Jewish stereotype characterized by a sense of otherness at both the physical and cultural level. As eastern European Jews failed to assimilate fully into the dominant white population, hopes of regeneration and wholesale acculturation faded. This led to the Jewish image now being cast in an essentially racial mold. Outward appearance and moral assumptions were inextricably intertwined. By 1914, favorable perceptions of the Anglo-German Jew had eroded substantially and the eastern European Jew by and large had come to define by sheer weight of numbers the essence and nature of Jewishness. Even those who separated the acculturated and urbane Jew from the eastern European newcomer exaggerated Jewish power and influence. Herein lay the convergence between the philosemitic and antisemitic view.

Wartime accusations of shirking, followed by the association of Jews with Bolshevism, consolidated the anti-Jewish stereotype. In the context of the postwar economic depression and the burgeoning of black radicalism, the Jew emerged as the archetypical subversive. Thus the Rand Rebellion of 1922 could be construed as a Bolshevik revolt. As eugenicist and nativist arguments—imported from abroad, especially the United States—increasingly penetrated South African discourse, eastern European immigrants were perceived as a threat to the Nordic character of South African society. Their outward appearance, it was argued, reflected an inherent or biological essence putting "paid" to nineteenth-century expectations of acculturation and assimilation.

Despite pervasive negative perceptions of the Jew, antisemitism in the crude and programmatic sense was still rejected in the mid-1920s. This was best illustrated by the failure of the League of Gentiles and in responses—spanning both party and language divides—to its crude proposals. Antisemitism, in short, remained confined essentially to the realm of literary and cultural stereotyping and to rhetoric that did not necessitate serious consideration. However, the 1930 Quota Act ushered in a change that took a far more invidious form in 1933 with the formation of the South African Christian National Socialist Movement— better known as the "Greyshirts"—under the leadership of Louis T. Weichardt. *Greyshirts* referred to the upper part of the uniform worn by the militant sector or advance guard of the movement, which was responsible for maintaining order at political meetings and protecting the leader.[3]

The Greyshirts were patently inspired by Hitler's success and tactics, particularly brownshirt thuggery and Nazi propaganda.[4] Weichardt had in fact joined up to fight for Germany in the First World War, and it was he who fashioned the movement's racist, antisemitic, and fascist philosophy. Although centered in Cape Town, the Greyshirts had cells throughout the country. At its peak the movement had 2,000 members and its success inspired a number of similar organizations to mushroom across the country.[5] Clearly, at this time South Africa was riddled with extremism and racist bigotry.

Although inspired by Nazi forms and racist or "Volkish" discourse,[6] the substantive message of South Africa's fascist movements related to the South African experience: Jews had fomented the South African War, inspired blacks against white civilization, controlled the press, exploited Afrikaners, dominated society, and so forth. These ideas were, as often noted in this study, well entrenched in a large part of the national consciousness; in the crises of the early 1930s they were embraced far and wide. Anti-Jewish activities, noted a report of the 11th Congress of the South African Jewish Board of Deputies in May 1935, had reached an unparalleled height.[7]

Hostility was further fueled by the entry of 1,044 German-Jewish refugees in the three years following Hitler's ascent to power, and Patrick Duncan was quite correct when he predicted a major "immigration problem before long" in a letter to Lady Selborne in August 1936.[8] He had undoubtedly sensed the rising mood of bigotry, its particular character, and the political ammunition it was providing for the *Gesuiwerdes* [purified nationalists] who were, after all, losing their radical right-wing to the "shirtist" movements.

The groundswell of anti-Jewish feeling, especially demands for action and threats against the existing Jewish community, now prompted the United party to introduce stiffer educational and financial requirements for purposes of immigration during the 1936 parliamentary session. These were to take effect on 1 November and resulted in an interim increase in German-Jewish immigration. The situation, noted Duncan, "could easily get quite out of hand."[9] His fears were well founded. By the end of October 1936, well-attended meetings, led by a group of Stellenbosch University professors, protested against the impending arrival of the *Stuttgart* carrying some 570 German-Jewish immigrants.[10] It is not surprising therefore that Weichardt was able to predict that his party was about to make a strong and rapid advance. "Everywhere," he exhorted, "our meetings are crowded and our message is eagerly welcomed by the people." Weichardt was especially encouraged by "the extent to which the intelligentsia and the working classes are embracing the ideals of National Socialism. Large numbers of professional men, university professors, lecturers and students, civil servants, school teachers, etc. belong to the Party, if not in open, at any rate as secret members. The workers, too, despite all attempts of the Jews to catch them with the poisoned bait of Communism and Bolshevism, are everywhere getting their eyes opened."[11] It seems that anti-Jewish feeling had enabled a worker-intellectual alliance to be cemented.

The rhetoric of protest and opposition to Jewish immigration was riddled with racist assumptions and antisemitic generalizations. Jews were aliens, disloyal and bent on exploitation. The professors, however, denied anti-Jewish motivations and explained their behavior rather in terms of economic competition and their fear that young Afrikaners would be unable to enter the professions for which they were being trained. These were issues raised long before the 1930s. The prospect of economic competition had always played a part in anti-Jewish sentiment, especially on the part of urbanizing Afrikaners. However, hostility was now primarily a product of exclusivist or "Volkish" ideas, central to Afrikaner nationalism at this time. Nationalist sentiment, in other words, sharpened perceptions of the Jew as a quintessential alien. For the Afrikaner, he symbolized all that was foreign and oppressive. Moreover, as English speakers for the most part, Jews were political enemies.

The Jew also helped to consolidate an all-embracing Afrikaner identity, understood in terms of cultural unity, national roots, and opposition to the foreigner. In this way antisemitism helped to cover or paper over class divisions and antagonisms within Afrikaner society. The Afrikaner's inferior status in society and his poverty could be explained in racial or national terms. Moreover, by employing the discourse of race to exclude and denigrate Jews, the Afrikaner was in turn elevated. As Robert Miles notes, "The act of representational exclusion is simultaneously an act of inclusion, whether or not Self is explicitly identified in the discourse."[12]

Consequently, it is no coincidence that antisemitism continued to suffuse specifically right-wing Afrikaner political discourse and programs—this despite the upturn in the economy from the mid-1930s. It must not, however, be forgotten that the Jew was a readily available scapegoat precisely because an anti-Jewish stereotype, in which the Jew symbolized subversion and exploitation, had been elaborated and diffused for decades. Major political parties now had to take cognizance of the groundswell of anti-Jewish feeling.[13] South Africans for the first time confronted a Jewish Question in its broadest sense.

By November 1936 Malan's Purified Nationalists were calling for the unequal treatment of Jews. Their arguments were predicated upon Jewish unassimilability and fears of Jewish power and domination. As a political program they wanted to curtail Jewish professional activity, limit their involvement in certain occupations, and proscribe name-changing.[14] Such ideas had of course been aired long before the 1930s, but by the mid-1930s these notions, influenced by the rise of rightist politics in central and eastern Europe, had become part of an acceptable political discourse, evident in Malanite ideology and policies.

In an obvious response to flourishing antisemitism, coupled with a private bill introduced by Malan to restrict Jewish immigration and stiffen naturalization laws, the United party introduced an Aliens Bill in January 1937. This was designed to restrict Jewish immigration—particularly from Germany—without mentioning Jews by name.[15] Immigrants were to be permitted entry by a Selection Board on the grounds of good character and the likelihood of assimilation into the European population. However, the bill failed to satisfy the Purified Nationalists; for them any Jewish immigration was unacceptable. This, they argued, was in the interests of the Jewish community and the country. Debate surrounding the Bill once again illustrates the entrenched nature of the Jewish stereotype in all its dimensions. Significantly, the employment of these stereotypes was not restricted to Afrikaners, and Dr H. F. Verwoerd, editor-in-chief of *Die Transvaler* since its inception in 1937, was probably correct when he pointed out that the English were "applauding and encouraging Nationalists in silence."[16] Nevertheless, at the political level, only right-wing Afrikaner nationalists included the Jewish Question as a central plank in their political platform. Even Malan, at one time ambivalent in his attitude toward the Jew but now increasingly under pressure from the ultraright Greyshirts, focused on the Jew as an explanation for the Afrikaners' political misfortunes. This was spelled out with utmost clarity in a speech to a Stellenbosch audience on 12 April 1937:

> Coalition and Fusion were to a great extent the result of Jewish organisation. The Jews did everything in their power to keep the Afrikaners from uniting, as they feared that South Africans would rise

from their lowly and insignificant position to save South Africa for the South Africans. . . . Throughout the world the Jews availed themselves of democratic institutions for their own profit and that was why they joined the Labourites. There is yet another aspect of Jewish Communism in South Africa. The Jews oppose discrimination because they fear discrimination against them. In South Africa this means miscegenation.[17]

Notwithstanding Malan's vicious attack, it was Verwoerd who stood at the vanguard of anti-Jewish agitation. In "The Jewish Question from the Nationalist Point of View" he summarized the whole corpus of antisemitic discourse: Jewish domination in business and the professions, the unassimilability of Jews, Jewish alienation from the Afrikaners, questionable Jewish commercial morality, and the use of money by Jews to influence government through the English-language press.[18] Obviously the Jewish Question was no longer a concern solely of fringe fascist groups; by 1937 it was firmly entrenched within mainstream white politics. With antisemitism assuming a preeminent position in Afrikaner public opinion, much of the rhetoric associated with the shirtist movements was appropriated by the Purified Nationalists, fearful that they were losing political adherents who were being won over by extremist antisemitic propaganda. Where they differed from the shirtist movements, however, was in strategy. As Purified Nationalist spokesman J. G. Strijdom, leader of the party in the Transvaal and a later prime minister, put it, the shirtists "aim at the same things as we do but go about it in the wrong way."[19] In short, the Purified Nationalists hoped to use parliament or other means which were legal to attain their ends.

Malan's Purified Nationalists predictably stressed the Jewish Problem in the 1938 general election campaign. Party propaganda was underpinned by an insistence on the prospect of Jewish domination (see fig. 9).[20] In Afrikaner nationalist eyes, these fears were confirmed by the May election result: a cartoon in *Die Burger* depicted Hoggenheimer carrying Smuts and Hertzog to victory (see fig. 10). The election year also saw the emergence of a new paramilitary authoritarian movement, the *Ossewabrandwag* (ox-wagon sentinel). Born out of the centenary celebrations of the Great Trek, the *Ossewabrandwag* (officially formed in 1939) "attacked British-Jewish-Masonic" imperialism and capitalism, "British Jewish" democracy, Jewish money-power and Jewish disloyalty.[21] With its "führer-prinzip," authoritarian philosophy, and anti-

Jewish stance, the movement was a Nazi clone. By 1941 the *Ossewa-brandwag* claimed to have a membership of over 300,000, drawn mainly from the Afrikaner petty bourgeoisie.[22]

Thus, by the late 1930s antisemitism had become an integral part of "volkish" Afrikaner nationalism. Many of the key theoreticians within the movement had studied in Germany, where they imbibed views of the corporate state, an idealist worldview, and a sense of exclusivist nationalism. These ideas propelled a powerful republicanism rooted in notions of divine election, a leitmotif within the Afrikaners' civil religion.[23] Like their European counterparts on the Right, Afrikaner nationalists were opposed to liberalism, Marxism, and laissez-faire capitalism.[24] The last, associated with British imperialism, was exemplified in Hoggenheimer, who was, as Moodie reminds us, "English-speaking, imperialist and clearly Jewish."[25]

Antisemitism was given further impetus following the South African parliament's very narrow decision to support the Commonwealth war effort to resist Germany in 1939. A powerful antiwar movement was orchestrated by the *Ossewabrandwag* in which the appeal of fascism and with it the rhetoric of antisemitism was strong. Indeed, a range of major National party publications issued in the early 1940s demonstrated the formative influence of Mussolini and Hitler on the exclusive nature of an insurgent Afrikaner nationalism in which the Jew had no place.[26] However, the struggle against Hitler gradually eroded the warm reception accorded to Nazi and fascist ideas. Although the Jewish tragedy in Europe was minimized in Nationalist newspapers, which depicted Buchenwald as just another concentration camp, ultimate knowledge of the Final Solution demonstrated unequivocally the logical culmination of bigotry and racism.[27]

Longterm Continuities

The 1930s had witnessed the transformation of what Endelman refers to as "private" antisemitism into "public" antisemitism.[28] That is to say, antisemitism moved from the private or ideational sphere into the public or party-political realm. The transformation was unquestionably related to specific traumas in the 1930s: the intensification of poor-whiteism following the impact upon South Africa of the world depression, the emergence of Nazism in Europe, and the rise of an exclusivist Afrikaner nationalism. All these processes do not, however, explain fully why anti-Jewish rhetoric resonated so resoundingly in South Africa. Nor do they explain why antisemitism provided such a useful means of political mobilization. To suggest, as historians have done hitherto, that antisemitism in South Africa was simply a product of specific upheavals in South African society and of Nazi propaganda is to ignore deeply entrenched anti-Jewish sentiment before 1930. In a pertinent model proposed by Marrus and Paxton that "conceives of anti-Semitism in the modern period as a series of concentric rings," the outermost ring was certainly well established in the South African case by 1930:

> In the outermost is a wide band of anti-Jewish feeling, the product of many factors which together produce a vague, often mild, antipathy. This anti-Jewish feeling is but one of many constellations of dislike that circulate within most societies, and that usually express themselves in social choices to associate or not to associate with particular groups or individuals. Closer to the center is a second band of feelings and responses which are more intense and volatile. Defensive and hostile, this area becomes particularly wide and active in times of trouble—most commonly economic trouble but also political trouble such as national collapse brought about by war. Third at the hard core, is the region of the anti-Jewish fanatic, which is also capable of growth and which has an impact upon the other two. This hard core is fuelled by the irrational, unprompted by events, and unaffected by what Jews do or do not do. But it too acts differently according to historical circumstances.[29]

Specific historical circumstances, including a profound sense of grievance in Afrikaner poor whites and workers, and a sense of outrage, alienation and powerlessness on the part of Afrikaner intellectuals, certainly activated anti-Jewish manifestations in South Africa during the 1930s and early 1940s. However, historians analyzing this period have failed to examine the emergence and consolidation of anti-Jewish sentiments that had long since penetrated deeply into the national consciousness. Without this preparation, Weichardt's vicious oratory and shirtist propaganda in general would not have been embraced at the popular level.[30] It was in fact because of the popular response to this that Malan was forced to incorporate specifically anti-Jewish policies into the Purified Nationalist's program. The illiberal and anti-modernist nature of Afrikaner nationalism during the 1930s is also vital in explaining why public antisemitism in South Africa was an essentially Afrikaner phenomenon and why it appealed across the whole spectrum of Afrikaner nationalist opinion.[31] In this sense South African antisemitism confirms those arguments that seek to explain German antisemitism in terms of antimodernism and illiberalism.[32]

The public antisemitism of the 1930s, then, was not simply a product of political, social, and economic traumas coupled with the impact of Nazi propaganda. Nor is it correct to describe antisemitism during the 1930s and 1940s as a deviation from "traditional attitudes of tolerance and fairplay."[33] On the contrary, there is a connection and a continuity between anti-Jewish sentiment as manifested in images of the Jew before 1930 and the anti-Jewish outbursts and programs of the 1930s and early 1940s. Without the specific traumas of the 1930s, the earlier sentiments may not have been translated into public or political policy. Nevertheless, as this study had demonstrated, the foundations of South African antisemitism in the 1930s and early 1940s were firmly laid in the prior South African experience.

Antisemitism and South African Culture

With the benefit of hindsight we know that programmatic antisemitism, associated with an insurgent and exclusivist Afrikaner nationalism, was shortlived, albeit threatening for those Jews who lived through the 1930s and early 1940s. Insofar as the National party remained in opposition until 1948, it was unable to translate ideology into action; once it attained power its attention was focused primarily on the country's mounting race problems. Nonetheless, its period in opposition demonstrates that ideological antisemitism can only become a serious danger for Jews once it informs and captures the organs of state.

The realities of South African antisemitism parallel the American experience rather than that of Europe. In both societies a range of remarkably similar Jewish stereotypes evolved from the late nineteenth century.[34] Immigration debates in the early 1920s also bore uncanny similarities: concern about radical subversion, fears of biological pollution, and accusations of Jewish unassimilability.[35] Exclusionary calls emanated from both countries against a background of labor instability and rapid industrialization. Afrikaner antipathy toward the Jews certainly had much in common with turn-of-the-century populist anger in the United States. Both groups shared an aversion toward the "unproductive" middleman, the parvenu, and the international financier. And, of course, they both loathed the city, symbolic of evil, manipulation, and modernity. "Poor white" and "populist" alike looked nostalgically back to an imagined past of "productive" labor and simple living. The rabid Jew-baiting of Henry Ford in the 1920s, and Father Coughlin in the 1930s, mirrored the worst of South Africa's ultraright extremists in the years immediately before and during the Second World War. Both elements sympathized with the domestic and foreign policies of Hitler and Mussolini. More importantly, both groups appealed to an anti-Jewish sentiment rooted in their own specific experiences. However, Afrikaner antisemitism presented a greater threat to the Jew since it informed the policies of an official parliamentary opposition in an essentially two-party system. One can only wonder to what extent Jewish rights would have been curtailed had the National party attained power during the fascist era and not after Hitler had been universally demonized and antisemitism rendered unacceptable in civilized society. In any event, a new agenda—that of dealing with the country's mounting race problems—had captured the center stage.

Both the United States and South Africa experienced a rapid decline in antisemitism after the war. In the former, a changing culture defined by a new consumerism meant, in the words of Higham, the "integration of rural America into an urbanised national culture" in which old "suspicions of the city as a place of alien intrigue" were eroded.[36] In South Africa a new Afrikaner bourgeoisie—well educated, confident and more optimistic than their forebears—enjoyed the economic fruits of racist exploitation and political power. Afrikaners, like agrarian American populists, developed a newfound respect for enterprise and material success. The very scaffolding that had underpinned their sense of inferiority was thus removed as they began to experience power and social mobility. A sense of competition with, and fear of, the Jew declined.

Even so antisemitism was never a defining feature of South African culture. Although Jews were the recipients of negative cultural and literary stereotyping, they faced little formal exclusion and ostracism. Only occasionally did they suffer in practical terms. Blackballing was seldom practiced and there was certainly less social exclusion in South Africa than in the United States, where Jews invariably found themselves barred from clubs and exclusive institutions of higher learning.[37] We cannot ignore the great number of Jews who achieved public prominence as mayors, politicians, entrepreneurs, athletes, and entertainers. Indeed, notwithstanding antagonism toward, and fear of, "Jewish power," South Africans accorded the Jewish fortune-seeker a grudging respect; frontier societies appear to put a premium on rugged individualism. Moreover, many South Africans genuinely appreciated the role played by Jews in the country's preindustrial economy. This appreciation, coupled with a persistent strain of philosemitism, acted as a counterweight to crass anti-Jewish bigotry. Another factor mitigating against antisemitism was the absence of encrusted traditions of privilege and power among whites, again a product of frontier conditions. This encouraged Jewish integration. Comparative studies suggest that Jewish immigrants confront greater obstacles as latecomers to a community.[38] In many mining towns such as Kimberley and Johannesburg, Jews were certainly there at the beginning. In the final analysis, however, the relative security of Jews was ensured by the presence of other target groups. As in the American South, blacks served as the lightning rod for racism.

Thus antisemitism was only one dimension, and a limited one at that, of South African prejudice and bigotry. A cardinal divide in South African society has always been one of color. Despite some observers' equating Jews with the much-maligned Indians, who similarly challenged the mercantile establishment, the white status of the Jew was never seriously questioned or threatened. Thus could Indians be progressively excluded from, and Jews gradually integrated into, society. The Anglo-German Jewish establishment certainly enjoyed privilege, power, authority, and even acclaim from earliest times, and the upward mobility of the eastern European Jew was patently obvious. The pariah was indeed transformed into the parvenu.

In the postwar years a new generation of Jews—no longer as alien and culturally removed as their forebears—was able to enjoy, often with guilt, the comforts, benefits, and opportunities accorded to whites in apartheid South Africa. Blacks, on the other hand, could never escape the color of their skin in a society defined by pigmentation. Together with Coloreds and Indians they were deliberately excluded from society. Pigmentation became the arbiter of opportunity and privilege.

Classic Jew-baiting since the war has been restricted to a fringe ultraright element. Although the government occasionally reminded Jews in the 1950s and 1960s that their disproportionate involvement in antiapartheid activities was unwelcome, they had little cause for discomfort.[39] Their security and well-being were further enhanced by Pretoria's very close ties with Jerusalem from the 1970s. The only disturbing feature has been a burgeoning anti-Zionism, evident in the last decade among the black, and more particularly, the Muslim population. That hostility was informed largely by a Third World weltanschauung, an equating of Zionism with racism, allegations of military collusion between South Africa and Israel, and an empathy with the Palestinian people.

In part, however, black hostility was built upon ambivalence toward the Jew, identified over two decades ago by Melville Edelstein from a sample of matriculation students in Soweto. Edelstein showed that blacks experienced a greater "social distance" in relation to Jews than toward English speakers in general although less than towards Afrikaners.[40] They told him that an African who was loth to part with his money was described as being as "stingy as a Jew." Edelstein thought that such prejudice arose from New Testament teaching in school and church.[41] It may well be that there is an added cause: the resentment of blacks (including Coloreds and Indians) against Jewish traders in town and country. Recently, Marcia Leveson has examined Jewish stereotypes in the fiction of black writers, and although much work remains to be done, it is clear that some blacks (including Coloreds and Indians) see Jews as exploitative and powerful.[42] Very recently a study conducted by the Human Sciences Research Council confirmed substantial black antipathy toward the Jew as opposed to the virtual absence of white antisemitism.[43]

It would be wrong, however, to assume that popular hostility among blacks is irreversible and all-pervasive. It must not be forgotten that the majority of South African blacks are Christians with a deep attachment to the Bible and the Holy Land. Such sentiment could generate an element of philosemitism or at least a position of neutrality. Perhaps more importantly, black nationalism is inclusive in orientation and nonracial in content. In this sense it differs fundamentally from exclusivist Afrikaner nationalism, so strident in the 1930s and 1940s.[44] It was this brand of nationalism, coupled with a legacy of negative stereotyping, that gave rise to a Jewish Problem in the 1930s and 1940s, thereby ensuring that South Africa, too, was not immune to that scourge which has plagued and tormented the Jewish past.

Notes

Bibliography

Index

Notes

Introduction

1. General South African historiography has paid little, if any, attention to the Jews. For example, T. R. H. Davenport's standard history mentions Jews only with reference to immigration legislation in the 1930s and the Nazi-type Greyshirt movement (*South Africa: A Modern History,* p. 335). This is similarly the case for Leonard Thompson's new *History of South Africa.* Jews are a factor in specialist works dealing with the 1930s and 1940s: see, e.g., Stultz, *Afrikaner Politics in South Africa 1934–1948;* Vatcher, *White Laager;* and, more recently, Furlong, *Between Crown and Swastika.*

2. Because *semite* denotes peoples originating in southwestern Asia and therefore includes Arabs and Jews, some scholars have dropped the hyphen and capital *S* for a more precise term. In this study I have chosen the nonhyphenated term although both are acceptable.

3. See, e.g., Millin, *The South Africans,* pp. 175–81; Abrahams, *The Birth of a Community;* Herrman, *History of the Jews in South Africa;* Saron and Hotz, eds., *The Jews in South Africa: A History.* Similar ideas have been appropriated by non-Jewish historians: see, e.g., Stultz, *Afrikaner Politics in South Africa 1934–1948,* pp. 44–45.

4. The origin of the word *smous* (vb. *smouse*) is not certain. The word may be a corruption of the name *Moses* brought over from Holland in the Dutch East India Company's days. The corruption arose from the manner in which the Dutch Jews themselves pronounced the name. It has been suggested that the word derives from *Mauschel,* the equivalent of Jewish trader. Another explanation claims that the word is derived from the German *schmuss* (talk, patter) and from the Hebrew *Sh'mu* (tales, news), the reference being to the persuasive eloquence of Jewish traders. While the former explanation seems plausible in a folk-etymological sense, *Sh'mu* is problematic. The author may have meant *Sh'mu'a,* which means rumor, report, news, tidings, gossip, tradition. Certainly *smous* usually referred to a Jewish trader or merchant.

5. Abrahams, "Western Province Jewry," pp. 27–28; Saron, "Boers, Uitlanders, Jews," p. 183; Abrahams, "Western Province Jewry," pp. 27–28; Aschman, "Oudtshoorn in the Early Days," p. 136; *ZR,* 4.6.1947 (quoted in Shimoni, *Jews and Zionism,* p. 45).

6. A similar process is evident in American and English Jewish historiography: see Sarna, "Anti-Semitism and American History" and Cesarani, "Dual Heritage or Duel of Heritages?" In Canada, Richard Menkis has drawn attention to the work of B. G. Sack, who overemphasized the specifically Jewish contribution to New France (Menkis, "Historiography, Myth and Group Relations").

7. Saron, "Epilogue 1910–1955," pp. 381–82. In a recent study Hagemann has shown that Nazi propaganda in South Africa was limited ("Rassenpolitische Affinitat und Machtpolitische Ravalitat").

8. Cohen, "Anti-Jewish Manifestations in the Union of South Africa"; Bradlow, "Immigration into the Union, 1910–1948"; Shimoni, *Jews and Zionism,* see esp. chs. 4, 9, 10, 11; Shain, *Jewry and Cape Society.* Charles van Onselen, Riva Krut, and Greg Cuthbertson have also indirectly touched upon conflict between Jew and Gentile: see Van Onselen, "Randlords and Rotgut, 1886–1903"; Krut, "The Making of a South African Jewish Community in Johannesburg, 1886–1914"; and Cuthbertson, "Jewish Immigration as an Issue in South African Politics, 1937–1939."

9. There were, indeed, many instances of goodwill. In Calvinia, for example, in 1878 the coinciding of *Nachtmaal* (Holy Communion) and the Jewish New Year meant that L. Rosenblatt, a Calvinia businessman, would lose the traditional Nachtmaal business. After the Reverend Joel Rabinowitz had written to Professor N. J. Hofmeyr of the Stellenbosch Seminary explaining the position, the *Kerkraad* (church council) postponed· Nachtmaal to accommodate Rosenblatt's interests (Abrahams, "Western Province Jewry," p. 30). Numerous reports from South Africa in the 1890s appearing in the eastern European press similarly indicate respect toward Jews on the part of the Boers (Simonowitz, "The Background to Jewish Immigration to South Africa," p. 88).

10. Shimoni, *Jews and Zionism,* p. 64. When touching on Jewish-Afrikaner relations, general historians have similarly identified an affinity between the Afrikaner, steeped in Calvinism, and the "Chosen People"; see, e.g., Patterson, *The Last Trek,* p. 290. A recent article by André du Toit demonstrates convincingly that "neo-Calvinist" rather than "Calvinist" appropriately characterizes the Afrikaner's worldview in the late nineteenth century ("Puritans in Africa?").

11. Furlong, *Between Crown and Swastika,* p. 47. On the question of Nazi propaganda during the war, see Marx, "Dear Listeners in South Africa."

12. The only organized anti-Jewish movement was the shortlived and unsuccessful League of Gentiles, founded in the mid-1920s. See ch. 5.

13. *ELDD,* 3.2.1930; *DB,* 30.1.1930; *ST,* 2.2.1930; *Ca,* 7.2.1930; *DR,* 10.2.1930; see also *OV,* 1.2.1930, and *CA,* 8.2.1930. Although the Immigration Quota Act made no specific mention of Jews, they were undoubtedly the most prominent foreigners and were certainly the targets of this legislation.

14. Schachar, "Studies in the Emergence and Dissemination of the Modern Jewish Stereotype in Western Europe," p. 18. For Lippmann see Allport, *The Nature of Prejudice,* pp. 191 ff.

15. Jordan, *White over Black,* p. vii.

16. This includes the *Jewish Chronicle* (London), founded in 1841; the *South African Jewish Chronicle,* founded in 1902; the *Zionist Record,* founded in 1908; and various Yiddish newspapers. The last-named have been exhaustively examined by Moshe Pesach Grosman ("A Study in the Trends and Tendencies of Hebrew and Yiddish Writings").

17. Marrus, *The Politics of Assimilation,* p. 3. A Jewish presence has been shown to be unnecessary for perpetuating the stereotype (Glassman, *Anti-Semitic Stereotypes without Jews*). Werner Cahnman's comments are also pertinent: "Moreover, if a

patterned arrangement of social forces repeats itself generation after generation, an image is formed in the minds of men which in continued cultural transmission becomes itself a factor of structural potency. The image of the Jew in the minds of occidental peoples has served to justify his position in the social structure and his position in turn has served to illuminate the image" ("Socio-Economic Causes of Anti-semitism," p. 21).

18. See Lewsen, "The Cape Liberal Tradition—Myth or Reality," p. 65.

19. Banton, *Race Relations*, p. 300. For a succinct overview of the literature on stereotypes see Ashmore and Delboca, "Conceptual Approaches to Stereotypes and Stereotyping."

20. *International Encyclopaedia of the Social Sciences*, S.V. "Stereotype"; Gay, *Freud, Jews and Other Germans*, p. 16.

Chapter One

1. For the early history see Herrman, *History of the Jews in South Africa*, chs. 1–6, and Abrahams, *The Birth of a Community*, ch. 1.

2. Booth, ed., *The Journal of an American Missionary in the Colony*, p. 28; Krauss, "A Description of Cape Town and Its Way of Life 1838–1840." For Benjamin Norden's welcome see Shain, *Jewry and Cape Society*, p. 1. In the Battle of Boomplaats, Smith had forced the Voortrekker leader, Andries Pretorius, to retreat. The fact that Norden supported Smith was indicative of Jewish allegiance to the British Empire.

3. *CT*, 28.10.1848. According to Herrman the right of a Jew to hold a public office was questioned as late as 1840 (*History of the Jews in South Africa*, p. 91). Philosemitism, albeit based on a variety of motives, ran deep within the Puritan tradition (Katz, *Philosemitism and the Re-admission of Jews to England 1603–1655*, pp. 232–44). British tolerance, as Cohen notes, was "nurtured by the eighteenth century British Enlightenment" ("Anglo-Jewish Responses to Antisemitism," p. 88). Liberal values were evident in the Cape Colony long before Smith's arrival as governor. In 1830, e.g., the *CGHL* expressed pleasure at Hebrew being taught at Cape Town's South African College (16.6.1830).

4. Barrow, *An Account of Travels into the Interior of Southern Africa*, p. 387; Mandelbrote, "Joseph Suasso de Lima: A Bibliography," p. 3.

5. *SACA*, 13.10.1849.

6. *CGGG*, 11.10.1849; Rosenthal, "Jews in the Boer Republics: Some Colourful Personalities."

7. Eybers, *Select Constitutional Documents Illustrating South African History 1795–1910*, pp. 45 ff., 188 ff.; *Cape of Good Hope Statutes*, Act 16, 1860 and Act 11, 1968.

8. Froude, "Visit to the Diamond Fields," p. 273.

9. Cited in Rosenthal, "On the Diamond Fields," p. 118. Barkly may well have been influenced by his earlier experience as governor in Jamaica, where he established close relations with Jewish sugar merchants: see Macmillan, *Sir Henry Barkly*, p. 63.

10. G42–1876 *Results of Census*, Colony of the Cape of Good Hope, 1875; Rosenthal, "On the Diamond Fields," p. 117. According to a Free State Census of 1880,

Jews numbered 67 out of 1,688 white inhabitants of Bloemfontein (Aronstam, "A Historical and Socio-Cultural Survey of the Bloemfontein Jewish Community," p. 67). For the Transvaal, see Sowden, "In the Transvaal till 1899"; for Natal, see Abelson, "In Natal," and Cohen, "A History of the Jews of Durban 1825–1918," ch. 2.

11. Williams, "The Anti-Semitism of Tolerance," p. 74. The "emancipation contract" referred to a Gentile assumption that in return for emancipation Jews ought to assimilate. As Caron writes, "Tensions between Christians and Jews in the nineteenth century were due in no small measure to conflicting interpretations over precisely what assimilation entailed" (*Between France and Germany,* p. 5). The emancipation contract as understood in the European context has been the subject of considerable analysis: see Baron, *Modern Nationalism and Religion,* pp. 219–20, and "Newer Approaches to Jewish Emancipation"; Hertzberg, *The French Enlightenment and the Jews,* chs. 8–10; Katz, "Misreadings of Anti-Semitism."

12. Shimoni, *Jews and Zionism,* pp. 5–7. For the background to Jewish immigration and the migration saga, see Krut, "Building a Home and a Community," ch. 1.

13. *DN,* 4.10.1881.

14. Standard Bank Archives, Private Correspondence, L. Michell to General Manager, 17.4.1882 (Henry Files) (quoted in Turrell, *Capital and Labour,* p. 117).

15. Turrell, *Capital and Labour,* p. 177; *Kn,* 22.10.1884; *La,* 21.2.1885; *CP,* 9.5.1888; Bellairs, *The Witwatersrand Goldfields,* p. 15; Osborne, *In the Land of the Boers,* p. 296. "Cape Boys" were persons of mixed descent. The association of Jews with illicit dealing persisted long after the initial discovery of diamonds. It was popularly associated with the legendary success of Barney Barnato, the Jewish lad who rose from humble beginnings in Whitechapel, London, to dominate the diamond industry by the early 1880s. An American Boer War correspondent, Hillegas, in elucidating the success of South Africa's early financiers was quite unguarded when commenting on the mercurial Jewish industrialist: "Illicit diamond buying was the easiest path to wealth and was travelled by almost every millionaire whose name has been connected with recent South African affairs. Mr Rhodes is one of the few exceptions, and even his enemies corroborate this statement. 'You don't steal diamonds', said Barney Barnato to Mr Rhodes fifteen years ago, 'but you must prove it when accused. I steal them, but my enemies must prove it. That's the difference between us'" (*Oom Paul's People,* p. 161).

16. According to one correspondent in the Stockenstroom district, the plight of eastern Cape farmers was a result of "merchants" and "law agents" (Bundy, "Vagabond Hollanders and Runaway Englishmen," p. 106); *BC,* 26.6.1865 (cited in Bundy, pp. 101–2).

17. See Campbell, "The South African Frontier, 1865–1885," pp. 34–35; Boyle, *To the Cape for Diamonds,* p. 82. Boyle may well have been referring to the substantial number of German Jews brought to South Africa by the Mosenthal brothers (Herrman, *History of the Jews in South Africa,* p. 216). For the *Era,* see Addleson, "In the Eastern Province," p. 307; *DAP,* 31.1.1877; *DZAVV,* 13.8.1881. For accusations against English and Jewish shopkeepers see Grundlingh, "The Parliament of the Cape of Good Hope, with Special Reference to Party Politics, 1872–1910," p. 182.

18. *UT,* 13.9.1883. The Afrikaner Bond was a political movement founded in the Cape Colony in 1880 to further the interests of Afrikaners.

19. Boon, *Jottings,* p. 163. A sense of Boon's antisemitic sentiment is further reflected in his *Immortal History of South Africa:* see, e.g., p. 142.

20. Boon, *The Immortal History of South Africa,* p. 59, and *The History of the Orange Free State,* p. 54.

21. Boon, *Jottings,* p. 168; idem, *The Immortal History of South Africa,* pp. 517, 343. "Lev-us-see" was a snide reference to Moritz Leviseur, a prominent Jewish resident in Bloemfontein.

22. *CP,* 4.7.1883.

23. *DZA,* 6.10.1887, 18.10.1887. This was probably a reference to the influence in Kruger's Republic of the Jewish industrialist Sammy Marks.

24. These sentiments were reciprocated by the newcomers who considered the Anglo-German Jewish establishment assimilated and "heathenish" (Herrman, *History of the Jews in South Africa,* pp. 263–64).

25. For an illuminating discussion on the eastern European Jew as a factor in the emergence of modern antisemitism in Germany, see Aschheim, "Caftan and Cravat."

26. *La,* 20.3.1880. Significantly, the *Cape Argus* took exception to such generalizations. "Jews in this Colony," the newspaper noted, "are the supporters of every philanthropic movement, and are never behind their Christian compatriots in any works of public usefulness or in any of the obligations of private life" (25.3.1880).

27. In 1887, e.g., Lady Robinson, wife of the British high commissioner, opened a Jewish bazaar to raise funds for the Cape Town Hebrew Congregation (Abrahams, *Birth of a Community,* p. 49). A similar sense of tolerance is evident in the *Oudtshoorn Courant*'s report on Oudtshoorn Jewry's decision to build a synagogue in 1886 (20.10.1886). The list of contributors toward funds for building the synagogue included the names of Afrikaners (2.12.1886). Two prominent Jews were Simeon Jacobs, attorney general of the Cape Colony from 1874 to 1882, and Ludwig Weiner, a parliamentarian in the Cape Legislative Assembly from 1883 to 1898.

28. *CT,* 16.2.1882. Such sentiments were recurrently echoed by Gentiles. In 1891, e.g., Kimberley's mayor, E. H. Jones, led an interdenominational protest against Jewish persecution in Russia, in which Catholics, Presbyterians, and Wesleyans all supported a resolution deploring Russian behavior and the absence of religious liberty (*Pr,* 26.11.1891).

29. *SAJC,* 21.6.1928; *CA,* 3.10.1883; *OC,* 1.2.1888.

30. Ambivalence is evident in Olive Schreiner's "autobiographical" *Undine,* published in 1929 but completed in the early 1870s (Schoeman, *Olive Schreiner,* p. 300). In her description of passengers on board a ship to South Africa she writes of two opulent and polite German Jews who were unlike "the little snivelling weasel-like creatures" who obsequiously exploit the Dutch farmers and yet help the farmer when necessary (pp. 152–53). For Schreiner's ambivalence, see also her *From Man to Man.* Although published in 1926, it is apparent from Schreiner's diary that "The Jew" section of the novel was written during 1883 (Levesen, "The Jewish Stereotype in Some South African Fiction," pp. 265–66). Schreiner, who spent some time in Cradock and on the diamond fields, was obviously influenced by the presence of Jewish traders and fortune-seekers.

31. *EPH*, 21.9.1883.

32. *UT,* 27.9.1883.

33. Boon's writing, of course, was underpinned by racist assumptions. In the late nineteenth century, however, he was the exception rather than the rule.

34. Katz, *Out of the Ghetto,* pp. 57–64, 71–73.

Chapter Two

1. Bryce, *From Impressions of South Africa,* p. 385. For the early history of Johannesburg Jewry, see Kaplan and Robertson, eds., *Founders and Followers.*

2. One need only consider such prominent financiers as George Albu, Alfred Beit, Lionel Phillips, Solly and Woolf Joel. A sense of Jewish economic power (from the earliest days) is evident in the *Critic's* comments wishing its Jewish readers a Happy New Year: "The Stock Exchange is closed in celebration of the event and it may be safely asserted that less business is transacted in town to-day than on any 1st January. This shows the members of the Jewish religion are the backbone of our industry and commercial pursuits" (15.9.1893).

3. According to the 1896 census carried out by the Johannesburg Sanitation Committee, there were 6,253 "Israelieten" out of 102,098 whites in the three-mile radius from the city's Market Square (Z.A.R. *Johannesburg Gezondheids Comite Sanitare Departement, Census 15 July 1896*).

4. Memoirs and contemporary studies are replete with references to the Jewish presence in Johannesburg during the city's formative years; see, e.g., *DVs,* 28.9.1886, and Mackenzie and Stead, *South Africa, Its History, Heroes and Wars,* p. 366.

5. Ritner, "Salvation through Separation," p. 23. See also Moodie, *The Rise of Afrikanerdom* and Du Toit, "No Chosen People" and "Puritans in Africa?"

6. Eybers, *Select Constitutional Documents,* pp. 362 ff. The constitution of the other Boer Republic—the Orange Free State—was something of an anomaly. Based in part on the constitution of the United States of America, church and state were separated. However, the Volksraad was to promote and support the Dutch Reformed Church (ibid., pp. 285 ff.). Prior to Ordinance 16 of 1877, Jews were forbidden to serve on a jury (Aronstam, "A Historical and Socio-Cultural Survey of the Bloemfontein Jewish Community," p. 68).

7. Saron, "Boers, Uitlanders, Jews," p. 185.

8. The South African Republic was established by the Trekkers in the mid-nineteenth century. In 1877 Britain annexed the Republic as part of a confederation scheme, only to return independence to the Boers after the latter had taken up arms in the Transvaal War of Independence (1880–81).

9. *TL,* 6.3.1905. Notwithstanding pressure from Catholics and Jews, articles 20, 36, 37, and 140 of the revised Grondwet of 1896 continued to discriminate against non-Protestants (Simonowitz, "The Background to Jewish Immigration to South Africa," p. 72).

10. *DVs,* 17.8.1892; *S&DN,* 16.9.1892.

11. Nathan, *Paul Kruger, His Life and Times,* p. 276. For Kruger's relationship with the Jewish community see Kruger, "Pres. Kruger en die Jode"; Hotz, "Paul Kruger en die Jode"; Twyman, "Paul Kruger en Johannesburg," pp. 122 ff.; Heyden-

rych, "Paul Kruger en die Joodse Gemeenskap van Johannesburg: Fabels en Feite." For the relationship between Kruger and Marks see Mendelsohn, *Sammy Marks,* ch. 5, and Gordon, *The Growth of Boer Opposition to Kruger 1890–1895.*

12. *LV,* 20.8.1889. Leo Weinthal, a South African–born Jew, whose parents had immigrated from Germany, was the editor from mid-1891 to mid-1897.

13. The identity of "Afrikanus Junior" was never revealed, but according to Gordon he was a Transvaal-born Afrikaner who had "rendered great service to his country in war and in the political field" (*The Growth of Boer Opposition,* p. 196). *LV,* 5.5.1891, 12.5.1891, quoted in Gordon, pp. 195–96); *LV,* 29.12.1892. Eckstein, a German, was not Jewish.

14. Joubert Papers, quoted in Gordon, *The Growth of Boer Opposition,* p. 130; *S&DN,* 7.10.1892.

15. Osborne, *In the Land of the Boers,* pp. 82 ff. A sense of the ambience within the Jewish "winkel" (shop) comes across in Pauline Smith's *The Beadle.* For the humorous dimension see Osborne, *In the Land of the Boers,* pp. 82 ff., and J. H. Corbett, "Barney's Salt Pork," in *Ow,* 8.2.1901.

16. G39–1893 Cape of Good Hope Labour Commission—1893; *Annexures to the Votes and Proceedings of the House of Assembly.*

17. *Pr,* 11.3.1893.

18. For their involvement and influence, see Aschman, "Oudtshoorn in the Early Days" and Mabin, "The Making of Colonial Capitalism," p. 110.

19. *OC,* 2.2.1893.

20. Inspector's Report, Oudtshoorn, 1892, INSP 1/1/120, Standard Bank Archives.

21. Inspector's Report, Oudtshoorn 1893 and 1894, INSP 1/1/121, Standard Bank Archives.

22. *DVb,* 23.2.1893.

23. Scully, *Further Reminiscences of a South African Pioneer,* p. 208.

24. Scully, *Between Sand and Sun,* p. 120.

25. Ibid., p. 29. See Leveson, "The Jewish Stereotype in Some South African Fiction," pp. 263–64.

26. Cape of Good Hope, *Legislative Assembly Debates,* 3.7.1894 (Du Toit); 25.8.1896 (Molteno); 8.8.1893 (Venter); 28.5.1896 (Theron, Jones and Upington).

27. *CT,* Xmas Special, 17.12.1900.

28. Cahnman contends that the consumer always has to be on his guard with the merchant. What "the neighbour as kinsmen, would have to offer free of charge, if only he had it, can indeed be had from the merchant, but he does not offer it free of charge, he sells, and since he sells, he stands under the assumption that he takes his advantage" ("Socio-Economic Causes of Anti-Semitism," p. 23).

29. For similar processes in the United States during the 1890s see Hofstadter, *The Age of Reform,* p. 73.

30. *Cr,* 3.3.1893.

31. Van Onselen, "Randlords and Rotgut, 1886–1903," p. 74.

32. *JT,* 1.4.1896. The term *Peruvian* is probably an acronym for Polish and Russian Union—a Jewish club established in Kimberley in the early days. It has also been suggested that the term refers to those immigrants who had sojourned in

Argentina under Baron de Hirsch's settlement scheme before coming to South
Africa. If that is the origin of the term, the lack of a geographical distinction
between Argentina and Peru needs to be explained. It is interesting to note,
however, that in a short story in the *Owl* (8.2.1901) by J. E. Corbett, the author refers
to the English Jews struggling to compete against "Hebrews from Peru and Argentina." Similarly the *Johannesburg Times* description of the Peruvian mentions the
"generosity of Baron Hirsch." Another theory is that the term is derived from
"Peruvia," a mistaken reference to the ancient Latin term for Poland.

33. *Pr*, 16.2.1892. The Reverend James Gray was not exaggerating the wicked
state of Johannesburg described by one contemporary as "a Monte Carlo super-
imposed upon a Sodom and Gomorrah" (Butler, *Sir William Butler: An Autobiography*, p. 415).

34. As early as 1890 the Reverend Martins's presidential address to the Dutch
Reformed Synod had noted that the liquor trade was in the hands of foreigners who
disregarded the sabbath, "much to the grief of all true Christians" (*Pr*, 13.5.1890).

35. See, e.g., *Cr*, 9.12.1892, 31.7.1894.

36. *S&DN*, 5.11.1894.

37. *LV*, 9/16.7.1896 and *TC*, 21.5.1897, 30.7.1897, 13.8.1897, 19.11.1897, 26.11.1897,
14.1.1898, 10.6.1898. *Land en Volk* was clearly expressing concern for the emergent
Afrikaner proletariat on the Witwatersrand. These unfortunate victims of drought,
the cattle disease rinderpest, locusts, and rural transformation were ill equipped for
city life; see Van Onselen, "The Main Reef Road into the Working Class" and Stals,
ed., *Afrikaners in die Goudstad*. On the Temperance crusade, see *Pr*, 3.12.1895,
11.12.1895.

38. According to the *S&DN* (2.6.1898), the first criminal landdrost of Johannesburg, N. P. van den Berg, had declared that he "preferred to credit the word of a
Kafir to that of a Jew" when dealing with illicit liquor laws. The issue was taken up
in the columns of the paper. In one letter (7.6.1898), C. M. Faigan recalled that van
den Berg had once told him in court not to speak so loudly, because "you are not
Boerverneuking." Although the paper found van den Berg's behavior objectionable, there was some support for the magistrate. For instance, F. W. Athersoble
separated the "low vile Russian Jew" from the "respectable English, Frank and
German Jew." He was surprised "that any respectable Jew or newspaper can be
forced to defend such a low and degrading class as the Russian Jew" (6.6.1898).

39. *LV*, 7.12.1898.

40. *TL*, 2.5.1899. It was not only the *Transvaal Leader* that focused on the
Appelbe case. As the *Transvaal Critic* put it, "Because of its origin in the illicit liquor
conspiracy the case attracted a great deal of notice" (12.5.1899). *Land en Volk* also
criticized "Prins" Nathanson for assuming money would buy him out of trouble
(6.6.1899).

41. *TL*, 5.5.1899.

42. *TL*, 9.5.1899, 15.5.1899. For further confirmation of the popular association of
"Peruvian" Jews with the illicit liquor trade, see Rose, *The Truth about the Transvaal*,
p. 48.

43. *S&DN*, 7.12.1898. See also *TC*, 11.6.1899, 18.6.1897. It should be noted that
the manager of the *Standard and Diggers News* was a Jew, Emanuel Mendelssohn.

For insights into the rather controversial Mendelssohn, see Mendelsohn, "Oom Paul's Publicist." For the Johannesburg underworld, see Van Onselen, "Prostitutes and Proletarians, 1886–1914." Johannesburg's Jewish leaders were also disturbed at increasing Jewish vice: see Robertson and Kaplan, "Johannesburg's First Organised Social Welfare Work," ch. 5.

44. *St*, 10.7.1897.

45. *St*, 15.7.1897; *TL*, 13.5.1899.

46. *SAZ*, 4.3.1893, and *Ow*, 23.1.1897. For the Jewish underworld see Van Heyningen, "Public Health and Society in Cape Town 1880–1910," p. 381; Feldman, "Social Life of Cape Town Jewry, 1904–1914," pp. 31–32; Hallett, "Policeman, Pimps and Prostitutes," p. 7. The *Owl* was started by an Englishman, Charles Penstone, in Johannesburg shortly before the Jameson Raid. The raid, having more or less shattered the prospects of the weekly in Johannesburg, forced Penstone to restart the weekly in Cape Town (*CT*, 6.8.1896). In 1902 the *Owl* had a circulation of 16,000 (13.6.1902). It rapidly became the chief exponent of Cape Town's anti-Jewish press.

47. G42–1897 Cape of Good Hope, Reports of District Surgeons upon Public Health and Sanitation. *Annexures to the Votes and Proceedings of the House of Assembly.* For concern about public health see Van Heyningen, "Public Health and Society in Cape Town 1880–1910," p. 251.

48. For a grotesque depiction of the Jew see Griffith, *Knaves and Diamonds,* p. 2. On dishonesty see the short stories "Sam Saulinski" and "Old Diamond-Field Days: The Pioneer Talks," *Ow*, 6.11.1897, 8.6.1900.

49. *CT*, 30.3.1898, 1.4.1898. For language and accent, see the humorous exchange between Isaac and Cohen in *M&S*, 13.12.1897. As Gilman puts it in his discussion of European stereotypes, "The spoken language of the Jews kept alive the old charges of an inherently 'Jewish' way of understanding the world as mirrored in the special language of the Jews" (*Difference and Pathology*, p. 182).

50. Aschheim, *Brothers and Strangers*, p. 252. For eugenicist thought, see Stepan, *The Idea of Race in Science*, p. 113, and Semmel, *Imperialism and Social Reform*, ch. 2.

51. *DK*, 18.1.1897. Jacob Katz has argued that modern or racist antisemitism was medieval or religious antisemitism transformed into a secular or modern idiom; for an account of the metamorphosis see his *From Prejudice to Destruction,* esp. the introduction and ch. 26.

52. *DK*, 24.3.1898; *LV*, 7.12.1898.

53. *LV*, 7.12.1898, 18.1.1899.

54. *Pr*, 12.12.1898; *CT*, 1.4.1899.

55. *CT*, 3.4.1899. By introducing the caveat "cultivated" the paper was in essence underlining the emancipation contract and its expectations.

56. One correspondent thought the dean's comments were an April Fool's joke (*CT*, 3.4.1899); *JC*, 28.4.1899; *CT*, 4.4.1899.

57. It has been argued that Paul Kruger defended Jews in the "naive hope" that they would eventually come to the "true faith of Christ" if they are "properly defended" (Simonowitz, p. 90; Nathan, *Paul Kruger,* pp. 36 ff.). This view was spelled out very clearly in Kruger's detailed manifesto in 1899 as to why Jews should be given citizenship: see *St*, 15.8.1899.

58. Simonowitz, pp. 78 ff.; *LV* and *HD*, quoted in *S&DN*, 19.10.1897, 22.7.1897.

59. Cape of Good Hope, *Legislative Assembly Debates*, 27.7.1894; Bryce, *From Impressions of South Africa*, p. 384.

60. Cumberland, *What I Think of South Africa*, p. 12. "Cumberland" was a pseudonym of Charles Garner.

61. *JC*, 13.8.1897; *RR*, Oct. 1899; *JT*, 1.7.1897; Schreiner, "Words in Season."

62. The Bleichroders, Rothschilds, and Oppenheims indeed exemplified what Eric Hobsbawn has referred to as "the age of capital" (*The Age of Capital, 1848–1875*). The high profile of Jews in European banking and finance made them readily available targets for vilification, both from the Left and the Right.

63. The London-born Jew Barney Barnato was a vital part of that process. Born Barnett Isaacs, he came to dominate the diamond industry by the early 1880s. Thereafter, following a titanic struggle, he was eclipsed by Cecil John Rhodes. Hirschfield, "The British Left," p. 96.

64. Ogden, ed., *The War against the Dutch Republic in South Africa*, p. 32.

65. Hirschfield, "The British Left," p. 96.

66. *Blackwoods Magazine*, quoted in *RR*, 1.8.1896; *Pr*, 1.1.1896; *St*, 31.12.1895; Meir Zivan in *Hameliz*, 1896, quoted in Grosman, "A Study," pp. 101–2.

67. *CR*, 1.8.1896, reprinted in *RR*, 1.9.1896.

68. *Pr*, 31.3.1896.

69. "Statham, F. R.," *Dictionary of South African Biography*; Mendelssohn, *South African Bibliography*, II:423. Statham came to South Africa in 1877 at the age of thirty-three to take up the editorship of the *Natal Witness*. He had at that time had only one year's experience as a journalist, having been an evangelical lay preacher and before that a stockbroker. Worger's study of early Kimberley confirms De Beers's domination of the city, which was a company town ("The Making of a Monopoly," p. 312).

70. Statham, *South Africa as It Is*, pp. 196–97.

71. Rothschild's involvement is confirmed in Innes, *Anglo*, pp. 35–36. Rudolf Glanz, commenting on a similar "Rothschild myth" in America, attributed the legend of his name to a "need to express the essence of capitalism in one great human example that was, moreover, no individual fortune doomed to extinction, but a family undertaking, continuing from generation to generation" ("The Rothschild Legend," pp. 5–6).

72. See, e.g., Schreiner and Cronwright-Schreiner, *The Political Situation* and Olive Schreiner's *Trooper Peter Halket of Mashonaland*.

73. Statham, *South Africa as It Is*, p. 279.

74. P. Fitzpatrick to J. Wernher 12.12.1898, in Duminy and Guest, eds., *Fitzpatrick*, p. 171.

75. Steyn, quoted in *RR*, 1.3.1898; *M&S*, Mar. 1898.

76. *TL*, 16.6.1899. In point of fact, Jews had the franchise in England long before 1870.

77. Quoted in Porter, *Critics of Empire*, p. 201. The idea of Jews exploiting South Africa and having little commitment to the country went back to at least 1896. In that year the Jewish communal leader Samuel Goldreich was accused in the Transvaal Volksraad of making money and taking it out of the country (*St*, 26.7.1896).

78. Hobson, *The War in South Africa*, p. 11. This antisemitic polemic was based on Hobson's reports to the *Manchester Guardian*.

79. Quoted in Lewsen, *John X. Merriman,* p. 209.

80. Merriman, quoted in correspondence from Campbell Bannerman to James Bryce, 10.11.1899, cited in Galbraith, "The Pamphlet Campaign in the Boer War."

81. See Davey, *The British Pro-Boers, 1877–1902* and Porter, *Critics of Empire,* pp. 101, 114. Condemnation of the war was not accepted by all Fabians. George Bernard Shaw, for example, wrote a pamphlet "Fabianism and Empire" supporting the war, while the Webbs also took an imperial line. Ultimately the society split over the war issue. (I am indebted to Jeffrey Butler for this information.)

82. According to Ruth First and Ann Scott, Olive Schreiner had actually helped to inspire Hobson's thesis (*Olive Schreiner,* pp. 240–41). In view of Schreiner's position on the Jews, it is unlikely that the antisemitic component of Hobson's work can be attributed to her.

83. Denoon, *A Grand Illusion,* p. 15. For caricatures, see, e.g., *Ow,* Xmas Number, 1901.

84. *SAN,* 16.12.1899; *JC,* 12.1.1899; *JG,* 26.12.1900.

85. Reitz, *A Century of Wrong,* pp. 37, 42. The book, translated from Dutch into English, was actually written by Jacob Roos and Jan Smuts but issued in the name of F. W. Reitz, the Transvaal state secretary; see Thompson, *The Political Mythology of Apartheid,* p. 33. Kitchener quoted in Denoon, "Capitalist Influence and the Transvaal Government," p. 301.

86. For the increase in Cape Town's Jewish population, see *JC,* 22.10.1899. According to Van Heyningen approximately 20,000 to 25,000 refugees arrived in Cape Town in the latter half of 1899 ("Public Health and Society in Cape Town 1880–1910," p. 286). This would mean Jewish refugees comprised between 20 and 25 percent of all refugees. Milner, quoted in Cammack, "The Politics of Discontent," p. 248.

87. Milner, *My Picture Gallery 1886–1901,* p. 138; Van Heyningen, "Refugees and Relief in Cape Town," p. 81.

88. Jewish refugees were also conspicuous in Port Elizabeth where, according to the *Star,* "boarding houses will not take them in" (9.10.1899).

89. Van Heyningen, "Public Health and Society in Cape Town 1880–1910," chs. 5, 7; *CT* (weekly), 1.11.1899.

90. G66–1902 Cape of Good Hope, Report on Public Health for the Year 1901, *Annexures to the Votes and Proceedings of the House of Assembly.*

91. G66–1903 Cape of Good Hope, Report on Public Health for the Year 1902, *Annexures to the Votes and Proceedings of the House of Assembly.*

92. See Professor W. J. Simpson, "Lecture on Plague," cited in Van Heyningen, "Public Health and Society in Cape Town 1880–1910," p. 302.

93. Its crude stereotyping and journalism shock the modern-day reader, sensitive to the consequences of prejudice and bigotry. At that time, however, this Cape Town weekly took exception to charges of antisemitism. Indeed, it argued that a range of ethnic groups fell within its scope. However, even a cursory reading demonstrates that the Peruvian was its favorite target.

94. *Te,* 13.1.1900.

95. *CT,* 20.3.1902.

96. Quoted in Van Heyningen, "Refugees and Relief in Cape Town, 1899–1902," p. 92.

97. Cammack, "Class, Politics and War," p. 57, and *The Rand at War 1899–1902*, p. 158.

98. *SB*, 12.2.1902; *WS*, 15.2.1902; *FBA*, 12.2.1902, all quoted in *SAJC*, 7.3.1902.

99. *SAJC*, 18.7.1902.

100. *SAJC*, 7.8.1903.

Chapter Three

1. Anti-Jewish rhetoric in the Cape Colony was sufficiently serious to provoke Jewish figures in the Cape Colony to establish a Jewish Board of Deputies. Modeled on the British Jewish Board of Deputies, the organization was specifically designed to safeguard the interests of the community: see Shain, *Jewry and Cape Society*, chs. 2–5. In the Transvaal a similar body was established to deal with Jewish immigration, and a vigilance society was founded to deal with prostitution and the "white slave traffic" (Bristow, *Prostitution and Prejudice* and Kaplan and Robertson, "Johannesburg's First Organised Social Welfare Work"). In Johannesburg the South African Zionist Federation, founded in 1898, considered anti-Jewish rhetoric in 1907 sufficiently serious to convene a special meeting to discuss the wave of anti-Semitism in the country (*SAJC*, 8.3.1907).

2. Grosman, "A Study in the Trends and Tendencies," p. 188.

3. *SAR*, 6.2.1903.

4. *TL*, 29.5.1903. For antialienism in the Cape Colony see Shain, *Jewry and Cape Society*, ch. 3.

5. Between 1880 and 1910 approximately 40,000 Jews entered the country. In the Union's first census published in 1911, Jews numbered 46,926 (*Census for the Union of South Africa 1911*, Pretoria, Government Printing and Stationery Office, 1913; Shimoni, *Jews and Zionism*, p. 5).

6. G63–1904 Report on the Working of the Immigration Act 1902–1904, *Annexures to the Votes and Proceedings of the House of Assembly, Cape Colony*.

7. *JC*, 24.7.1903.

8. *SAR*, 25.3.1904.

9. It should be noted that Milner was even unhappy with the British Tommy as an immigrant and wanted instead a massive influx of "good class" British-speakers: see Davenport, *South Africa*, p. 227, and Streak, *Lord Milner's Immigration Policy for the Transvaal 1897–1905*, ch. 1.

10. *CT*, 5.2.1904; H. Farmer, "What Is Wrong with South Africa," quoted in *SAJC*, 30.10.1908.

11. *Ca*, 3.1.1908. For an account of Jewish life in District Six, Cape Town, see Feldman, "Social Life of Cape Town Jewry," pp. 19–22. For similarly unfavorable descriptions see "The Jewish Quarter," by Helen Blackmore, in *Ca*, 6.8.1909, and *ST*, 10.3.1907.

12. TK 169 *Census of the Transvaal Colony and Swaziland—1904*, Transvaal Archives Depot; *SAJC*, 15.4.1904; *ST*, 10.3.1907.

13. Cesare Lombroso (1836–1909) founded the science of criminal law: see Mosse, *Towards the Final solution*, pp. 83–87, and Bradlow, "Immigration into the Union, 1910–1948," p. 187.

14. *Ow,* 17.7.1903, 13.2.1903; *Natal Legislative Assembly Debates,* 25.6.1903.

15. *SAR,* 6.2.1903; Inspector's Report, Paarl 1908, INSP 1/1/254 Standard Bank Archives.

16. Merriman to Smuts, Merriman Papers 187/25. 13.1.1908.

17. *SAJC,* 17.1.1908. For anti-Indian legislation, see Bhana and Brain, *Setting Down Roots. TC,* 10.1.1908. See also the *Transvaal Critic* for articles on "Our White Slave Traffic," which associated the menace with continentals, including Russian Jews (9.3.1906, 16.3.1906, 30.3.1906, 18.5.1906). It is important to note the presence of continentals other than eastern European Jews. Indeed, two years later a major article in the *Transvaal Critic* (7.2.1908), "Illicits and Crime" in Johannesburg, referred to continentals without mentioning Jews or Peruvians.

18. *TL,* 4.3.1907; *ST,* 10.3.1907. The regular use of the epithet "Jew" was taken up by the Jewish Board of Deputies for Transvaal and Natal: see Morris Alexander Papers, BC 160 May 1903–April 1923, 20.11.1907.

19. *Report of the Liquor Commission 1908. SACJ,* 29.7.1904.

20. As Krut notes, the Board of Deputies for Transvaal and Natal Jewry "set about an active but visible program that combined patronage with policing, coaxing with rigid control." The essential intention was to "Anglicize" the "aliens" ("The Making of a South African Jewish Community," pp. 150–51).

21. *CT,* 18.3.1904. The writer pointed out that Peter the Great had appreciated the deleterious influence of Jews on the peasantry.

22. *CT,* 27.10.1905.

23. *ME,* 1.12.1905. For the origins of the Cape Jewish Board of Deputies see Shain, *Jewry and Cape Society,* chs. 1–4.

24. C3–1906 Report on the Select Committee on Labour Settlement for Indigent Whites, Minutes of Evidence, *Annexures to the Votes and Proceedings of the House of Assembly,* Cape of Good Hope, p. 27.

25. TG13–1908 Transvaal Indigency Commission Minutes of Evidence, pp. 187, 283.

26. Quoted in *Ow,* 27.1.1905.

27. Ibid. In keeping with its antisemitic outlook, the *Owl* lost no opportunity to comment upon Jewry's emergent hegemony, even if that meant noting the numerical preponderance, political influence, commercial and financial power of New York Jews (14.6.1905; see also 27.10.1905).

28. See, e.g., the comments of J. N. P. de Villiers (North Western Province), M. J. Pretorius (North Eastern Province), and P. W. Michau (North Eastern Province) (*Cape Legislative Council,* 19.7.1906).

29. In the immediate postwar period the demand for black labor on the mines outstripped the supply—a result of new railway construction projects and the rebuilding of farms attracting black labor: see Richardson, *Chinese Mine Labour in the Transvaal,* ch. 1.

30. *Cape Legislative Council,* 21.7.1903; *Cape Legislative Assembly,* 30.9.1902.

31. Hancock, *Smuts,* pp. 133, 183; Denoon, "Capitalist Influence and the Transvaal Government," p. 301.

32. *TC,* 3.4.1903, 26.6.1903, 24.7.1903.

33. *Ow,* 3.7.1903, 3.4.1903.

34. It should be noted that the *SAJC* also castigated Jews of the "goldbug" type for being interested only in "heaping wealth upon wealth" (5.6.1903).

35. *Ow,* 4.4.1903.

36. "The Jew's Lament," *Ow,* 4.4.1903; *Ow,* 29.5.1903, 18.9.1903, 11.6.1903. Even a cartoon in the *Burgersdorp Stem* (reported in *Ow,* 4.10.1904) depicted the Chinese, Jew, and clergyman bypassing the interests of the British Empire.

37. *CT,* 5.1.1904. Carver's address also included a poem, published in the *London Speaker* and reproduced in *De Zuid Afrikaan* (7.1.1904) which identified Jewish names with postwar domination. In similar vein, George Woolends, a popular Cape Town outdoor agitator, harangued Jewish capitalists during sessions at the Van Riebeeck fountain (*SAN,* 21.5.1904). Another laborite, Corley, ridiculed "talk about British supremacy" in the light of power wielded by intriguing foreign financiers (ibid., 4.2.1904).

38. *Cape Legislative Council,* 22.4.1904, 26.4.1904; *CT,* 5.1.1904.

39. *NM,* 14.1.1904.

40. *SAN,* 26.4.1904; *CT,* 6.1.1904.

41. See Herrman, "Hoggenheimer," pp. 559–60, and Hocking, *Oppenheimer and Son,* p. 99.

42. It is quite evident that Jews took no exception to the production. As the *Transvaal Critic* put it: "The Jews who dominate every department of society in this community are too strong and sensible to be sensitive to broad burlesque and low-class caricature and they can afford to laugh at it" (13.11.1903).

43. For reviews see *SAN,* 23.9.1903; *TL,* 10.11.1903; *St,* 10.11.1903; *NM,* 23.2.1903.

44. *SAN,* 24.9.1903. Before the production of *The Girl from Kays* Boonzaier had depicted a mining magnate in cartoon form: see, e.g., *SAN,* 15.8.1903. Those associating international capital with the cosmopolitan Jew would have identified the magnate as being of semitic extraction. The association ensured the parvenu quality of the character, an image recognizable from the moment W. W. Walton strode the stage of the Good Hope Theatre. Commented one critic: "Hoggenheimer is, alas, a type only too well known in this country" (*SAN,* 15.9.1903).

45. Boonzaier's cartoons were so popular that the *South African News* published them collectively in book form. The newspaper warned prospective buyers that "to prevent disappointment orders should be forwarded at once" (*SAN,* 9.12.1903).

46. See Schoonraad and Schoonraad, *Companion to South African Cartoonists,* pp. 64–72.

47. Boonzaier Papers, MSC 4, II: Letters from J X Merriman to Boonzaier, 22.8.1905 and 1905–17, Merriman to Boonzaier, 22.8.1905; *SAN,* 26.4.1904. For the association of Hoggenheimer with Milner, see, e.g., *Ow,* 27.11.1905.

48. See Shain, "Hoggenheimer—the Making of a Myth."

49. *CT,* 1.11.1903; *NW,* 21.3.1906; *SAJC,* 9.10.1903.

50. *Ow,* 27.11.1903.

51. Krut, "Building a Home," pp. 152–56. For the United States see Higham, *Send These to Me.*

52. *CT,* 16.7.1906. The full text of the speech is reprinted in *Jewish Affairs:* see Schreiner, "A Letter on the Jew."

53. *CT,* 7.12.1905; *TL,* 5.7.1906, 8.12.1906.

54. *PH*, 7.2.1903, quoted in *SAJC*, 21.2.1903; *SAJC*, 8.4.1904.

55. *SAJC*, 27.10.1905 and 15.5.1908; Bruce, *The New Transvaal*, pp. 71–72; *SAJC*, 12.5.1905. For an example of Jews being conceived as a race, see article by "Quivus" (*Ow*, 12.2.1904).

56. Even the Cape Colony with its well-established Anglo-German Jewish population had 11,667 Russian born residents (presumably all Jewish) out of a population of 19,509 Jews in 1904 (G19–1905 *Census of the Colony of the Cape of Good Hope, 1904*).

57. *ST*, 28.3.1907; Inspector's Report, Fordsburg 1908, INSP 1/1/214 Standard Bank Archives; *SAJC*, 13.11.1908, 16.10.1907; Inspector's Report, Cape Town 1904, INSP 1/1/199 Standard Bank Archives; Inspector's Report, Oudtshoorn 1905, INSP 1/1/253 Standard Bank Archives.

58. *CT*, 16.7.1906.

59. *SAJC*, 3.8.1906.

60. Ibid., 18.8.1908, 10.1.1908.

61. Ibid., 7.8.1903.

62. Parry, "'In a Sense Citizens, but Not Altogether Citizens,' Rhodes, Race and the Ideology of Segregation," pp. 384–88, and Martin, "Political and Social Theories of Transkeian Administrators," p. 82.

63. *SAJC*, 13.11.1908; *TL*, quoted in *SAJC*, 7.8.1903.

64. *SAJC*, 3.9.1909. In the context of heated debate as to whether Yiddish was acceptable as a European language in terms of the Cape Colony's Immigration Restriction Act of 1902, there remained some question as to whether "Hebrews" were "Europeans." Censuses in the Cape Colony had always differentiated between "Europeans" and "Hebrews."

65. *TL*, 29.9.1910.

66. G35–1904 Report of the Medical Officer of Health for Cape Colony, 1904, *Annexures to the Votes and Proceedings of the House of Assembly*.

67. *SAJC*, 27.10.1905.

68. *SAJC*, 4.9.1908.

69. *GRA*, 30.10.1907.

70. *SAJC*, 3.6.1910.

71. For reviews see the *CT*, 2.3.1910; *Ca*, 4.3.1910; *SAJC*, 3.6.1910, which even suggested that the author had omitted other pertinent features of the negative stereotype; *RDM*, 30.5.1910.

72. *RDM*, 30.5.1910.

73. *NPBN*, quoted in *SAN*, 25.6.1910; *House of Assembly Debates*, 13.3.1911; *SAJC*, 29.11.1912.

74. Report of the Medical Officer of Health, Johannesburg, 1913, cited in Krut, "The Making of a South African Jewish Community," p. 157; *SAJC*, 6.2.1914.

75. Significantly, when a Jewish Land Settlement Association was formed in 1913, the *SAJC* commented with approval, noting that it had "long been a reproach levelled against our community that we are today a nation of hucksters and small traders" (30.5.1913).

76. *SAJC*, 9.1.1914, 23.1.1914.

77. Sartre, *Anti-Semite and Jew*, p. 13.

78. Much the same process happened in Germany at that time: see Mosse, *The Crisis of German Ideology,* p. 137.

79. Mosse, *Towards the Final Solution,* pp. 83–84.

80. *CT,* 3.2.1904, 23.1.1903.

81. Inspector's Report, Paarl 1908, INSP 1/1/254, Standard Bank Archives.

82. These are the words of Arnold Rose, an American sociologist, who explained antisemitism in terms of hatred of the city ("Anti-Semitism's Roots in City Hatred"). Jews have been historically associated with the city from the late middle ages, and Western literature has, of course, incorporated an antiurban bias: see Hadden and Barton, "An Image That Will Not Die." I am grateful to Jane Carruthers for drawing my attention to the former article.

83. We have seen indications of religious ideas fueling perceptions of the Jew, but on the whole religiously based animosity was unacceptable to mainstream opinion. Early in the twentieth century, e.g., Prof. C. F. J. Muller's (misreported) comments at a Dutch Reformed Synod about Jews being a "curse" to South Africa were answered by the *South African News*. The newspaper detested the "practice of affixing race and creed labels" and concluded with a plea against "that blighting curse of the Continent, anti-Semitism" (12.11.1903).

84. Pinsker, "Auto-emancipation: An Appeal to His People by a Russian Jew (1882)," p. 185; Schermerhorn, *Comparative Ethnic Relations,* p. 6.

85. See, e.g., Holmes, *Anti-Semitism in British Society, 1879–1939,* pp. 231–32.

Chapter Four

1. In 1917, e.g., Stephen Black's *Helena's Hope Ltd* once again elicited no sympathy for the "unscrupulous speculator and company promoter" Abraham Goldenstein (*CT,* 3.1.1917). For reviews, see *RDM,* 30.1.1917; *CT,* 3.1.1917; *CA,* 2.1.1917. Jews similarly continued to be associated with IDB and ridiculed for their petty trading practices: see *SAJC,* 14.5.1920. The postwar also witnessed the emergence of the Afrikaans smous joke: see, e.g., *DH,* Jan., Aug., Sep., Nov., Dec. 1919. The shrewd business instinct of the Jew was best captured in a Labour party newspaper, the *Guardian,* when discussing the character of J. W. Jagger, minister of railways and harbours. He had, noted the newspaper, "die slimheid van die Skot en die handelsinsig van die Jood" (the brains of a Scot and the business acumen of a Jew) (quoted in *DB,* 6.1.1922). The stereotype was also personified in Schlimowitz, a character in Stephen Black's novel *The Dorp*. The philosemitic dimension of the stereotype was also evident. The minister of mines, F. S. Malan, e.g., praised Jews for their industry and enterprise. Commercially and industrially, he argued, Jews "ruled the roost" (*RDM,* 14.11.1917).

2. Kentridge, *I Recall,* pp. 55 ff. Kentridge was one of several leading Jewish Laborites. See also Alexander, *Morris Alexander,* p. 76; *RDM* and *ST,* cited in *SAJC,* 30.12.1915, 15.12.1915.

3. *RDM,* 8.12.1915.

4. See, e.g., the letters of "Proud Khaki" (*NA,* 22.8.1916); "Too Old" (*NA,* 28.8.1916); and "One Who Has Fought and Suffered for Country" (*NA,* 5.9.1916).

5. *RDM,* 30.1.1917.

6. Quoted in *SAJC,* 9.2.1917.

7. *CT,* 1.2.1917.

8. *CT,* 3.2.1917.

9. *RDM,* 6.3.1917, 8.3.1917.

10. *Ca,* 5.10.1917, 12.10.1917, 19.10.1917.

11. *RDM,* 12.3.1917; *Ca,* 23.11.1917.

12. *RDM,* 24.3.1917; *AJW,* 11.10.1917; *SAJC,* 23.11.1917. Negative sentiments toward Russian Jews were, of course, influenced by the belief that most Communists were Jewish.

13. Morris Alexander Papers, BC 160, List III, Letter Book 1911–25; Alexander to Percy Cowan, general secretary, South African Jewish Board of Deputies, 10.9.1917; *SAJC,* 27.3.1918. It is estimated that Jews comprised approximately 6 percent of the Union's defense forces (Alexander, *Morris Alexander,* p. 76).

14. *SAJC,* 27.3.1918. Despite his evidence, Alexander supported the charge that Goldsmid's article was antisemitic. For the *Natal Advertiser* debate see 11.3.1918, 23.3.1918, 7.3.1918, 16.3.1918, 19.3.1918, 22.3.1918, 25.3.1918, 22.3.1918.

15. See, e.g., *DB,* 11.3.1917. See also the cartoons in the *CT,* 4.2.1919 and 22.2.1919.

16. *CT,* 19.2.1919.

17. Bonner, "The Transvaal Native Congress 1917–1920," p. 274. On the International Socialist League see Johns, "Marxism-Leninism in a Multi-Racial Environment," pp. 70, 82.

18. *DB,* 13.5.1919.

19. See Mantzaris, "The Promise of the Impossible Revolution."

20. See Johns, "Marxism-Leninism in a Multi-Racial Environment," p. 165.

21. *CT,* 9.1.1919; *Ca,* 10.1.1919.

22. *CT,* 16.1.1919. Comparing Bolshevism to the great influenza epidemic that had only recently devastated South Africa (including Cape Town) was an enormously emotive, if not invidious comparison. For insights into the traumatic impact of the Spanish flu in South Africa see Phillips, "'Black October,'" ch. 8. For a similarly invidious and indeed apocalyptic view of Bolshevism see the letter from "A Watchman in Zion," *ST,* 19.1.1919.

23. *Ca,* 7.2.1919.

24. According to their hosts, Lapitsky was a "barrister at law at the University of Petrograd, ex-Secretary of the Minister of Labour, Attorney General in the Ukraine," while Sosnovic was a "journalist, Knight of the Order of St. George, delegate for the Soldiers Council in Petrograd, ex-Assistant Minister of War in the Ukraine, member of the Peoples' Tribunal of Justice" (*St,* 27.3.1919).

25. *CT,* 29.3.1919.

26. *St,* 27.3.1919.

27. Duncan to Selborne, BC 294. D5.13.6: 3.3.1919, Patrick Duncan Papers, University of Cape Town.

28. *CT,* 29.3.1919, 15.4.1919; *St,* 29.3.1919; *RDM,* 29.3.1919.

29. *CA,* 13.4.1919; *CT,* 15.4.1919, 18.4.1919; *RDM,* 10.4.1919. For the Johannesburg municipal strike see *RDM,* 1.4.1919.

30. See Harrison, *Memoirs of a Socialist,* pp. 65–72.

31. *CT,* 31.3.1919; *Ca,* 4.4.1919; *CT,* 30.4.1919.

32. See Mantzaris, "The Promise of the Impossible Revolution," p. 150.

33. As one Jewish correspondent to the press, Benzion Hersch, put it: "It is an undisputed fact that when a 'Russian' was referred to in this country the Jew of Russian origin was meant, and this was to a certain extent justified by the fact that the vast majority of Russians in this country were Jews. To-day, however, when a Russian is spoken of the inference in the mind of the average citizen is not only that the Jew was intended, but also that it was a Bolshevist" (*St*, 21.4.1919). Hersch had been appointed an immigration officer at the Cape Town docks by the South African Jewish Board of Deputies in 1913. The office was terminated in 1915 due to lack of funds but reestablished in 1923: see Bradlow, "Immigration into the Union, 1910–1948," pp. 194–95, 207.

34. *St*, 18.4.1919. "Observer" similarly pointed out "local Russian Bolsheviks . . . in England large numbers are being deported"; see also letters from "Britisher" (*CT*, 22.4.1919), "TBB" (*CT*, 26.4.1919), and "Observer" (*St*, 18.4.1919). The press, moreover, took every opportunity to remind readers of the Russian origins of Kentridge, who was Labour's key spokesman: see, e.g., *St*, 22.3.1919, and the *PN*, 9.5.1919).

35. For evidence of Jewish concern see letters from Benzion Hersch, *CT*, 24.4.1919, and "A British Jew," *St*, 23.4.1919.

36. The *Cape Times* (26.4.1919), e.g., had accused the minister of justice, N. J. de Wet, of burying his head in the sand while Bolshevik clouds were brewing. *ST*, (4.5.1919) commented editorially on the question of aliens inciting the native population of South Africa; see also *DB*, 13.5.1919.

37. *CT*, 12.6.1919; *ZR*, 14.7.1919; *CT*, 20.6.1919.

38. *St*, 3.5.1919; *ST*, 4.5.1919; *CT* comments cited in *St*, 12.6.1919. An interesting series of letters is included among the evidence to the Martial Law Commission of 1922 making it quite clear that South African security chiefs were concerned at this time about Bolshevik agitation and wished to supervise immigration more stringently: see Col. Sir Walter Hamilton Fowle Kell, 13.6.1919, Martial Law Commission, K4, Transvaal Archives Depot.

39. Central Archives CIA M 212 Sec. for Interior to Principal Immigration Officer, 12.5.1919, and Central Archives CIA 215, Deputy Commissioner CID to Principal Immigration officer, 7.6.1919 (cited in Bradlow, "Immigration into the Union, 1910–1948," p. 196).

40. *Ca*, 29.8.1919. For editorials discussing the civil war in Russia and the excesses of Bolshevism, see, e.g., *CT*, 18.8.1919.

41. *ZR*, 14.9.1919.

42. *Ca*, 12.12.1919.

43. *CT*, 22.11.1919.

44. *Ca*, 30.4.1920. The *Cape* was wrong in claiming Duncan had lived all his life in South Africa. In fact he came to the country in 1901 as part of Milner's youthful team, known as the "kindergarten."

45. *CT*, 9.12.1920; *St*, 4.12.1920. On the Industrial Socialist League see Johns, "Marxism-Leninism in a Multi-Racial Environment," p. 200; for strike details see *Union of South Africa: Official Year Book, No. 7—1924*, pp. 260, 262.

46. *Volksblad* article cited in *St*, 15.1.1921.

47. The *Cape* was a good example. It relentlessly attacked Solly Joel as a symbol

of exploitation: see the poem "Solly! or a Magnate from the Golden Rand," in *Ca*, 21.12.1919. In the *Cape*'s so-called political alphabet, "Y" stood for Yid, "with his bags full of cash" (6.2.1920). See also comments following the publication of the will of Sammy Marks in *Ca* (16.4.1920) and *ST* (16.4.1920).

48. *House of Assembly Debates*, 25.6.1921, 8.8.1921, 14.10.1921, 16.8.1921; *GRA*, 8.8.1921, 14.10.1921; *CT*, 16.8.1921; Bradlow, "Immigration into the Union, 1910–1948," p. 199. Marwick was born in Richmond, Natal, in 1875. Having originally been involved in Native administration he became a senior partner in the firm of Marwick and Morris, Employers of Native Labourers on Transvaal Gold Mines and Natal Collieries. Marwick was at one time a member of the committee of the Anthropological Section, British Association of Science (*South African Who's Who*).

49. *Ca*, 2.12.1921.

Chapter Five

1. *DB*, 6.2.1922, 21.1.1922, 13.3.1922, 31.1.1922. In 1925 Afrikaans replaced Dutch as an official language in South Africa (*House of Assembly Debates*, 25.2.1922, 28.2.1922). Although *Die Burger* was an Afrikaans daily, many of its articles at this time still appeared in Dutch.

2. *RDM*, 6.2.1922, 19.1.1922, 6.2.1922, 18.2.1922.

3. *DB*, 23.2.1922. *House of Assembly Debates*, 23.3.1922. It should be noted that Madeley was no enemy of the Jews. However, in evoking images of international finance and Hoggenheimer he was, willy-nilly, reinforcing prewar notions of Jewish finance capitalism.

4. Duncan to Lady Selborne, BC 294. D5.16.1, 21.2.1922.

5. See, e.g., *RDM*, 6.2.1922; *QD*, 5.2.1922, and *NM*, 7.2.1922; Herd, *1922: The Revolt on the Rand*, p. 34. Waterston's resolution was rejected by an assembly of seventeen National and Labour party MPs at a meeting in Pretoria.

6. *GRA*, 6.2.1922; *CA*, 6.2.1922; *EPH*, 8.2.1922. Kentridge, Kreschmar, and Buirski were Jewish and involved in left-wing agitation. See Mantzaris, "The Promise of the Impossible Revolution," pp. 147–55.

7. *DB*, 10.2.1922. Afrikaner nationalists, as we know, shared with the South African party a fear of Bolshevism. The Russian state, explained *De Kerkbode* (21.2.1922), official organ of the Dutch Reformed Church, was godless. The Council of Action was formed in February 1921 following a clash between the Mineworkers' Union and a group of communists in the union. See Johns, "Marxism-Leninism in a Multi-Cultural Environment," p. 252.

8. *De Prins Albert Vriend*, 1.3.1922, cited in *DVs*, 7.3.1922; *St*, 2.3.1922; *House of Assembly Debates*, 2.3.1922; *RDM*, 3.3.1922; *DFA*, 2.3.1922.

9. Editorial, "A Day of Horrors," *RDM*, 11.3.1922. For an outline of events on the Rand see Johns, "Marxism-Leninism in a Multi-Cultural Environment," pp. 268–74.

10. *RDM*, 13.3.1922; *GRA*, 13.3.1922; *CA*, 13.3.1922; *St*, 13.3.1922. The *Star* (20.3.1922) appealed for intelligence surveillance to be tightened. *DK*, 16.3.1922.

11. *NM*, 19.3.1922; *DB*, 16.3.1922, 24.4.1922; *QD*, 24.4.1922.

12. *NM*, 31.3.1922. See also Julius Jeppe's speech as chairman of the Johannesburg

Hospital Board, *RDM*, 1.4.1922. The conspiratorial view was vividly captured in an article in the *Cape Argus* (15.4.1922): "The Complete Bolshevist—by a Long-Suffering Johannesburg." On the "Bolshevik insect" see *DB*, 23.3.1922. The report of the Commission of Inquiry into the events certainly corroborated the conspiracy thesis: see Union of South Africa, UG–35 *Report of the Martial Law Inquiry Judicial Commission 1922*, p. 32.

13. Duncan to Selborne, BC 294. D5.16.4, 15.3.1922.

14. *St*, 6.3.1922.

15. *EPH*, 14.3.1922.

16. *ELDD*, 13.3.1922, 16.3.1922, 14.3.1922; *NA*, quoted in *St*, 16.3.1922.

17. *OC*, 15.3.1922; *CT*, 16.3.1922, 21.3.1922. For examples of correspondence, see *ELDD*, 21.3.1922, *NM*, 21.3.1922. For editorial comments, see *St*, 20.3.1922; *DFA*, 20.3.1922; *ELDD*, 21.3.1922; *WS*, 25.3.1922.

18. The impact of American nativist sentiment is evident in Col. Mackenzie's address to the South African party congress in August 1923 (*CT*, 16.8.1923). For insight into domestic segregationist discourse, see Dubow, "Race, Civilisation and Culture," pp. 75–78.

19. *DFA*, 17.3.1922.

20. *CT*, 18.3.1922. The editor, B. K. Long, was referring to the acceptance of Yiddish as a European language for purposes of the Immigration Act.

21. *ST*, 19.3.1922.

22. Duncan to Lady Selborne, BC 294. D5.16.5, 23.3.1922. For Jewish economic activity see Kaplan, *Jewish Roots in the South African Economy*, chs. 7–12, and Arkin, "Economic Activities," pp. 58–59.

23. *ZR*, 31.3.1922.

24. *RDM*, 24.3.1922.

25. *ST*, 26.3.1922.

26. *A Pictorial View of Recent Events*.

27. See, e.g., *DB*, 28.3.1922. Skepticism about a conspiratorial plot was increasingly expressed: see *DB*, 29.3.1922, and *ELDD*, 3.4.1922. In parliament T. Boydell asked for a judicial commission to establish the accuracy of Smuts's reported allegation that "the recent crisis was due to the influence of Bolshevik propaganda, with a view to establishing a local Soviet Government in South Africa" (*House of Assembly Debates*, 5.4.1922). The Nationalist member for Rustenburg, P. Grobler, similarly expressed skepticism of a "Bolshevik revolution" (ibid., 18.4.1922; see, e.g., the report of a strike meeting in *DB*, 13.4.1922).

28. *DK*, 13.4.1922.

29. *RDM*, 31.3.1922. According to the 1913 act, entry was forbidden to "any person who when an immigration officer dictated to him not less than fifty words in the language selected by such an officer, fails to write out those words in that language to the satisfaction of that officer." If immigrants were thought suitable this test would be put in a language he knew and there would be no difficulty in his entering the country (Bradlow, "Immigration into the Union, 1910–1948," p. 29).

30. Of course, the Immigration Restriction Act of 1902 in the Cape Colony was an attempt to exclude Yiddish-speaking immigrants. However, pressure from Jew-

ish leaders ensured Yiddish being accepted as a "European language" for purposes of the act (Shain, *Jewry and Cape Society,* pp. 27–32).

31. Higham makes the same point with regard to antisemitism in the United States during the late nineteenth century ("American Anti-Semitism Historically Reconsidered," in Stember, *Jews in the Mind of America,* pp. 244–45). The "Bolshevik" crisis, then, was a deviation from real problems and in this sense bears some comparison with the "mugging" crisis in Britain during the early 1970s as expounded by Stuart Hall et al., *Policing the Crisis,* pp. vii–viii.

32. *ELDD,* 1.4.1922.

33. Duncan to Selborne, BC 294. D5.16.8, 20.4.1922.

34. This is not to argue, however, that the bogey was entirely and cynically manipulated. In his evidence to the Martial Law Commission, the commissioner of police, Col. T. G. Truter, referred to a large number of Bolsheviks who had conspired to overthrow the government and proclaim a republic (*RDM,* 11.5.1922).

35. These included V. Kent, chairman of the Wanderers Cricket Club (*RDM,* 12.4.1922); A. E. King, secretary of the S.A. National Union (*CT,* 10.4.1922); the executive of the Johannesburg Chamber of Commerce (*CA,* 1.6.1922), and a number of politicians.

36. *House of Assembly Debates,* 13.4.1922.

37. Ibid., 20.4.1922; *RDM,* 10.4.1922; *House of Assembly Debates,* 24.4.1922.

38. Charles H. Frude to General J. Smuts, 26.6.1923, Archives of the South African Jewish Board of Deputies; *Ca,* 28.4.1922.

39. Brutus [H. F. Viljoen], *Never Again.* The writer has been unsuccessful in tracing the identity of Viljoen.

40. *ZR,* 30.6.1922.

41. *CT,* cited in *QDR,* 17.8.1922; *SAJC,* 3.11.1922; for Duncan's warning, see Bradlow, "Immigration into the Union, 1910–1948," p. 208; *House of Assembly Debates,* 29.5.1923. It is quite clear that the opposition was attempting to attract Jewish support.

42. S. A. Jewish Board of Deputies. Executive Report, *SAJC,* 24.7.25; Bradlow, "Immigration into the Union, 1910–1948," pp. 24–29, 211; *ZR,* 31.3.1924; S. A. Jewish Board of Deputies, Executive Report; *SAJC,* 24.7.1925.

43. *QDR,* cited in *CT,* 2.5.1924; Bradlow, "Immigration into the Union, 1910–1948," p. 211.

44. South African party [Election Pamphlets] 1924, South African Library, *CA,* 30.5.1924; *DK,* 6.4.1924, 14.5.1924.

45. *BF,* 11.7.1924. Bradlow, "Immigration into the Union, 1910–1948," p. 215.

46. Significantly the newspaper did not resort to the eastern European–Anglo-German dichotomy. This of course is another indication that by the early 1920s Jews in general were defined by the eastern European Jew.

47. *House of Assembly Debates,* 21.8.1924.

48. *DK,* 4.7.1923. On Smuts see *CT,* 15.3.1923.

49. *ZR,* 26.9.1924.

50. This is well illustrated in contemporary jokes: see, e.g., the story of the Englishman, Dutchman, Jew, and Indian in *Die Huisgenoot,* Oct. 1923.

51. *SAJC,* 10.8.1923. Raphaely's explanation—and that taken throughout this

chapter—is shared by Yudelman: "Smuts perpetuated the idea that the 1922 revolt was a foreign-led aberration rather than the product of genuine indigenous tensions. Russian immigrants to South Africa, the argument goes, were responsible for a Bolshevik-type Rand Revolt." Despite Smuts being a firm supporter of Jewish and Zionist aspirations, "he refused the private entreaties of the Jewish Board of Deputies to scotch allegations that Russian Jews were responsible for the revolt, even though they clearly were not and he knew they were not" (*The Emergence of Modern South Africa*, p. 184).

Chapter Six

1. In 1924 the United States introduced the Johnson Act, which sought to safeguard the "Nordic" character of American society (Higham, *Strangers in the Land*, pp. 316–22). A cursory glance at immigration debates in South Africa reveals quite palpably that the American act influenced South African legislators.

2. Saron and Hotz, eds., *The Jews in South Africa*, p. 378.

3. Houghton, "Economic Development, 1865–1965," p. 25.

4. *St*, 17.12.1924. Maritz had been close to the currents of European fascism. In 1938 he published *My Lewe en Strewe* (My life and struggle), a viciously antisemitic diatribe which included substantial sections lifted from the notorious *Protocols of the Elders of Zion* (Cohen, "Anti-Jewish Manifestations in the Union," p. 63).

5. The *Rand Daily Mail*, e.g., expressed disgust at his "vicious attack on an important section of the community" (18.12.1924). See also *St*, 17.12.1924.

6. *DB*, 16.12.1924; *St*, 22.12.1924.

7. *PN*, 22.12.1924.

8. *PN*, 22.12.1924. Roos had apparently referred to Jews as "the most law-abiding race in the country" (*PN*, 22.12.1924). According to the *Cape* (23.1.1925), Roos's office was inundated with demands from indignant Jews who wished to know whether he agreed with the sentiments uttered by his fellow Nationalist, Maritz. For Kemp's response see *St*, 22.12.1924.

9. *DVs*, 27.12.1924; *Ca*, 23.1.1925.

10. *RDM*, 14.5.1925.

11. *RDM*, 15.5.1925, Report of the Sixth Biennial Congress of the S.A. Jewish Board of Deputies Congress, Durban; *SAJC*, 9.8.1925. In other words Jews were regarded as responsible for animosity toward themselves: see correspondence, *RDM*, 18.5.1925; *ST*, 17.5.1925.

12. *Special Report Series of the Census Department, Immigration 1920–25, No.25*. J. E. Holloway became chairman of the Native Affairs Commission, a body which provided an important arsenal for significant policies in South Africa: see Dubow, *Racial Segregation and the Origins of Apartheid in South Africa, 1919–36*, pp. 36–37.

13. *RDM*, 11.9.1925.

14. See Dubow, *Racial Segregation and the Origins of Apartheid in South Africa, 1919–36*, pp. 45–51.

15. This was certainly a viewpoint held by some English eugenicists: see Stepan, *The Idea of Race*, p. 129. Of course, eugenicist discourse was not necessarily antisemi-

tic. At the turn of the century, e.g., many eugenicists in Britain wrote favorably of the Jews' pride in family and race, seeing it as a kind of eugenical model for other groups (ibid., p. 125). Significantly, the writings of a prominent Jew, Sarah Gertrude Millin, were informed, as Dubow puts it, by "the language and imagery of biological degeneration" ("Race, Civilization and culture: The Elaboration of Segregationist Discourse," p. 77). See also Coetzee, "Blood, Flaw, Taint, Degeneration: The Case of Sarah Gertrude Millin."

16. *St*, 17.9.1925.

17. *CT*, 11.9.1925.

18. *DB*, 15.9.1925.

19. *St*, 27.11.1925; *RDM*, 27.11.1925.

20. *RDM*, 28.11.1925. Although the myth of Jewish men threatening Gentile women was a well-known theme in European antisemitism, this dimension of the anti-Jewish stereotype never flourished in South Africa.

21. *NM*, 28.11.1925.

22. *RDM*, 30.11.1925, 29.11.1925; *St*, 28.11.1925; Executive Council Minutes 1925–1927, Archives, S.A. Jewish Board of Deputies, Johannesburg.

23. *St*, 3.11.1925, 30.11.1925.

24. See "JPR," *RDM*, 30.11.1925, and "An Old Johannesburger," *RDM*, 2.12.1925. Madeley added his voice to the protest (*NM*, 2.12.1925). For response see *RDM*, 1.12.1925; *DB*, 1.12.1925.

25. *CT*, 1.12.1925.

26. *ELDD*, 28.11.1925.

27. *EPH*, 4.12.1925.

28. This optimistic assumption echoed assimilationist hopes of the nineteenth century. It certainly contradicted the determinist paradigm informing most of the article. The idea was taken even further when *OV* (4.12.1925) argued that the Jews' racial pettiness would not continue to the next generation.

29. *OV*, 4.12.1925.

30. *EPH*, 4.12.1925.

31. Besides an anti-Jewish pamphlet campaign on the Witwatersrand during the Christmas period (*SAJC*, 15.1.1926), little was heard of the league.

32. *House of Assembly Debates*, 17.2.1926.

33. *CT*, 4.3.1926.

34. *CT*, 13.3.1926.

35. *House of Assembly Debates*, 3.5.1926.

36. Ibid., 3.5.1926.

37. *SAJC*, 1.1.1926.

38. *DB*, 8.10.1926; *CT*, 29.10.1926, cited in Bradlow, "Immigration into the Union, 1910–1948," p. 222. On the structural similarities of philo- and antisemitism see Todd Endelman's review of Paul Johnson's *A History of the Jews* ("A question of influence") in *TLS* (26.6.1987).

39. *ZR*, 12.11.1926.

40. *ZR*, 3.12.1926.

41. Higham's comments about the American value system which "celebrated the businessman as provider, community builder, and industrious trader" but "was

more uncertain about the merits of bankers and creditors" has relevance here: see *Send These to Me,* p. 180.

42. *ZR,* 3.12.1926.

43. E. B. Grosskopf, "Die Rolprent Spekulasie" (The film speculation), *DH,* 14.8.1925; Willem C. W. Kemp, "Oom Gielie en die Smous" (Uncle Gielie and the Smous), *DH,* 8.4.1925; B. J. Kloppers, "Die Smous en Slaaplied" (The smous and the lullaby), *DH,* 1.2.1927. A regularly repeated joke, e.g., concerned the smous who saw no problem in his new home being without water because he would be there for only half a year; see, e.g., *DH,* 8.5.1925. Negative views are even evident in nonfiction: see C. G. W. Schuumann, "Iets oor die Handel en Handelstudie" (Something about commerce and commercial study), *DH,* 26.3.1926. Schuumann was a Stellenbosch academic who subsequently played a prominent role in right-wing Afrikaner antisemitism and intellectual life.

44. Coetzee, *White Writing,* p. 78; Van Bruggen, "Bywoners," in Van Bruggen, *Op die Veld en Rante; Malherbe, Die Meulenaar.* For the portrayal of Jews in Afrikaans literature during the 1930s and 1940s see Pheiffer, "The Jew in Afrikaans Literature" and Tannenbaum, "Jewish Characters in Afrikaans Fiction."

45. See Dundes, *Cracking Jokes,* p. viii. For examples of smous jokes see *DH,* 23.1.1925, 27.2.1925, 3.4.1925, 17.4.1925, 1.5.1925, 22.5.1925, 15.1.1926, 22.1.1926.

46. *SAJC Rosh Hashana Number,* 1928.

47. *Ca,* 21.5.1926.

48. *SAJC,* 28.9.1928, 5.10.1928. See also the comments of Sir Abe Bailey (*SAJC,* 13.1.1928).

49. For evidence of this clustering in the 1930s, see Sonnabend, "Statistical Survey of Johannesburg Jewish Population."

50. *SAJC,* 9.7.1926. The writer has been unable to establish the identity of Mackintosh.

51. *SAJC,* 14.1.1927. The pamphlet was allegedly distributed by the League of Gentiles, the first and last manifestation of its existence since the fanfare of its inception in November 1925. Two months later a pamphlet modeled on the notorious Protocols of the Elders of Zion was distributed: see *SAJC,* 11.3.1927.

52. Sonnabend's survey of Johannesburg Jewry in 1935 showed that 8.39 percent of Jewish males were engaged in the professions, as compared to 4.34 percent of the general white population ("Statistical Survey" and Arkin, "Economic Activities").

53. *SAJC,* 13.1.1928; *Ca,* 25.1.1929.

54. *CT,* 29.10.1927.

55. *House of Assembly Debates,* 9.5.1928.

56. *CT,* 28.8.1929, 21.10.1929.

57. Bradlow, "Immigration into the Union, 1910–1948," p. 224.

58. *House of Assembly Debates,* 12.2.1930, 10.2.1930.

59. Ibid. During the Hitler period Malan acknowledged that this was the case: see Bradlow, "Immigration into the Union, 1910–1948," pp. 276–77.

60. *House of Assembly Debates,* 12.2.1930, 12.2.1930.

61. Ibid., 10.2.1930.

62. Ibid.

63. Ibid., 12.2.1930, 17.2.1930. For vilification of the Jew, see the comments of Christie and MacCallum, *House of Assembly Debates,* 12.2.1930.

64. *BF,* 31.1.1930; *House of Assembly Debates,* 10.2.1930.

65. *House of Assembly Debates,* 10.2.1930.

66. It should be noted that southern Europeans were also included in the Quota Act for similar reasons as applied to Jews, i.e., religious unassimilability (Roman Catholics) and "racial" distinctiveness.

67. Bradlow, "Immigration into the Union, 1910–1948," p. 244.

Chapter Seven

1. During an interview with *Die Burger* in Nov. 1931, Malan warned those Jews agitating against the Quota Act that it was very easy to rouse a "feeling of hate towards the Jews" in South Africa (2.11.1931).

2. The new United South African National party (the United party) led by Hertzog witnessed defections to the Left and Right; in the main, the latter formed the "Purified" National party under Dr. D. F. Malan.

3. Cohen, "Anti-Jewish Manifestations in the Union of South Africa," pp. 65–68, and Shimoni, *Jews and Zionism,* pp. 110–11. For further details about Weichardt, see Scher, "Louis T. Weichardt and the South African Greyshirt Movement."

4. This is particularly evident in the Greyshirts' fortnightly bilingual newspaper, *Die Waarheid—The Truth,* published from Feb. 1934 to July 1938, and its monthly, *Die Blanke Front* (The white front), published from July 1947 to May 1948. For an outline of its anti-Jewish policy, see Van Heerden, "Nasionaal-Sosialism," pp. 76–80.

5. These included the South African National Democratic party; Die Volksbeweging, or Blackshirts; the People's Movement; the National Workers Union, or Brownshirts; the South African Fascists, and the Gentile Protection League. For details see Cohen, "Anti-Jewish Manifestations in the Union of South Africa," pp. 67–69.

6. The Greyshirts, e.g., spoke of "pure Europeans of Aryan descent," an "organic Volk-state," and a "national-socialist republic": see Shimoni, *Jews and Zionism,* pp. 111–14.

7. A Greyshirt handbill, "South Africa Awake," exhorted Christians to deal only with their coreligionists. It maintained that because the percentage of Jewish doctors, dentists, wholesalers, shopkeepers, and attorneys was so high, Gentiles would within ten years be unable to advance in the face of Jewish competition. An Afrikaner trade unionist, L. J. Naude, similarly told 600 people celebrating Dingaan's Day at Taaibospruit in 1936 that Jews were bent on controlling South Africa's commerce and industry as well as the spiritual, social and economic assets of the Boer (Cohen, "Anti-Jewish Manifestations in the Union of South Africa," pp. 87, 77).

8. Quoted in Bradlow, "Immigration into the Union, 1910–1948," p. 252.

9. Quoted ibid., p. 265.

10. See ibid., p. 266. Dr. H. F. Verwoerd, a professor of psychology, was one of the most vocal. A professor of Roman law at the University of Cape Town, J. Kerr

Wylie, rallied to the support of the Afrikaner professors. Jews, he argued, were disloyal and sought only their own ends. They also took no part in productive work, being interested only in speculation, money-lending and propagating communism among blacks (Cohen, "Anti-Jewish Manifestations in the Union of South Africa," p. 43).

11. *Fascist Quarterly,* Oct. 1936, quoted in Cohen, "Anti-Jewish Manifestations in the Union of South Africa," pp. 85–86.

12. Miles, *Racism,* p. 39.

13. In his study of Afrikaner nationalism, Dunbar Moodie argues that anti-Jewish agitation in the late 1930s "resulted from grassroots pressure rather than from initiative by the leaders" (*The Rise of Afrikanerdom,* p. 167).

14. Bradlow, "Immigration into the Union, 1910–1948," pp. 272–73, and Shimoni, *Jews and Zionism,* pp. 119 ff.

15. That this was the real intention of the bill was disclosed by Hertzog during the parliamentary debate, much to the embarrassment of Deputy Prime Minister Smuts (Cohen, "Anti-Jewish Manifestations in the Union of South Africa," p. 126, and Bradlow, "Immigration into the Union, 1910–1948," p. 283).

16. Shimoni, *Jews and Zionism,* p. 125. English-speakers, however, were by and large opposed to vulgar, crude, and programmatic antisemitism, and a number were prominent in efforts designed to combat rampant antisemitism (ibid., ch. 5). Patrick Duncan is a good example of one who realized where the new antisemitic discourse would end.

17. Quoted in Furlong, *Between Crown and Swastika,* p. 65.

18. *DT,* 1.10.1937.

19. Shimoni, *Jews and Zionism,* p. 122.

20. Cohen, "Anti-Jewish Manifestations in the Union of South Africa," pp. 148–49.

21. Shimoni, *Jews and Zionism,* p. 130.

22. O'Meara, *Volkskapitalisme,* p. 128.

23. See Moodie, *The Rise of Afrikanerdom,* p. 21.

24. They did, however, believe in parliamentary government, which was patently not the case for the Ossewabrandwag. For the intellectual underpinnings of Afrikaner nationalism, see Simson, *The Social Origins of Afrikaner Fascism and Its Apartheid Policy,* ch. 6, and Furlong, *Between Crown and Swastika,* ch. 3.

25. Moodie, *The Rise of Afrikanerdom,* p. 15.

26. Vatcher, *White Laager,* pp. 68–75, and Furlong, *Between Crown and Swastika,* ch. 8. In 1940 Jews were debarred from membership of the Transvaal National party. This did not apply to the other provinces (Bunting, *The Rise of the South African Reich,* p. 64).

27. Friedman, "Jews, Germans and Afrikaners," ch. 4.

28. Endelman, "Comparative Perspectives on Modern Anti-Semitism in the West," p. 104. Private antisemitism in this view refers "to expressions of contempt and discrimination outside the realm of public life" while public antisemitism refers to the "eruption of anti-Semitism in political life—the injection of anti-Semitism into matters of policy and the manipulation of anti-Semitism for partisan political ends."

29. Marrus, "The Theory and Practice of Anti-Semitism." The theory was originally developed in Marrus and Paxton, *Vichy France and the Jews.*

30. The only analysis that does locate Afrikaner antisemitism (and English acquiescence) in the specifically South African experience was an article "Die Juden-frage in Südafrika," published in *Der Weltkampf* (Oct. 1938), a German periodical. Hannah Arendt made extensive use of this article in the South African section of her monumental *The Origins of Totalitarianism;* see pp. 197–207.

31. Besides this being illustrated in party politics, evidence is also provided in a survey of anti-Jewish opinion conducted in 1944 by Simon Herman, then of the Department of Psychology at the University of the Witwatersrand. For a full copy of his analysis, which was based on interviews with 112 persons who held "strategically" important positions in various sectors of South African public life, see Albrecht Hagemann, "Antisemitism in South Africa during World War II: A Documentation."

32. See Volkov, *The Rise of Popular Antimodernism in Germany;* Gay, *Freud, Jews and Other Germans;* Stern, *The Failure of Illiberalism.*

33. Saron, "Epilogue 1910–55," p. 381.

34. See Dobkowski, *The Tarnished Dream.*

35. Feingold, *A Midrash on American Jewish History,* pp. 179–88.

36. Higham, *Send These to Me,* p. 193.

37. Ibid., pp. 150–51.

38. See Higham, *Send These to Me,* pp. 164–65.

39. For details see Shimoni, "South African Jews and the Apartheid Crisis," p. 27.

40. Edelstein, *What Do Young Africans Think?*

41. Edelstein, "The Urban African Image of the Jew."

42. Leveson, "The Jewish Stereotype in Some South African Fiction," pp. 278–82.

43. "The Attitude of White and Black Elites towards Anti-Semitism," Opinion Surveys Research for a New South Africa, Pretoria 8–14 Aug. 1990, cited in Dubb and Shain, "South Africa," p. 419.

44. Exclusivist nationalism has historically had explosive implications for the Jew: see Almog, *Nationalism and Antisemitism in Modern Europe, 1815–1945.*

Bibliography

A. Manuscript Sources

Charles H. Frude to General J. Smuts	Archives of the South African Jewish Board of Deputies, Johannesburg
Executive Council Minutes 1925– 1927: South African Jewish Board of Deputies	Archives of the South African Jewish Board of Deputies, Johannesburg
Inspectors' Reports	Standard Bank Archives, Johannesburg

- (i) Oudtshoorn 1893, INSP 1/1/120
- (ii) Oudtshoorn 1893, INSP 1/1/121
- (iii) Oudtshoorn 1894, INSP 1/1/121
- (iv) Paarl 1898, INSP 1/1/254
- (v) Cape Town 1904, INSP 1/1/199
- (vi) Middelburg 1905, INSP 1/1/246
- (vii) Oudtshoorn 1905, INSP 1/1/253
- (viii) Fordsburg 1907, INSP 1/1/214
- (ix) Fordsburg 1908, INSP 1/1/214
- (x) Paarl 1908, INSP 1/1/254

John X. Merriman Papers	South African Library
Morris Alexander Papers	BC 160, Manuscript Division, Jagger Library, University of Cape Town
Patrick Duncan Papers	BC 294, Manuscript Division, Jagger Library, University of Cape Town
Records of the Cape Town Municipality	3 CT 1/1/5/10 Cape Archives Depot
South African Party [Election Pamphlets] 1924	South African Library

B. Printed Government Documents

Natal Legislative Assembly Debates
Cape of Good Hope, Legislative Assembly Debates
Cape of Good Hope, Legislative Council Debates
Notulen—Eersten Volksraad 1899

Cape of Good Hope Government Gazette

Cape of Good Hope, Statutes, Act 16, 1860

Cape of Good Hope, Statutes, Act 11, 1868

G42—1876 *Results of Census. Colony of the Cape of Good Hope*

G39—1893 *Cape of Good Hope Labour Commission*

Z.A.R. *Johannesburg Gezondsheids Comite Sanitare Departement. Census 15 July 1896*

G42—1897 *Cape of Good Hope, Reports of District Surgeons upon Public Health and Sanitation*

G66—1902 *Cape of Good Hope, Report on Public Health for the Year 1901*

G66—1903 *Cape of Good Hope, Report on Public Health for the Year 1902*

G35—1904 *Cape of Good Hope, Report of the Medical Officer of Health for Cape Colony for the Year 1904*

G63—1904 *Report on the Working of the Immigration Act 1902–1904*

G19—1905 *Census of the Colony of the Cape of Good Hope, 1904*

C3—1906 *Cape of Good Hope, Report of the Select Committee for Labour Settlement for Indigent Whites, Minutes of Evidence*

TK 169 *Census for the Transvaal Colony and Swaziland—1904.* Transvaal Archives Depot

TG 13—1908 *Transvaal Indigency Commission. Minutes of Evidence.* Transvaal Archives Depot

Report of the Liquor Commission 1908, Pretoria

Census for the Union of South Africa 1911.

UG—35 *Report of the Martial Law Inquiry, Judicial Commission, 1922*

Union of South Africa Official Year Book, no.7—1924. Special Report Series of the Census Department: Immigration 1920–25. No.25

House of Assembly Debates: Union of South Africa

C. Secondary Sources

I Books and Articles

Abelson, Deborah. "In Natal." In Saron and Hotz, eds., *The Jews in South Africa.*

Abrahams, Israel. *The Birth of a Community: A History of Western Province Jewry from Earliest Times to the end of the South African War, 1902.* Cape Town, 1955.

———. "Western Province Jewry, 1870–1902." In Saron and Hotz, eds., *The Jews in South Africa.*

Addleson, Abraham. "In the Eastern Province." In Saron and Hotz, eds., *The Jews in South Africa.*

Alexander, Enid. *Morris Alexander: A Biography.* Cape Town and Johannesburg, 1953.

Allport, Gordon W. *The Nature of Prejudice.* Boston, 1954.

Almog, Shmuel. *Nationalism and Antisemitism in Modern Europe 1815–1945.* Oxford, 1990.

Arendt, Hannah. *The Origins of Totalitarianism,* New York, 1954.

Arkin, Antony. "Economic Activities." In *South African Jewry: A Contemporary Survey,* ed. Arkin. Cape Town, 1984.

Aronstam, Sheila Minnie. "A Historical and Socio-Cultural Survey of the Bloemfontein Jewish Community with Special Reference to the Conception of Jewish Welfare Work." Ph.d. diss., Univ. of the Orange Free State, 1974.

Aschheim, Steven E. *Brothers and Strangers: The East European Jew in German and German Jewish Consciousness.* Madison, Wis., 1982.

———. "Caftan and Cravat: The Ostjude as a Cultural Symbol in the Development of German Antisemitism." In *Political Symbolism in Modern Europe,* ed. Seymour Drescher, David Warren Sabean, and Allan Sharlin. New Brunswick and London, 1982.

Aschman, George. "Oudtshoorn in the Early Days." In Saron and Hotz, eds., *The Jews in South Africa.*

Ashmore, Richard D., and Francis K. Delboca. "Conceptual Approaches to Stereotypes and Stereotyping." In *Cognitive Processes in Stereotyping and Intergroup Behaviour,* ed. David L. Hamilton. Hillsdale, N.J., 1981.

Banton, Michael. *Race Relations.* London, 1967.

Baron, Salo W. *Modern Nationalism and Religion.* New York, 1947.

———. "Newer Approaches to Jewish Emancipation." *Diogenes* 29 (Spring 1960): 56–81.

Barrow, John. *An Account of Travels into the Interior of Southern Africa in the Years 1797 and 1798, vols I and II.* London, 1801.

Beck, Henry Houghton. *History of South Africa and the Boer British War.* Philadelphia, 1900.

Bellairs, Kenneth F. *The Witwatersrand Goldfields: A Trip to Johannesburg and Back.* London, 1889.

Bhana, Surendra, and Joy B. Brain, *Setting Down Roots: Indian Migrants in South Africa, 1860–1911.* Johannesburg, 1990.

Bickford-Smith, John Vivian. "Commerce, Class and Ethnicity in Cape Town, 1875 to 1902." Ph.d. diss., Cambridge Univ., 1988.

Black, Stephen W. *Die Dorp.* London, 1920.

Bonner, Philip. "The Transvaal Native Congress 1917–1920: The Radicalisation of the Black Petty Bourgeoisie on the Rand." In *Industrialisation and Social Change in South Africa: African Class Formation, Culture and Consciousness 1870–1930,* ed. Shula Marks and Richard Rathbone. London, 1982.

Boon, Martin James. *Jottings by the Way or Boon's madness on the Road. Being a Philosophical View of Life, Past, Present and to come, in the Orange Free State, Natal and Cape Colony.* London, 1884.

———. *The Immortal History of South Africa.* 2 vols. London, 1885.

———. *The History of the Orange Free State.* Vol. 1. London, 1885.

Booth, A. R., ed. *The Journal of an American Missionary in the Cape Colony, 1835.* Cape Town, 1967.

Boyle, Frederick. *To the Cape for Diamonds.* London, 1873.

Bozzoli, Belinda, ed. *Class, Community and Conflict: South African Perspectives.* Johannesburg, 1987.

Bradford, Helen. *A Taste of Freedom: The ICU in Rural South Africa 1924–1930.* Johannesburg, 1988.

Bradlow, Edna. "Immigration into the Union, 1910–1948: Policies and Attitudes." Ph.d. diss., Univ. of Cape Town, 1978.

Bristow, Edward J. *Prostitution and Prejudice: The Jewish Fight against White Slavery 1870–1939.* New York, 1983.

Bruce, M. C. *The New Transvaal.* London, 1908.

"Brutus" [H. F. Viljoen]. *Never Again: The Psychology and Lesson of the Rand Revolt 1922.* Johannesburg, 1922.

Bryce, James. *From Impressions of South Africa.* London and New York, 1897.

Bundy, Colin. "Vagabond Hollanders and Runaway Englishmen." In *Putting a Plough to the Ground: Accumulation and Dispossession in Rural South Africa 1850–1930,* ed. William Beinart, Peter Delius, and Stanley Trapido, Johannesburg, 1986.

Bunting, Brian. *The Rise of the South African Reich.* Harmondsworth, 1964.

Butler, William Francis. *Sir William Butler: An Autobiography.* London, 1911.

Cahnman, Werner J. "Socio-Economic Causes of Anti-semitism." *Social Problems* 5, no. 1 (1957): 21–29.

Cammack, Diana. "The Politics of Discontent: The Grievances of the Uitlander Refugees, 1899–1902." *Journal of Southern African Studies* 8 (1982): 243–70.

———. "Class, Politics and War: A Socio-Economic Study of the Uitlanders of the Witwatersrand, 1897–1902." Ph.d. diss., Univ. of California, 1983.

———. *The Rand at War 1899–1902: The Witwatersrand and the Anglo-Boer War.* Pietermartizburg, 1990.

Campbell, Waldermar B. "The South African Frontier, 1865–1885: A Study in Expansion." *Archives Year Book for South African History.* Vol. 1. 1959. Elsies River, 1960.

Caron, Vicki. *Between France and Germany: The Jews of Alsace-Lorraine, 1871–1918.* Stanford, 1988.

Cesarani, David. "Dual Heritage or Duel of Heritages? Englishness and Jewishness in the Heritage Industry." In *The Jewish Heritage in British History: Englishness and Jewishness,* ed. Tony Kushner. London, 1992.

Coetzee, J. M. "Blood, Flaw, Taint, Degeneration: The Case of Sarah Gertrude Millin." *English Studies in Africa* 23, no. 1 (1980): 41–58.

———. *White Writing: On the Culture of Letters in South Africa.* New Haven and London, 1988.

Cohen, Michael. "Anti-Jewish Manifestations in the Union of South Africa during the Nineteen-Thirties." B.A. (Hons) diss., Univ. of Cape Town, 1968.

Cohen, Stephen A. "A History of the Jews of Durban 1825–1918." M.A. diss., Univ. of Natal, 1977.

Cohen, Stuart A. "Anglo-Jewish Responses to Antisemitism." In *Living with Antisemitism: Modern Jewish Responses,* ed. Jehuda Reinharz. Hanover and London, 1987.

Couper, James Robertson. *Mixed Humanity: A Story of camp life in South Africa.* London, 1892.

Cumberland, Stuart C. *What I Think of South Africa: Its People and Its Politics.* London, 1896.

Cuthbertson, Greg C. "Jewish Immigration as an Issue in South African Politics, 1937–1939." *Historia* 26 (1981):119–33.

Davenport, T. R. H. *South Africa: A Modern History.* 3d ed. Johannesburg, 1987.

Davey, Arthur. *The British Pro-Boers, 1877–1902.* Cape Town, 1978.

Denoon, D. J. N. *A Grand Illusion: The Failure of Imperial Policy in the Transvaal Colony during the Period of Reconstruction 1900–1905.* London, 1973.

———. "Capitalist Influence and the Transvaal Government during the Crown Colony Period, 1900–1906." *Historical Journal* 11 (1968): 301–31.

Dobkowski, Michael N. *The Tarnished Dream: The Basis of American Anti-Semitism.* Westport, Conn., 1979.

Dubb, Allie A., and Milton Shain. "South Africa." In *American Jewish Year Book.* 1992. Ed. David Singer. Philadelphia, 1992.

Dubow, Saul. "Race, Civilisation and Culture: The Elaboration of Segregationist Discourse in the Inter-war years." In *The Politics of Race, Class and Nationalism in Twentieth Century South Africa,* ed. Shula Marks and Stanley Trapido. London and New York, 1987.

———. *Racial Segregation and the Origins of Apartheid in South Africa, 1919–36.* London, 1989.

Duminy, Andrew Hadley, and William R. Guest, eds. *Fitzpatrick: South African Politician, Selected Papers 1888–1906.* Johannesburg, 1976.

Dundes, Alan. *Cracking Jokes: Studies of Sick Humor Cycles and Stereotypes.* Berkeley, 1987.

Du Toit, André. "Puritans in Africa? Afrikaner Calvinism and Kuyperian Neo-Calvinism in Late Nineteenth Century South Africa." *Journal for Comparative Study of Society and History* 27 (1985): 209–40.

Du-Val, Charles H. "All the world around!!! With Pencil, Pen and Camera." In *Johannesburg Pioneer Journals 1888–1909,* ed. Maryna Fraser. Cape Town, 1985.

Edelstein, Melville L. *What Do Young South Africans Think?* Johannesburg, 1972.

———. "The Urban African Image of the Jew." *Jewish Affairs* 27, no. 2 (1972): 6–8.

Endelman, Todd M. *The Jews of Georgian England 1714–1830, Tradition and Change in a Liberal Society.* Philadelphia, 1979.

———. "Comparative Perspectives on Modern Anti-Semitism in the West." In *History and Hate: The Dimensions of Anti-Semitism,* ed. David Berger. Philadelphia, 1986.

———. "A Question of Influence." *TLS* 26.6.1987, p. 684.

———. *Radical Assimilation in English Jewish History 1656–1945.* Bloomington, Ind., 1990.

Eybers, George von Werfling. *Select Constitutional Documents Illustrating South African History 1795–1910.* New York, 1918.

Farrelly, Michael James. *The settlement after the war in South Africa.* Cape Town, 1900.

Feingold, Henry L. *A Midrash on American Jewish History.* Albany, 1982.

Feldman, Bonny Irma. "Social Life of Cape Town Jewry, 1904–1914, with Special Reference to the Eastern European Immigrant Community." B.A. (Hons) diss., Univ. of Cape Town, 1984.

Festinger, Leon. *A Theory of Cognitive Dissonance.* Evanston, Ill., 1957.

First, Ruth, and Ann Scott. *Olive Schreiner: A Biography.* London, 1989.

Friedman, Sharon Lynne. "Jews, Germans and Afrikaners—Nationalist Press Reaction to the Final Solution." B.A. (Hons) diss., Univ. of Cape Town, 1982.

Froude, James Anthony. "Visit to the Diamond Fields." Photocopy. African Studies Library, Univ. of Cape Town.

Furlong, Patrick J. *Between Crown and Swastika: The Impact of the Radical Right on the Afrikaner Nationalist Movement in the Fascist Era.* Johannesburg, 1991.

Galbraith, John S. "The Pamphlet Campaign in the Boer War." *Journal of Modern History* 24 (1952): 111–26.

Gay, Peter. *Freud, Jews and Other Germans: Masters and Victims in Modernist Culture.* New York, 1978.

Gerber, David A. "Anti-Semitism and Jewish-Gentile Relations in American Historiography and the American Past." In *Anti-Semitism in American History,* ed. Gerber.

———, ed. *Anti-Semitism in American History.* Urbana, Ill., 1986.

Gilman, Sander L. *Difference and Pathology: Stereotypes of Sexuality, Race and Madness.* Ithaca, 1985.

Glanz, Rudolph. "The Rothschild Legend in America." *Jewish Social Studies* 19 (1957): 3–28.

Glassman, Bernard. *Anti-Semitic Stereotypes without Jews: Images of the Jew in England 1290–1700.* Detroit, 1975.

Gordon, C. T. *The Growth of Boer Opposition to Kruger 1890–1895.* Cape Town, 1970.

Griffith, George Chetwynce. *Knaves and Diamonds: Being Tales of Mine and Veld.* London, 1899.

Grundlingh, M. A. S. "The Parliament of the Cape of Good Hope, with Special Reference to Party Politics, 1872–1910." *Archives Year Book for South African History.* Vol. 2. 1969. Johannesburg, 1973.

Grosman, Moshe Pesach. "A Study in the Trends and Tendencies of Hebrew and Yiddish Writings in South Africa since the Beginning of the Early Nineties of the last Century to 1930." Ph.d. diss., Univ. of the Witwatersrand, 1973.

Hadden, Jeffrey K., and J. J. Barton. "An Image That Will Not Die: Thoughts on the History of Anti-urban Ideology." In *The Urbanization of the Suburbs.* Vol. 7 of *Urban Affairs Annual Review,* ed. Louis H. Masotti and Jeffrey K. Hadden. Los Angeles, 1975.

Hagemann, Albrecht. "Antisemitism in South Africa during World War II: A Documentation." *Simon Wiesenthal Center Annual.* Vol. 4. New York, 1987.

———. "Rassenpolitische Affinitat und Machtpolitische Revalitat: Das 'Dritte Reich' und die Sudafrikansche Union 1933–1945." Ph.d. diss., Bielefeld Univ., 1987.

Hall, Stuart, Charles Critcher, Tony Jefferson, John Clarke, and S. Roberts. *Policing the Crisis: Mugging, the State and Law and Order.* London, 1978.

Hallett, Robin. "Policemen, Pimps and Prostitutes—Public Morality and Police Corruption: Cape Town, 1902–1904." In *Studies in the History of Cape Town,* ed. Christopher S. Saunders. Vol. 1. Univ. of Cape Town, 1979.

Hancock, William Keith. *Smuts: The Sanguine Years 1870–1918.* Cambridge, 1962.

Harrison, Wilfred H. *Memoirs of a Socialist in South Africa.* Cape Town, 1949.

Hepple, Alexander. *Verwoerd.* Baltimore, 1967.

Herd, Norman. *1922: The Revolt on the Rand.* Johannesburg, 1966.

Herrman, Louis. *History of the Jews in South Africa.* London, 1930.

———. The Cape Town Hebrew Congregation: A Centenary History 1841–1941. Cape Town, n.d.

———. "Hoggenheimer," *Standard Encyclopaedia of South Africa.*

Hertzberg, Arthur. *The French Enlightenment and the Jews: The Origins of Modern Anti-Semitism.* New York, 1968.

Heydenrych, L. "Paul Kruger en die Joodse Gemeenskap van Johannesburg: Fabels en Feite." *Historia* 31, no. 2: 26–39.

Higham, John. "American Anti-Semitism Historically Reconsidered." In *Jews in the Mind of America,* ed. Charles Herbert Stember et al. New York, 1966.

———. *Send These to Me: Jews and Other Immigrants in Urban America.* New York, 1975.

———. *Strangers in the Land: Patterns of American Nativism 1860–1925.* 2d. ed. New York, 1981.

Hillegas, Howard Clemens. *Oom Paul's People.* New York, 1899.

Hirschfield, Claire. "'The British Left' and the 'Jewish Conspiracy': A Case Study of Modern Anti-Semitism." *Jewish Social Studies* 43 (Spring 1981): 95–112.

Hobsbawn, Eric. *The Age of Capital, 1848–1875.* London, 1975.

Hobson, John Atkinson. *The War in South Africa: Its Causes and Effects.* London, 1900.

———. "Before and after the Jameson Raid." In H. J. Ogden, ed. *The War against the Dutch Republic in South Africa.*

Hocking, Anthony Courtney. *Oppenheimer and Son.* Johannesburg, 1973.

Hoffman, Tzippi, and Alan Fischer. *The Jews of South Africa: What Future?* Johannesburg, 1988.

Hofmeyr, Jan. *Christian Principles and Race Problems.* Hoernlé Memorial Lecture. Johannesburg, 1945.

Hofstadter, Richard. *The Age of Reform: From Bryan to F.D.R.* New York, 1956.

Holmes, Colin. *Anti-Semitism in British Society, 1879–1939.* London, 1979.

Hotz, Louis. "Paul Kruger en die Jode." *Die Joodse Gedagte,* Dec. 1962, pp. 4–6.

Houghton, D. Hobart. "Economic Development, 1865–1965." *The Oxford History of South Africa.* Vol. 2, *South Africa 1870–1966,* ed. Monica Wilson and Leonard Thompson. Oxford, 1971.

Innes, Duncan. *Anglo, Anglo-American and the Rise of modern South Africa.* Johannesburg, 1984.

Johns, Sheridan Waite. "Marxism-Leninism in a Multi-Racial Environment: The Origins and Early History of the Communist Party of South Africa, 1914–1932." Ph.d. diss., Harvard Univ., 1965.

Jordan, Winthrop D. *White over Black: American Attitudes towards the Negro 1550–1812.* Chapel Hill, 1968.

Kaplan, Mendel, *Jewish Roots in the South African Economy.* Cape Town, 1986.

Kaplan, Mendel, and Marian Robertson, eds. *Founders and Followers: Johannesburg Jewry 1887–1915.* Cape Town, 1991.

———. "Johannesburg's First Organised Social Welfare Work." In Kaplan and Robertson, eds., *Founders and Followers.*

Katz, David S. *Philosemitism and the Readmission of Jews to England 1603–1655.* Oxford, 1982.

Katz, Jacob. *Out of the Ghetto: The Social Background of Jewish Emancipation 1770–1870.* New York, 1978.

———. *From Prejudice to Destruction: Anti-Semitism, 1700–1933.* Cambridge, 1980.

———. "Misreadings of Anti-Semitism." *Commentary* 74, no. 1 (1983): 39–44.

Kentridge, Morris. *I Recall: Memoirs of Morris Kentridge.* Johannesburg, 1959.

Krauss, Ferdinand. "A Description of Cape Town and Its Way of Life 1838–1840." *Quarterly Bulletin of the South African Library,* vol. 21, 1966–67.

Kruger, D. W. "Pres. Kruger en die Jode." *Die Huisgenoot* 28 (Nov. 1955): 9, 11.

Krut, Riva M. "Building a Home and a Community: Jews in Johannesburg, 1886–1914." Ph.d. diss., Univ. of London, 1985.

———. "The Making of a South African Jewish Community in Johannesburg, 1886–1914." In Belinda Bozzoli, ed., *Class, Community and Conflict: South African Perspectives.* Johannesburg, 1987.

Levesen, Marcia. "The Jewish Stereotype in Some South African Fiction: A Preliminary Investigation." In *Waters Out of the Well: Essays in Jewish Studies,* ed. Reuben Musiker and Joseph Sherman. Johannesburg, 1988.

Lewsen, Phyllis. "The Cape Liberal Tradition—Myth or Reality." *Race* 13, no. 1 (1971): 65–80.

———. *John X. Merriman: Paradoxical South African Statesman.* Johannesburg, 1982.

Mabin, Alan Spence. "The Making of Colonial Capitalism: Intensification and Expansion in the Economic Geography of the Cape Colony, South Africa." Ph.d. diss., Simon Fraser Univ., 1984.

Mackenzie, William Douglas, and Alfred Stead. *South Africa, Its History, Heroes and Wars.* Chicago, 1900.

Macmillan, Mona. *Sir Henry Barkly: Mediator and Moderator 1815–1898.* Cape Town, 1970.

Malherbe, Daniel François. *Die Meulenaar.* Bloemfontein, 1926.

Mandelbrote, Joyce C. "Joseph Suasso de Lima: A Bibliography." *Quarterly Bulletin of the South African Library* 3, no. 2 (1948): 2–22.

Mantzaris, Evangelos A. "The Promise of the Impossible Revolution: The

Cape Town Industrial Socialist League, 1915–1921." In *Studies in the History of Cape Town*. Vol. 4, ed. Christopher S. Saunders, Howard Phillips, and Elizabeth van Heyningen. Univ. of Cape Town, 1984.

Marrus, Michael R. *The Politics of Assimilation: The French Jewish Community at the Time of the Dreyfus Affair*. New York, 1971.

———. "The Theory and Practice of Anti-Semitism." *Commentary* 74, no. 2 (1982): 38–42.

Marrus, Michael R., and Robert O. Paxton, *Vichy, France and the Jews*. New York, 1981.

Martin, Samuel John Russell. "Political and Social Theories of Transkeian Administrators in the Late Nineteenth Century." M.A. diss., Univ. of Cape Town, 1978.

Marx, Christopher. "'Dear Listeners in South Africa': German Propaganda Broadcasts to South Africa 1940–1941." *South African Historical Journal* 27 (1992): 148–72.

Mendelsohn, Richard. *Sammy Marks: "The Uncrowned King of the Transvaal."* Cape Town and Athens, Ohio, 1991.

———. "Oom Paul's Publicist: Emanuel Mendelssohn, Founder of the First Congregation." In Kaplan and Robertson, eds., *Founders and Followers*.

Mendelssohn, S. *South African Bibliography*. Vol. 2. 2d. ed. London, 1957.

Menkis, Richard. "Historiography, Myth and Group Relations. Jewish and Non-Jewish Quebeçois and Jews and New France." *Canadian Ethnic Studies* 33, no. 2 (1991): 24–38.

Miles, Robert. *Racism*. London and New York, 1989.

Millin, Sarah Gertrude. *The South Africans*. London, 1926.

Milner, Violet Georgina. *My Picture Gallery, 1886–1901, by the Viscontess Milner*. London, 1951.

Moodie, T. Dunbar. *The Rise of Afrikanerdom: Power, Apartheid, and the Afrikaner Civil Religion*. Berkeley and Los Angeles, 1975.

Mosse, George L. *The Crisis of German Ideology: Intellectual Origins of the Third Reich*. New York, 1964.

———. *Nazism: A Historical and Comparative Analysis of National Socialism, an Interview with Michael A. Ledeen*. Oxford, 1978.

———. *Towards the Final Solution: A History of European Racism*. London, 1978.

Nathan, Manfred. *Paul Kruger, His Life and Times*. Durban: 1941.

Ogden, H. J., ed. *The War against the Dutch Republic in South Africa*. Manchester, *National Reform Union*, 1901.

O'Meara, Dan. *Volkskapitalisme: Class, Capital and Ideology in the Development of Afrikaner Nationalism 1934–1948*. Johannesburg, 1983.

Osborne, Oliver. *In the Land of the Boers; or the Other Man and Myself.* London, 1893.

Pama, Cornelis. *Bowler's Cape Town: Life at the Cape Colony in Early Victorian Times 1834–1868*. Cape Town, 1977.

Parry, Richard. "'In a Sense Citizens, but Not Altogether Citizens': Rhodes, Race and the Ideology of Segregation at the Cape in the Late Nineteenth Century." *Canadian Journal of African Studies* 17 (1983): 377–91.

Patterson, Sheila. *The Last Trek: A Study of the Boer People and the Afrikaner Nation*. London, 1957.

Pencharz, Myer, and Dora L. Sowden. "In the Orange Free State." In Saron and Hotz, eds., *The Jews in South Africa*.

Pettman, Charles. *Afrikanderisms*. London, 1913.

Pheiffer, Roy. "The Jew in Afrikaans Literature." *Patterns of Prejudice* 11, no. 1 (1977): 23–27.

Pinsker, Leo. "Auto-emancipation: An Appeal to His People by a Russian Jew (1882)." In *The Zionist Idea, a Historical Analysis and Reader*, ed. Arthur Hertzberg. New York, 1984.

Porter, Bernard. *Critics of Empire: British Radical Attitudes to Colonialism in Africa 1895–1914*. London, 1968.

Phillips, Howard. "'Black October': The Impact of the Spanish Influenza Epidemic of 1918 on South Africa." *Archives Year Book for South African History*. Vol. 1. Pretoria, 1990.

A Pictorial View of Recent Events: Through the Red Revolt on the Rand, Including Photographs from the Star. N.p./n.d.

Pulzer, Peter. *The Rise of Political Anti-Semitism in Germany and Austria*. New York, 1964.

Reitz, Francis William. *A Century of Wrong*. London, 1900.

Richardson, Peter. *Chinese Mine Labour in the Transvaal*, London, 1982.

Ridpath, John Clark, and Edward Sylvester Ellis. *The Story of South Africa*. New York and Chicago, 1899.

Ritner, Susan Rennie. "Salvation through Separation: The Role of the Dutch Reformed Church in South Africa in the Formation of Afrikaner Race Ideology." Ph.d. diss., Univ. of Mich., 1975.

Rose, Arnold. "Anti-Semitism's Roots in City Hatred." *Commentary* 6 (1948): 374–78.

Rose, Edward B. *The Truth about the Transvaal*. London, 1902.

Rosenthal, Eric. "Jews in the Boer Republic: Some Colourful Personalities." Unp. paper, South African Jewish Sociological and Historical Society, South African Jewish Board of Deputies Archives. Johannesburg, n.d.

———. "On the Diamond Fields." In Saron and Hotz, eds., *The Jews in South Africa*.

———. *Heinrich Egersdörfer, An Old-time Sketch Book*. Cape Town, 1960.

Sarna, Jonathan D. "Anti-Semitism and American History." *Commentary* 71, no. 3 (1981): 42–47.

Saron, Gustav. "Epilogue 1910–1955." In Saron and Hotz, eds., *The Jews in South Africa*.

———. "Boers, Uitlanders, Jews." In Saron and Hotz, eds., *The Jews in South Africa*.

———. "The Long Road to Unity." In Saron and Hotz, eds., *The Jews in South Africa*.

Saron, Gustav, and Louis Hotz, eds. *The Jews in South Africa: A History*. Cape Town, 1955.

Sartre, Jean Paul. *Anti-Semite and Jew*. Trans. George J. Becker. New York, 1965.

Schachar, Isaiah. "Studies in the Emergence and Dissemination of the Modern Jewish Stereotype in Western Europe." Ph.d. diss., Univ. of London, 1967.

Scher, David M. "Louis T. Weichardt and the South African Greyshirt Movement." *Kleio* 18 (1986): 15–27.

Schermerhorn, R. A. *Comparative Ethnic Relations: Framework for Theory and Research.* New York, 1970.

Schoeman, Karel. *Olive Schreiner: 'N Lewe in Suid Afrika 1855–1881.* Cape Town, 1989.

Schoonraad, Murray, and Elsabe Schoonraad. *Companion to South African Cartoonists.* Johannesburg, 1989.

Schreiner, Olive Emily Albertina. *Trooper Peter Halket of Mashonaland.* London, 1897.

———. "Words in Season: An English South African's View of the Situation." *Standard and Diggers News,* 29.5.1899.

———. *From Man to Man.* London, 1926.

———. *Undine.* London, 1929.

———. "A Letter on the Jew." *Jewish Affairs* 31, no. 8 (1976): 6–11.

Schreiner, Olive Emily Albertina, and Samuel C. Cronwright-Schreiner. *The Political Situation.* London, 1896.

Schulze, Ernest. "Der Judenfrage in Südafrika." *Der Weltkampf,* 1938, pp. 453–61.

Scully, William Charles. *Between Sand and Sun: A Tale of an African Desert.* London, 1898.

———. *Further Reminiscences of a South African Pioneer.* London, 1913.

Semmel, Bernard. *Imperialism and Social Reform: English Social Imperial Thought 1895–1914.* New York, 1968.

Shain, Milton. "Hoggenheimer—the Making of a Myth." *Jewish Affairs* 36 (1981): 112–16.

———. *Jewry and Cape Society: The Origins and Activities of the Jewish Board of Deputies for the Cape Colony.* Cape Town, 1983.

Shellack, Werner. "The Afrikaners' Nazi Links Revisited." *South African Historical Journal* 27 (1992): 173–85.

Shimoni, Gideon. *Jews and Zionism: The South African Experience (1910–1967).* Cape Town, 1980.

———. "South African Jews and the Apartheid Crisis." *American Jewish Year Book.* 1988. Ed. David Singer. Philadelphia, 1988.

Simonowitz, Gideon. "The Background to Jewish Immigration to South Africa and the Development of the Jewish Community in the South African Republic, between 1890 and 1902." B.A. (Hons) diss., Univ. of the Witwatersrand, 1960.

Simson, Howard. *The Social Origins of Afrikaner Fascism and Its Apartheid Policy.* Uppsala, 1980.

Smith, Kenneth W. *From Frontier to Midlands: A History of the Graaff-Reinet District 1786–1910.* Grahamstown, 1976.

Smith, Pauline. *The Beadle.* London, 1926.

Sonnabend, H. "Statistical Survey of Johannesburg Jewish Population." Unp.

paper, South African Jewish Board of Deputies Archives. Johannesburg, n.d.

Sowden, Dora L. "In the Transvaal till 1899." In Saron and Hotz, eds., *The Jews in South Africa.*

Stals, Ernest Ludewicus Paul, ed. *Afrikaners in die Goudstad.* Pretoria, 1987.

Statham, Francis Reginald. *Mr Magnus.* London, 1896.

———. *South Africa as It Is.* London, 1897.

———. *South Africa and the Transvaal: The Story of a Company.* Westminster, 1899.

Stepan, Nancy. *The Idea of Race in Science: Great Britain, 1800–1960.* London, 1982.

Stern, Fritz. *Gold and Iron: Bismarck, Bleichroder and the Building of the German Empire.* New York, 1977.

Streak, Michael. *Lord Milner's Immigration Policy for the Transvaal 1897–1905.* Johannesburg, 1969.

Stultz, Newell M. *Afrikaner Politics in South Africa 1934–1948.* Berkeley and Los Angeles, 1974.

Tannenbaum, E. "Jewish Characters in Afrikaans Fiction." *Jewish Affairs* 6, no. 5 (1951): 14–18.

Thompson, Leonard M. *The Political Mythology of Apartheid.* New Haven, 1985.

———. *A History of South Africa.* New Haven, 1990.

Turrell, Robert Vicat. *Capital and Labour on the Kimberley Diamonds Fields 1871–1890.* Cambridge, 1987.

Twyman, L. J. "Paul Kruger en Johannesburg." M.A. diss., Univ. of Pretoria, 1965.

Van Bruggen, Jochem. "Bywoners." In *Op die Veld en Rante,* ed. Jochem van Bruggen. Pretoria, 1930.

Van Heerden, F. J. "Nasionaal-socialism as Factor in die Suid-Afrikaanse Politiek, 1933–1948." D.Phil. thesis, Univ. of the Orange Free State, 1972.

Van Heyningen, Elizabeth B. "Refugees and Relief in Cape Town." In *Studies in the History of Cape Town.* Vol. 3. Ed. Christopher S. Saunders and Howard Phillips. Cape Town, 1980.

———. "Public Health and Society in Cape Town 1880–1910." Ph.d. diss., Univ. of Cape Town, 1989.

Van Onselen, Charles, ed. *Studies in the Social and Economic History of the Witwatersrand 1886–1914.* 2 vols. Johannesburg, 1982.

———. "Randlords and Rotgut, 1886–1903." In Van Onselen, ed., *Studies in the Social and Economic History of the Witwatersrand 1886–1914.* Vol. 1. *New Babylon.*

———. "Prostitutes and Proletarians, 1886–1914." In Van Onselen, ed., *Studies in the Social and Economic History of the Witwatersrand 1886–1914.* Vol. 1. *New Babylon.*

———. "The Main Reef Road into the Working Class." In Van Onselen, ed., *Studies in the Social and Economic History of the Witwatersrand 1886–1914.* Vol. 2. *New Ninevah.*

Vatcher, William Henry. *White Laager: The Rise of Afrikaner Nationalism.* London, 1965.

Volkov, Shulamit. *The Rise of Popular Antimodernism in Germany: The Urban Master Artisans, 1873–1896*. Princeton, 1978.

Worger, William Hewlett. "The Making of a Monopoly: Kimberley and the South African Diamond Industry 1870–95." Ph.d. diss., Yale Univ., 1982.

Williams, Bill. "The Anti-Semitism of Tolerance: Middle-class Manchester and the Jews 1870–1900." In *City, Class and Culture: Social Policy and Cultural Production in Victorian Manchester,* ed. A. J. Kidd and K. R. V. Roberts. Manchester, 1985.

Yudelman, David. *The Emergence of Modern South Africa: State, Capital and the Incorporation of Organized Labour on the South African Gold Fields, 1902–1939*. Cape Town and Johannesburg, 1984.

II Newspapers and Periodicals and Their Abbreviations

AJW	*African Jewish World*
BC	*Burghersdorp Chronicle*
BD	*Business Day*
BF	*Bloemfontein Friend*
Bu	*The Burlesque*
Ca	*The Cape*
CA	*Cape Argus*
CGHL	*Cape of Good Hope Literary Gazette*
CJC	*Cape Jewish Chronicle*
CP	*Cape Punch*
Cr	*The Critic*
CR	*Cape Register*
CT	*Cape Times*
CTM	*Cape Town Mail*
DAP	*Di Afrikaanse Patriot*
DB	*De Burger* (after 1922 *Die Burger*)
DBF	*Die Blanke Front*
DH	*De Huisgenoot*
DK	*De Kerkbode*
DN	*Diamond News*
DR	*The Daily Representative*
DS	*De Spektator*
DT	*Die Transvaler*
DVb	*De Volksbode*
DVs	*De Volksstem*
DW	*Die Waarheid—The Truth*
DWe	*Der Weltkampf*
DZA	*De Zuid Afrikaan*
DZAV	*Die Zuid Afrikaan Verenigd met Ons Land*
DZAVV	*De Zuid-Afrikaan Verenigd met die Volksvriend*
ELDD	*East London Daily Dispatch*
EPH	*Eastern Province Herald*
FL	*Free Land*

Index